Praise for

"A.C. Fisher Aldag brings magic out of the temple and into fields, forests, and kitchens. She brings knowledge wide and deep—of energy basics, lore, tools, and timing; of otherworldly entities, divination, and trance—that make access and understanding of magical principles from the common folk of yesteryear available to today's readers. Importantly, she addresses the issue of ethics in magical work. She tells us more about magick and spellwork than we ever knew we needed to know."

—M. Macha Nightmare (Aline O'Brien),
witch at large, author, activist, ritualist

"Steeped in history, *Common Magick* delves deeply into the roots of modern Paganism and witchcraft, allowing the reader a deeper view into what was, how we came to be, and how the lessons and practices of the past can lead us into a more honest and open spiritual future. There is a certain wisdom within the pages of this book that dually inspires and sets the groundwork for a modern interpretation of magick based upon tradition. Brilliant."

—Marcus F. Griffin, author of *Advancing the Witches Craft*

"*Common Magick* is one of those unique books that goes beyond the simple instructions in most Pagan books and gives history and practice about the true beginnings of Paganism … I highly recommend this book for everyone who wants to know the history and the majesty of Pagan origins and practice."

—Susan Wilson, Wiccan priestess and former
information officer for Cherry Hill Seminary

common
MAGICK

© Shirley Rigozzi

About the Author

A.C. Fisher Aldag (Bangor, Michigan) has practiced a folk magico-religion from the British Isles for over forty years. She has assisted in facilitating many local Pagan events and regularly teaches classes and workshops on folk magick. A.C. has written for *Llewellyn's Magical Almanac* and other Pagan publications.

To Write to the Author

If you wish to contact the author or would like more information about this book, please write to the author in care of Llewellyn Worldwide Ltd. and we will forward your request. Both the author and publisher appreciate hearing from you and learning of your enjoyment of this book and how it has helped you. Llewellyn Worldwide Ltd. cannot guarantee that every letter written to the author can be answered, but all will be forwarded. Please write to:

A.C. Fisher Aldag
℅ Llewellyn Worldwide
2143 Wooddale Drive
Woodbury, MN 55125-2989
Please enclose a self-addressed stamped envelope for reply,
or $1.00 to cover costs. If outside the U.S.A., enclose
an international postal reply coupon.

Many of Llewellyn's authors have websites with additional
information and resources. For more information,
please visit our website at http://www.llewellyn.com.

A.C. FISHER ALDAG

common
MAGICK

origins *and* practices *of*
BRITISH FOLK MAGICK

Llewellyn Publications
Woodbury, Minnesota

FIRST EDITION
First Printing, 2020

Book design by Samantha Penn
Cover design by Shira Atakpu
Interior art on pages 47, 143, 168, 249 by Eugene Smith
Interior art on pages 22, 120, 200 by Llewellyn Art Department

Llewellyn Publications is a registered trademark of Llewellyn Worldwide Ltd.

Library of Congress Cataloging-in-Publication Data
Names: Aldag, A. C. Fisher, author.
Title: Common magick : origins & practices of British folk magick / by A.C.
    Fisher Aldag.
Description: First edition. | Woodbury, MN : Llewellyn Publications, [2020]
    | Includes bibliographical references and index. | Summary: "This book
    is for anyone interested in learning about authentic magical folkloric
    traditions, with spells and rituals for health, love, home, happiness,
    protection, luck, money, and more"-- Provided by publisher.
Identifiers: LCCN 2020036773 (print) | LCCN 2020036774 (ebook) | ISBN
    9780738763132 (paperback) | ISBN 9780738763224 (ebook)
Subjects: LCSH: Magic--Great Britain. | Folklore--Great Britain. | Rites
    and ceremonies--Great Britain.
Classification: LCC BF1622.G7 A22 2020 (print) | LCC BF1622.G7 (ebook) |
    DDC 133.4/30941--dc23
LC record available at https://lccn.loc.gov/2020036773
LC ebook record available at https://lccn.loc.gov/2020036774

Llewellyn Publications
A Division of Llewellyn Worldwide Ltd.
2143 Wooddale Drive
Woodbury, MN 55125-2989
www.llewellyn.com

Printed in the United States of America

Other Books by A.C. Fisher Aldag
Cambria, Indiana
This Bright Land o' Blessing

Forthcoming Books by A.C. Fisher Aldag
Afalon, Ohio

To my family, for all of their support,
and to Heather Greene at Llewellyn
for granting me this wonderful opportunity.

CONTENTS

Disclaimer

This book is presented solely for educational and entertainment purposes. The author and publisher are not offering it as medical advice. This book is not meant to be used, nor should it be used, to diagnose or treat any medical condition. For diagnosis or treatment of any medical condition, readers are advised to consult or seek the services of a competent medical professional. The publisher and author are not responsible for any specific health or allergy needs that may require medical supervision. The publisher and author are not liable for any damages or negative consequences from any treatment, action, application, or preparation to any person reading or following the information in this book.

While best efforts have been used in preparing this book, the author and publisher make no representations or warranties of any kind. The author and publisher assume no liabilities of any kind with respect to the accuracy or completeness of the contents and specifically disclaim any implied warranties of fitness of use for a particular purpose. Neither the author nor the publisher shall be held liable or responsible to any person or entity with respect to any loss or damages caused, or alleged to have been caused, directly or indirectly, by the information contained herein. Every situation is different, and the advice and strategies contained herein may not be suitable for your situation.

References are provided for informational purposes only and do not constitute endorsement of any websites or other sources. Readers should be aware that the websites listed in this book may change.

This book is sold with the understanding that the publisher is not engaged to render any type of psychological, legal, or professional advice. Neither the publisher nor the author shall be liable for any physical, psychological, emotional, financial, or commercial damages, including, but not limited to, special, incidental, consequential, or other damages. Our views and rights are the same: You are responsible for your own choices, actions, and results.

one
INTRODUCTION TO
COMMON MAGICK

I t's around the first of May and you've been invited to a gathering. There are some familiar sights, like people dancing around a Maypole and enjoying a feast. There are also some unusual activities. A person costumed as a horse and rider is chasing a gaggle of laughing revelers. Three couples wearing bells are ecstatically dancing. Someone dressed in green, leafy tree branches cavorts next to a bush covered by rags, trinkets, and flowers. Children carrying decorated boughs are chanting, "We bring back life to the village." You have encountered a common magick gathering...or just another holiday celebration in a small British town.

Common magick is, quite simply, the magick of the common people. "Magick" is the process of using natural energies to create change or transformation on a physical, mental, or spiritual level. It is spelled with a *K* to differentiate it from stage magic performances. It is also called folk magick, folkloric nature spirituality or religion, earth spirituality or religion, "old-line" Paganism, traditional magick, traditional witchcraft, traditional folkways, or a folkloric magico-religion. Folk magick means that it uses folklore, or knowledge that was verbally communicated between generations. Nature spirituality is a belief system drawing upon entities, forces, and places that exist in our natural environment. A magico-religion is a practice that combines the use of magick with spiritual beliefs.

In this book we'll focus on the common magick embraced by the people of the British Isles, including Cornwall, England, Ireland, the Isle of Man, Scotland, Wales, and what used to be called Brittany, an area in the north of France.

1

Various magico-religious praxes (practices) were created by the regions' original inhabitants. They were also created or influenced by the Celts, Romans, Norse, Anglo-Saxons, and other people who have lived in the British Isles over time. It is sometimes called Brythonic folk magick. It is not possible to know the origins of some current folkways, nor is it possible to know exactly what rituals our predecessors enacted, although new discoveries happen frequently.

People might think of folk magick as being primitive superstition, yet that is not true. People may also believe that Christianity completely supplanted witchcraft and Paganism in modern Europe, but that isn't really true either. Many British ritualized dramas were photographed in the late 1800s. Older rites with Pagan origins were practiced right up until World War II. Since the 1970s there has been a tremendous resurgence of interest in traditional folkways. Some practices, such as folk arts and crafts, ritual theater, folk dances, folklore and storytelling, and folk magick are truly ancient. Other rituals are new creations, reconstructions, revivals, or even mergers with modern pop culture. Common magick remains a vibrant living tradition.

Many magico-religious folk customs are not at all hidden. They are highly visible, and they are everywhere. Some traditions became ingrained in society. We see and hear them in artwork, holiday celebrations, folk music, place names, ritualized actions like tossing a coin into a well or knocking on wood for luck, and other everyday activities. Some rites are even performed publicly to amuse tourists.

Folkloric magick is still relevant today. Writers fasten quartz crystals onto a computer's power source to keep it from crashing. People use burning herbs for cleansing a place, perhaps in order to dissipate the feelings of unease caused by an argument. Some practices have entered the public consciousness, like divination, candle-burning rites, using talismanic items for good luck, dream interpretation, and mindfulness exercises. Other folkways have lost their usefulness on a physical level but can still be used in a modern context; for example, using sigils for protecting horses to protect your car. The main objective of most magickal workings is to create change for a purpose by using or directing energy. This includes transformation of the self.

Some folkloric ceremonies evolved into the holiday celebrations still enjoyed in present times. People enact these rituals to connect with the seasons and to ensure beneficial conditions, like an abundant harvest. Some events, including folk dances or ritual theater, are performed to entertain. Many people participate in common magick rites for community unification, a municipal identity, and fun. Others enjoy expressing their heritage. Yet these activities also accomplish the goals of raising energy and attuning ourselves with deities, ancestors, and/or nature.

Some of the British folk customs made their way to Australia, the United States of America, and other British colonies during mass emigrations. Other practices came to the US during the years when Gardnerian Wicca was brought to the public's attention. In America, the British folkways were blended with other peoples' traditions, including various European immigrants, African American enslaved workers, and Native American populations. However, British folkways do not require that the participants belong to any specific race, nationality, heritage, or ethnicity—people need not be Welsh, English, Irish, or Cornish to participate in common magick.

Nor does one have to follow any specific religious path to practice folk magick. Some participants acknowledge an "old-line" form of Paganism or traditional nature spirituality. Others practice forms of shamanism, connecting with the natural world as well as unseen realms. Still others are Christians who identify with their folkways' ancient roots. Some folk magick and folkloric nature spirituality has been syncretized, or merged, with Christianity. For example, there are spells that use Bible verses. Other rites come from the folktales and folk beliefs of various cultures, such as the fairy faith. In recent years, British magico-religious folkways have been practiced in conjunction with Wicca, Druidry, Asatru, and other neo-Pagan religions.

This book will be useful for people who have an interest in magick, ancient religions, or folklore. They may like to read fairy tales, myths, and legends. They might have psychic abilities such as clairvoyance or healing touch. They could be involved in earth-based spirituality or feel an affinity with nature, a connection to animals, plants, stones, and other natural beings. Ritual theater might interest them. They may wish to use spells or other workings to create change in their surroundings. They may be aware of other magico-religious traditions such as Wicca, ceremonial magick, or neo-Paganism. Thus, common magick will be significant for these readers.

Folkloric magick is another way of using energy and interacting with ethereal beings. It taps into ancient powers—yes, really! Like other traditions, common magick can aid in personal growth and transformation. Folk magick takes some work, but it is also a lot of fun.

A Wee Bit o' History

To understand where folk magick traditions come from (and where they are going), I'll need to discuss just a little bit of the past.

In ancient times, people were concerned with basic survival in a harsh environment. Hunting, herding and slaughtering animals, fishing, and gathering food were crucial activities. Equally important were collecting enough fuel for warmth, creating adequate shelter, and providing a source of clean water. Human conditions of childbirth, puberty, sexuality, surviving an illness, and aging were not fully understood. Changes in climate made migrations imperative. Magickal rites, charmed objects, and ritualized activities were developed to facilitate these processes, linked with physical labor, or "acting in accord." Shamanic workings and deities who represented motherhood and the hunt arose during this time.

During subsequent eras of human history, new events required new magick. Planting, growing, and harvesting food were a drastic change from hunting and gathering. Discovering the uses for bronze and then iron meant new ways of dealing with the material world. Working-class people including farmers, healers, skilled tradespeople, soldiers, artisans, sailors, and merchants frequently employed magick to help them in their pursuits. Workers used rituals, talismanic items, and symbolic drawings for their endeavors. Modern-day Masonic rites have their origin in the rituals and symbology of builders' guilds.[1] Deities were believed to facilitate activities such as smithcraft, dairying, and sailing large vessels. Laborers developed spells, or words of power, to manifest their intent. Some of their verbal chants may have come to us as work songs, sea chanteys, and spoken lore.

People learned to look for certain signs in nature to predict events, such as watching birds migrate, which indicated a change of seasons. Sayings like "Red sky at night, sailor's delight" helped forecast the weather, which was important to farmers and seafaring people. From there, the common folks instituted other forms of divination in order to determine possible outcomes.

On the home front, homemakers were concerned with cooking and preserving foods safely, including animal products like sausage, lard, honey, and milk products. This was necessary before the advent of home canning and refriger-

---

1. "History of Freemasonry," Masonic Service Association of North America, accessed March 30, 2020, http://www.msana.com/historyfm.asp.

ation. Housework employed ritual implements and spells to aid in cleanliness. Keeping babies and small children healthy and safe was critical. Sigils and magickal objects were used to protect the home and its inhabitants from evil. Herbal mixtures kept people healthy. There was also a concern about harmony between family members. Folktales entertained and instructed children. Nursery rhymes such as "Fishy in the Brook," "Ride a Cock Horse to Banbury Cross," and "Jack Be Nimble" may have originally been spells which were chanted or sung to bring about beneficial conditions.

Population shifts meant new forms of magick were brought to Britain by Celts, Romans, the Scandinavian Vikings, Germanic peoples, and Christianized Normans. For example, our beautiful Maypoles, ubiquitous on May Day in England, may have come from a merger between Celtic and Norse cultures.[2] Ceremonial magick techniques such as tarot and horoscope came to the British Isles from elsewhere in Europe. Christianity did not make as much of an impact on our magickal practices as was previously thought. People still believed in fairies, put old shoes inside the wall to ward off harmful energies, drew protective sigils on their work tools, and held harvest dances, even during the worst of Puritan oppression.

All of these events contributed to our modern practice of common magick, and also to many other neo-Pagan traditions.

Modern Manifestations

For our purposes, common magick can be divided into various beliefs and practices. I define a "theistic" belief as revering, aligning with, and utilizing the powers and capabilities of energetic beings such as god-forms or spirits. Earth-based spirituality and nature religions have components of theistic belief. I consider a "nontheistic" belief as performing esoteric workings to create change, independent of the belief in deities or other entities. The practice of what is now called witchcraft is often nontheistic. As a magico-religion, sometimes common magick incorporates both theistic and nontheistic elements.

---

2. Prudence Jones and Nigel Pennick, *A History of Pagan Europe* (New York: Routledge, 1997).

Theistic Beliefs and Practices

Brythonic folk magick tradition usually draws upon esoteric beings that derive from the British Isles and the populations that inhabited these locations over history. There are many stories and considerable folklore about deities, heroes, and supernatural beings in British literature. Some entities are only seen in artwork or enacted in folkplays. Others are described in fairy tales or folktales but may have been "downgraded" from deific status to a hero or legendary figure.

Common magick practitioners sometimes revere or work with specific deities with whom we have an affinity. These god-forms may be personified, which I define as visualizing human traits in a nonhuman situation, such as winter. The deities may reflect a human condition such as war, poetry, or love. They may or may not be aligned with nature. The god of smithcraft, most often called Wayland, is aligned with human work but also has natural tendencies and powers, such as using fire and air to draw metal from rocks.

Attunement with nature and respect for natural beings, such as the spirits of the land, are important to many common magick practitioners. Many personify Nature with a capital N. This means that nature itself, along with natural beings and associated spirits, deities, and entities, are viewed as having a consciousness and experiencing thoughts and emotions.

Folkloric nature spirituality may incorporate some aspects of Animism, the belief that all natural things including animals, plants, landforms like mountains and lakes, and natural forces like the wind have a consciousness and spirit. An example is the being Aneira, the Welsh personification of snow, who is viewed as angry or gentle, depending on the type of snowfall.

Some practitioners may view spirit beings as separate and distinct from their location, as in the belief that a spirit dwells within an underground mine rather than the mine itself having a consciousness. An example is the Coblynau, a Welsh mining spirit. This entity was said to make knocking, creaking, or moaning noises to warn mineworkers that a tunnel was unsafe. The Romans, who left their stamp on the British Isles during 450-plus years of occupation, believed in *genius loci*, or a deity or spirit that occupied one particular location, like the goddess Sulis who dwelled in the hot springs in what is now Bath, England.

The fairy faith may be incorporated into common magick. This is a belief in beings known as "the Fae" or fairies, who may be viewed as a race of people, spirits of nature, supernatural or extra-natural entities, or the ghosts of the departed. The fairy tradition draws heavily upon folklore, folktales, and fairy tales.

Common magick users may practice a form of shamanism. The word *shaman* comes from the Tungusic language group.[3] People who lived in early British civilizations had their own terms for these practitioners such as the old Welsh word *dewin*, which means "wizard," or *hudwr*, "enchanter," which also translates as "howler." In vernacular Scots Gaelic, a magick user is sometimes called a "howdy," which can mean a midwife or a howler, as in someone who wails or chants spells.

A shaman strives to work with the forces and beings found in nature for the purposes of spiritual attunement and discovering knowledge. In this instance, shamanism can be considered theistic. Some shamans use magick and/or altered states of consciousness, often for healing or for creating harmony with the natural world. These praxes can be theistic or nontheistic.

Nontheistic Praxes

These include the use of magick itself. Common magick utilizes energy to bring the will into manifestation, just like other esoteric traditions. There are rites of healing and protection. Like many other metaphysical practitioners, we often seek to develop our intuitive powers or expand our knowledge through the use of divination or visualization. Common magick users sometimes endeavor to communicate with the departed. We consider all of these beliefs and practices to be natural and wonderful.

Folk magick workers may incorporate the practice of traditional witchcraft. In the past, the words *witch* and *witchcraft* were often pejorative terms. In this book, witchcraft is defined as the craft and art of using energy for a designated goal, which may be independent of religion. Other witches feel it is a spiritual or religious praxis. One very recognizable form of witchcraft is combining ingredients while speaking words of power in order to bring one's desires into reality. This is often called conjuring, doing a working, or casting a spell. Common magick practitioners often use everyday objects from the home or workplace, such as a spindle or pitchfork, or natural implements, like feathers or stones, for the purposes of spell-casting.

---

3. Berthold Laufer, "Origin of the Word Shaman," *American Anthropologist New Series* 19, no. 3 (July–September 1917): 361–71, https://doi.org/10.1525/aa.1917.19.3.02a00020.

In the course of enacting common magick, practitioners may utilize all, none, or a combination of the aforementioned praxes: Animism, belief in spirits, belief in deities, witchcraft, and shamanism. We might combine praxes from a variety of British cultures and eras or stick with just one way of doing things. Common magick is a truly eclectic approach.

What Common Magick Is and What It Ain't

British folk magick praxes do not have any specific sacred book or body of literature. Common magick users of the past were usually preliterate. Much of folkloric tradition has been handed down as an oral history within families or from neighbor to neighbor, kept alive by those who actually practiced the rites. Other praxes might have been discovered by working directly with deities and/or energies. Common magick can incorporate folktales, fairy tales, family recipes, and a great deal of experimentation. Yes, sometimes we make it up as we go along!

Common magick often utilizes "low magick" as opposed to "high magick." High magick mostly comes from books of esoteric knowledge written by early philosophers and scientists. It is formulaic, stylized, and usually calls upon certain entities that are somehow bound to the mage. Low magick is also called earth magick or natural magick. Working-class people learned to perform earth magick through close contact with the land. They devised ways to deal with the unseen worlds, including the forces of birth, illness, and death, as well as how to interact with supernatural beings. They also learned practical skills, such as how to work metal, grow crops, and perform healing, by actual practice.

Much of nature spirituality centers on natural cycles. Common magick users realize that certain energies might be stronger at specific times of the day, month, or year. Almost all of our holidays have to do with the seasons, nature, planting and harvest, hunting, herding, preserving food, craftsmanship, and honoring personifications of death, birth, and life. These holidays may or may not include the "big eight" Sabbats of Wicca, the Celtic holidays observed in modern Druidry, or the Scandinavian and Germanic sacred days celebrated by Asatrur. Some observances were syncretized with Christian holy days. Folkloric magico-religions celebrated seasonal festivals with rituals, games, feasting, dancing, and decorating a place with symbolic items.

An affinity for the earth is true for urban adherents as well as rural folks. In the past, those who lived in cities maintained a balance with nature and grew kitchen herb gardens, kept chickens, and used natural omens for divination, such as the thickness of animal pelts. They had to prepare for winter by gathering a fuel supply and making clothing to withstand the cold. Rituals accompanied each action. Some common magick praxes seem to have no basis in nature, such as the Mari Lwyd, or "old horse" procession. However, this ritual is enacted to honor and appease an anthropomorphized Death during the winter months.

Since common magick users view all natural spaces as holy, most outdoor places are seen as already sanctified and pure. For some practitioners, energy is not always contained and released. Instead, the magick can be free-flowing. The individual person is often a conductor between the source of power and its intended endpoint. Many people use wards or shields to protect themselves from undesirable conditions rather than delineating a particular space to separate themselves from outside forces.

However, some folkloric traditionalists believe in creating a hallowed place, or outlining a circle, to protect an area for ritual use. Some folk magick users circumnavigate a tree, standing stone, or ritual space three times. Celebrations may take place within that area, and workings can be done. Others do not use a circular area in their rituals at all. Many seasonal rites are performed in house-to-house processions, as a folk dance on the town square, or as a skit in a private building such as a restaurant or pub. These include ritualized dramatizations, or folkplays, which are very open to the public.

In common magick, energetic beings and forces may or may not be viewed as associated with a particular direction or element. Some entities might be seen as elementals, such as fairies or earth spirits. They may be significant to a working or celebration. Beings can be greeted, called upon, or simply acknowledged, but not necessarily invoked or asked to participate. People may politely request the entities' intervention in certain situations. The beings may be given offerings in reverence, supplication, or propitiation. Some people do not work with elements or their associated beings at all.

Common magick was and is practiced within a family or by individuals, communities of friends, or trade guilds. Rites are attended by a group of revelers, like-minded individuals from the same town, or an extended family or tribe, called a *teulu* in the Welsh language, or a *tribh* or *tuath* in Irish Gaelic. Some folk magick users practice as solitaries.

Groups who engage in folkloric traditions can have members who are all genders, sexual orientations, and expressions of sexuality. In the past, some witches, shamans, and old-line Pagans were gender-fluid or gender-nonconforming. This is still true today. When performing magick or participating in a folkloric ritual, intent often matters far more than biological sex or gender. However, in some rites, certain roles were traditionally given to specific people; for example, a young woman portraying a springtime goddess.

Common magick traditions are passed on by observation and participation through extended families or by individuals imparting knowledge to peers. Elders and adepts teach younger people or newbies. Rites of passage were and are performed, but there are no formal dedications or "degrees" earned by learning and practicing. There might be an apprenticeship which lasts for the traditional year and a day. When initiation ceremonies took place, they were based upon passing from one state of being to another, such as becoming a journeyman blacksmith, attaining adulthood, or becoming a first-time parent.

In past times, there really weren't any "clergy" within folkloric magico-religions. Some nature spirituality celebrations and workings have a designated leader, but few of them are expected to know everything—healing, divining, facilitating rites. Often people switch roles of leadership and participation. In a ritual drama, there are usually a narrator and performers rather than a specific leader. Sometimes musicians are the driving force for the rite and there is no narration at all. That said, modern people may want to gain legal clergy status for the purpose of officiating at weddings and for other reasons.

Many different methods of raising, storing, and directing energy are used within common magick. Anything that creates a physical change, including involving personal or natural life force, can bring about energetic change. Human actions such as dance, song, tying knots, sewing, physical work such as chopping weeds, and yes, lovemaking, can summon power. Natural forces, such as a thunderstorm or growth of crops, or a changing situation, such as sunrise or the first day of winter, can raise energy. Many practitioners simply tap in to existent natural forces, directing them from Point A, the source, to Point B, the desired outcome. Certain objects are believed to attract natural forces, including a wooden wand, a lodestone, a crystal, or a man-made representational item like a mask or drawing. While energy is not always contained in a magick circle, it can be stored in a power object such as a talisman or magickal tool.

In folk magick rites, altars are sometimes used, sometimes not. An altar is a place where magickal implements or venerated objects are stored and displayed. It can serve as a focal point for a ceremony. Natural places such as wellsprings, standing stones, tombs, and sacred trees were and are held in esteem. The workspace of a common magick user can be the hearth, the kitchen table, or a picnic bench in the backyard. Shrines dedicated to particular entities are also used.

Folkloric magick practitioners might put on distinctive garments, such as robes, to enact a ceremony. These outfits might be of a particular color related to the seasons or might represent a specific entity. The robe is viewed by some as a repository of energy and as a device to help people feel more prepared to perform rituals. Other folks feel more comfortable in ethnic or historic attire, or they might wear their everyday clothing, the uniform of their profession, or "fancy dress" as is worn to go to dinner or a job interview. For ritual dramas, people often constructed costumes from whatever was handy. Some costumes became very elaborate and were handed down from one generation to the next.

Some people prefer to work magick while "skyclad," wearing nothing but their own skin. Some practitioners find this empowering and feel that it brings them closer to nature. Some believe energy is easier to access when unencumbered by clothing. Since I live in Michigan, where the air is often quite cold in winter and full of biting insects the rest of the time, I usually forgo being skyclad.

A concept many folkloric magico-religions have in common with other faiths is the idea that people will live during another lifetime after this current incarnation. The concept of life after death was found amongst pre-Wiccan folk traditions of the British Isles. There are many examples in Celtic literature about a land of the dead, Summerland, or otherworld where souls went after death. Celtic legends tell of those who were reborn as, or transmigrated into, animals, landforms, or supernatural entities. The Germanic tribes believed in the concept of *wyrd*, which is not quite the same as reincarnation but has overtones of predestination, not unlike the Greek belief in fate. Of course, some believe in Valhalla, heaven, or permanent residence in a Summerland.

Like many other Pagan religions or magickal folkways, common magick is governed by ethics in the use of power. We endeavor to work our magick responsibly and mindfully with consideration toward the consequences of our actions.

Common magick can easily be performed in conjunction with Wicca, Druidry, heathenry, and/or neo-Paganism, including casting a ritual circle, invoking elements and deities, toasting the gods, using an altar, and having leadership of a priestess and priest. Folkloric rites are best used as the "body" of a Wiccan ceremony or during the same holiday as a separate celebration outside of a Wiccan ritual circle. Folkloric rituals can also stand on their own.

Unique Concepts

Folk magick traditionalists have several ways of looking at the world, and of performing esoteric workings, that are different from other magico-religious practices. We have some distinctive concepts that may seem unfamiliar.

Common magick not only means the rituals of the common people, it also alludes to the common sources of power. Folk magick taps into the deep pools of energy created by rituals that have been performed over hundreds of years, or the reserves of power found in nature. The energy pools are somewhat like the "collective unconscious" written about by Dr. Carl Jung.[4] Common magick also replenishes the energy taken from these reserves.

Folk magick users often believe in a concept called "priordination." (Note: This concept is not the same as "preordination," or the belief that events and circumstances are predetermined or destined by fate.) Priordination means manifesting a condition that had previously occurred by symbolically reenacting that situation during the present time. An example is doing a ritual hunting dance to create plentitude.

The spoken word is not always utilized in folk magico-religions. Ritual participants use imagery, movement, and music to bring about a desired situation, as much as or more than using words to speak their intent into reality. Many common magick ceremonies are acted out in the form of a skit or street theater called a folkplay. These rituals tap in to a deep wellspring of culture and heritage and connect participants with the divine. They are believed to cause priordination to occur. The folklorist Sir James George Frazer theorized that "ritual dramatizations" drew upon the concepts of sacrifice, death, and rebirth.[5]

However, common magick practitioners do sometimes use verbalization for spell work. This can include singing, chanting, and speaking words of power.

---

4. C. G. Jung, *The Archetypes and the Collective Unconscious*, vol. 9, *Collected Works of C. G. Jung*, trans. R. F. C. Hull (Princeton, NJ: Princeton University Press, 1969).

5. James George Frazer, *The Magic Art and the Evolution of Kings*, vol. 1 of *The Golden Bough: A Study in Magic and Religion* (London: Macmillan, 1976).

Many of us believe that we can actually speak events into manifestation via a direct communication with a magickal source.

Many nature-spirituality adherents believe that various entities have a personal relationship with human populations as ancestors, deities, heroes, guides, or helpful spirits. Common magick users may employ what Jung called archetypes such as the Mother, the Hero, the Villain, or the Healer.[6] These archetypes are akin to what Wiccans and neo-Pagans recognize as god and goddess forms. Like other magico-religions, folkloric spirituality traditionalists may practice "invoking" magickal entities or archetypes by talking to the beings and asking for assistance. "Aspecting" means that the individual strives to promote characteristics of the entity such as courage or nurturing. "Avataring" takes the process one step further. To avatar means temporarily contain the persona of a magickal entity, not only taking on their aspects, but allowing them to inhabit one's physical body and take over one's consciousness.

While performing in a ritual drama such as a folk dance or folkplay is incredibly fun, the action also presents a great opportunity to avatar a god-form or magickal entity. Doing so can bring about priordination of beneficial events and tap in to a reserve of magickal power. It can create an attunement with a deity and universal sources of energy. How to go about these processes will be explored within this book.

Of course, our preliterate forebearers did not actually use terms like *archetype*, *theistic*, *avatar*, or *priordination*. They were more likely to say, "I'm being Govannon now," before picking up their magickally charged venerated object—a hammer—to put shoes onto their horses' feet. Modern terms are used here simply as a method of explanation.

Folklore, Folktales, Legend, and Myth

Folkloric magico-religions are intimately connected to folk stories and legends. This is especially true of British common magick.

As mentioned, folkways contain information from a particular culture. Folklore is about peoples' actions and practices and the reasoning behind their activities. This is important because we often no longer have village elders or wise grandparent figures who are willing to share information and then demonstrate

---

6. Jung, *Archetypes and the Collective Unconscious.*

how to use it. Folklore can give advice about the weather; tips for farming, cooking, hunting, or craftsmanship; and instruction on how to practice magickal rituals, spells, and workings.

Although our forebears were, of necessity, practical people, they also enjoyed a rich heritage of myths, legends, folktales, and fairy tales. Legends and myths are inspiring tales of gods and glorious heroes. Folktales and fairy tales often contain supernatural beings such as spirits, fairies, and elementals. The tales with morals or axioms to live by are called fables. Readers might instantly recognize fairy tales cataloged by non-English authors Hans Christian Andersen, Charles Perrault, and the Brothers Grimm, yet many stories originated in the British Isles. There are Irish tales that are similar to the German "Rumpelstiltskin," Welsh sea maidens that resemble Andersen's "Little Mermaid," evil fairies like the one in "Sleeping Beauty," and helpful beings that have similarities to the fairy godmother in "Cinderella." Some fairy stories, such as "Goldilocks and the Three Bears," "Jack and the Beanstalk," and "The Three Little Pigs," came from England.

One of the most popular epics worldwide involves King Arthur and the Knights of the Round Table. Much of the body of literature surrounding Arthur came from Celtic legend. The quests represented magickal journeys and dream workings, while the stories provided insight into proper behavior. The notion of chivalry arose from Celtic codes of ethics, including honor and bravery.

Legends, myths, folktales, and fairy tales are important because they connect people through common experience. The tales are relatable—in any society, people need to feel brave, to assuage loneliness, or to acquire wisdom. Folktales can also provide a touchstone for cultural heritage. Reading or hearing these stories helps to foster understanding between communities. Myths and legends are still relevant today, including newly created tales such as those viewed in superhero movies.

There is some disagreement between folklorists, historians, and anthropologists about the "real" meaning of certain folktales…just as there are amongst modern Wiccans, witches, and Pagans. Our folklore naturally changed over time as certain portions were forgotten and others embellished. This is called mutation of a folkway. Some practices and beliefs merged with those of host cultures or invading populations. This is called syncretization. Some legends were translated from their native languages into Latin and then into English, losing certain parts of the plot or theme in the translation. Some tales were written down by Christian monks, and later by academics. Many writers were well-meaning and respectful, while others were disdainful of the common people and their folk-ways. Some authors of older anthropology books used terms like *rude, primitive, illiterate, vulgar, rustic,* and *quaint* to describe folk practices. However, if one reads between the lines, one can discover a wealth of folk customs, beliefs, and stories that contain genuine examples of magick.

Fairy tales are vital to a culture because they connect humans with the uncanny, the divine, or the spiritual world. They provide a sense of wonderment. Fairy tales can give insight into the behaviors of magickal beings. Many of them contain common magick beliefs, advisories about dealing with the unseen world, and even some spells and rituals.

My Own Personal Testimony—and a Disclaimer

I am very lucky to have been part of a family that still practiced some of the older folkloric magico-religious traditions of the British Isles. Some early memories include chasing an uncle who was wearing antlers on his head in commemoration of a sacred hunt. As a disabled child, this gave me a profound sense of empower-ment. I fell asleep listening to the music of fiddles and dulcimers, which brought good dreams and a feeling of peace. My grandmother prepared traditional foods like oatcakes, venison, and cabbage rolls, which nourished our young bodies and minds. Although we lived in a modern house during the winter, we did things like setting wards and driving pins into the window frames, which imparted a sense of security. When seeing spirits, my grandfather gave suggestions about how to interact with them. So many people of my generation were told that speaking to the departed was a figment of the imagination, or worse, a psychotic condi-tion. Members of an old-line Pagan tradition were often schooled in divining the future and dealing with spirit people, right alongside their arithmetic and geogra-phy lessons.

My family's folkways come from the folk traditions of the southeastern por-tion of Wales, bordering the western counties of England, which was called the Marches. People who emigrated from this region settled in Michigan's northern Lower Peninsula and the Upper Peninsula and became farmers, lumber workers, sailors, fisherfolk, and miners. Some of them were forcibly removed from the Brit-ish Isles as convicts during land grabs, others came as indentured servants, and still others moved to the US willingly. Their Cymric (Welsh) traditions merged with Cornish, Finnish, and Germanic folkways and the praxes of indigenous tribes in the region. These folks practiced some authentically older customs including hunting ceremonies, folk healing, honoring spirits of the land, seasonal celebrations, sweat cleansing, traditional dances and music, and folk magick. I have endeavored to pass on these folkways to my own descendants and to seekers at various events and gatherings.

So, Is Magick Real?

People sometimes wonder if magick actually works. They may think that practitioners are deluding themselves or seeking a correlation that isn't really valid. They attribute a ritual's fantastic outcome to the person's own subconscious or to coincidence. Some people even consider magick a type of scientific reaction that we do not yet understand. And I cannot argue, because they might be right. As of yet, we don't really understand what makes magick function. All that I know for certain is that magick does work. I will share some instances of successful workings and rites, although keep in mind these are subjective, as they cannot be proven.

In 2010 I was diagnosed with ovarian cancer. Lab tests revealed anomalies, and doctors assigned an elevated rating on the scale to measure such things. While I underwent the recommended surgery, I refused all of the prescribed drugs, chemotherapy, and radiation. Although ovarian cancer has a very high mortality rate and chance of recurring less than five years after surgery, as of this writing (2019) I am still surviving. Why? Myself and loved ones performed numerous ceremonies. I wore healing amulets, drank nasty-tasting herbal concoctions, did daily meditations, and thanked my gods. My familiar kitty slept with me and offered me comfort. Now, of course I do not recommend that anyone else refuse medicines or treatments prescribed by a knowledgeable healthcare provider in favor of charms and rites. This was a decision based on my own personal aversion to conventional Western medicine, the expense, and having to sit in bed rather than be outdoors. I knew the risks, which could have included pain and death. Other people may make a very different decision in regard to healthcare, and I respect their choices. Yet I feel magick helped me to heal.

Another incident involved my husband, who had to drive forty miles to work at three o'clock in the morning on dangerous country roads through swamps and forests. Some Michigan back roads are not plowed well during the winter and can accumulate deep snow and slippery ice. My husband had several accidents where he hit a deer, had one unfortunate encounter with a sloppy drunk driver, and had a large tree fall onto his truck during a wild thunderstorm. He escaped unscathed from each accident, although our insurance agent was quite displeased with him. Quitting his job was not an option; it was during the recession, employment was scarce, and he had to get to work. We implored the god of the woodlands for protection, put talismans in my husband's vehicle, and did a ceremony each morning before he left to drive to his job. The accidents stopped, and he was soon transferred to a closer work location. Again, I believe that magick was the reason.

I have witnessed people use magick for a healthy childbirth, to give them confidence in a job interview, to attain good grades in school, to protect their homes and workspaces, to keep them safe while serving in the military, to guard them while travelling, to win justice in a court case, to release an elder who desired to leave this life for the next, and to attract the perfect marriage partner. Some of these incidents might be explained by coincidence, self-hypnosis, or acting in accord. However, some of them have no tangible explanation other than magick. I have seen a person do a rite to calm the air spirits during a tornado, and their house was the only one on the block that remained undamaged. If that is a coincidence, it is a pretty amazing one.

Does magick always work? Not every single time we make a wish, or we'd all win the lottery and our pets would live forever. Magick cannot go against natural law, add numbers to a circumstance where the odds are zero, or make someone act against their own free will. The gods might have their own ideas about what lessons a person needs to learn or which course of action is best. Magick *can* increase the probability that something will occur. It can broaden possibilities. Energetic workings can change difficult circumstances for the better. Magick can also augment success in a current situation. Especially when we act in accord.

Attunement with the natural world and communication with spirits also have a very beneficial result. I have seen people perform divination and predict events that they could not possibly expect, given current conditions and use of ordinary logic. Mediums whom I have encountered gave insights into situations that they could not realistically have known about otherwise. Military veterans have used meditation and shamanic techniques to control post-traumatic stress. Trauma survivors have used magickal rites to raise confidence and to feel empowered. Again, can ceremonies fix everything? Not always, but I believe they certainly can help.

The Quest

This book explores the whys and wherefores of some British-based folk traditions and showcases many folkloric practices. Readers can bring these delightful folkways to their own spiritual practice. I list natural objects used in magick, tools that people can find in their home, garage, workplace, in nature, or at a local store; energetic beings such as fairies, animal spirits, and deities; some appropriate times and locations for esoteric rites; and many methods and techniques people have used for magickal workings. There is an outline of steps to take in performing spells and rituals and cautions about what not to do. People are perfectly capable of writing their own personalized spells, and because these workings are unique, they'll have much more power than anything I can discuss, whether it's ancient or not.

It's also suggested that people go outdoors, open themselves to the powers of the earth, do some divination, develop their own psychic interaction with magickal entities, and put the nature back in nature spirituality. Have fun on the quest!

two
MAGICKAL PRINCIPLES
AND ENERGY BASICS

In order for you to better understand common magick, I will first explore some basic esoteric principles that are universal among all magico-religious systems. Then I'll discuss how these magickal principles apply to folkloric nature spirituality.

Common magick of course utilizes magickal energy, or natural powers or forces which are not fully understood and cannot be scientifically explained. Practitioners have constructed methods of harnessing these powers and can use them to create change on the material level or for personal transformation within themselves.

Magickal energy is somewhat like electricity and shares many of its specific qualities. Like handling live electric wires, one must be careful while using magickal energy. Folklore has many examples of those who thoughtlessly used magick and suffered the consequences. And like electricity, magickal power has a source, a conduit, and a receptacle.

Source

While magick users acknowledge there is a source for magickal energy, we do not always agree on what or where that source is. It may include the powers of the universe or universal consciousness. The source may be viewed as the unseen world, the primal forces of nature, the otherworld, or spirit. Many old-line Pagans visualized the fount of power as a god or goddess, higher entities with divine qualities, or as energetic beings like elementals, fairies, or spirits.

Some traditional witches believe that there is a universal power or current that is not personified. This might be called a "life spark." After the discovery of atoms, some practitioners envisioned the source of energy as the electrons which occur in all organic beings. Regardless of your beliefs, there are many ways you can raise your energy.

Burning a candle or bonfire raises energy. Natural forces, such as the wind and the tides, also generate power. Human actions like drawing, writing, dancing, carving, and knitting raise your energy. Repetitive movements such as churning butter or tying knots in a piece of yarn can be utilized, as can walking in place—sometimes without saying a word. Performing ritual actions can raise energy. These sources of energy can be used as "fuel" for a magickal rite.

Conduit

Magickal energy can be directed with certain objects, sometimes called ritual tools, such as a wand, crystal, or ceremonial knife. An example is using the force generated during a thunderstorm to help someone heal from an illness. A wand is pointed toward the storm cloud while the practitioner gathers the energy. Then the magick user aims and guides the power into the intended recipient by pointing the wand at them. In this instance, the wand is considered a conduit that directs the energy.

The individual who is channeling or directing the energy is also a conduit for power. Like electricity, magickal energy has the strongest force near its origin—the person who is closest to the source of power. Hence, one's own will, intent, and focus are the most important part of any magickal action. Intent can be defined as the ability to make thoughtful choices about one's actions and behaviors. Will has the connotations of thought, personal strength, fortitude, and wisdom. Many old-line Pagans are firm believers in willpower. We believe we can work our will on the universe when employing magick. Intent is carefully considered, then energy is focused on attaining the true will. The person's intent is just as crucial for a magickal rite as the energy drawn and harnessed to bring it to life.

Energy itself is neither good nor bad, in the same way as electricity is neither good nor bad. Electricity can be used to power an appliance or to cause a painful shock. In its raw form, energy is like lightning: untamed, beautiful, and dangerous. The intent and purpose of the person directing the energy is what causes that power to be viewed as good, positive, beneficial, or helpful—or negative, harmful, or baneful.

Likewise, the result of the magickal working can be seen as good or bad depending on one's point of view. Emotions can be considered good or bad (for example, loving or hateful), and one's emotions concerning energy may affect its outcome. Malevolent or spiteful intent can cause harmful results. Good, loving, positive intent can cause a beneficial result.

Receptacle

The receptacle is the situation, object, or person that receives the magickal charge. In the above example, the person who receives the healing energy from the thunderstorm is the receptacle. A practitioner can also guide power into themselves.

Energy can be stored in various items for later use, just as electrical power can be stored in a battery. Many people use jewelry, a talisman, crystals, sculptures, or a magickal tool to contain energy that they might need later. Just like a battery, people, objects, places, and conditions can lose energy over time. They can be drained of power, but they can also be recharged.

Active and Passive Magick

Magick can be active (used to create change on the material level) or passive (used to acquire knowledge or to create change within oneself). "Active" and "passive" are not value judgments, merely ways of identifying the methods and outcome of the magickal working.

Active Magick

The ancient Greeks used the word *thaumaturgy* for the practice of using energy to cause adjustments to the physical world. Thaumaturgy translates as "wonderworking." It is a more active type of magick. Using the power of a thunderstorm to bring about healing is an example of thaumaturgy. Practitioners can use other objects and actions to raise, direct, and store energy; for instance, painting a sigil on a doorpost to repel harmful beings or wearing an amulet to attract prosperity. They can also use movement and gestures, such as dancing, to bring about a bountiful harvest. Verbalization, like speaking words of power, can ensure a safe journey.

Combining symbolic ingredients, using magickal tools, and performing physical actions and verbalizations for esoteric purposes are all examples of active magick. This is sometimes called casting a spell, performing a working, or practicing witchcraft. Magickally charged items and ritualized behaviors are used in conjunction with the practitioner's will and intent to create a desired condition in the material world.

Figure 1: Daisy wheel

Passive Magick

Many people who practice folkloric traditions have the goal of attunement with energetic forces or entities for personal empowerment and spiritual well-being. The ancient Greek word *theurgy* means performing magickal rituals for the purpose of connecting with deity, acquiring knowledge, and for self-improvement. Theurgy translates as "divine working" and is considered a more passive, receptive, intuitive type of magick.

Theurgy is similar to thaumaturgy in that it can also use words of power, gestures, and movement; physical objects, such as a crystal used for gazing during divination; or a statue as a focal point for communication with spirits. However, there is a different intention and outcome. Rather than directing magickal energy to cause noticeable alterations to the material world, passive magick creates internal change. This might mean calming the emotions or gaining insight.

Both passive and active magick use energy, will, intent, and focus for the purposes of creating change for beneficial purposes.

Spells, Workings, Rites, and Rituals

In this book, I will use the terms *working* or *spell* for a smaller act of magick, such as speaking a bedtime prayer aloud, drawing a symbol in the condensation in the window, or mixing herbs together. A rite or ritual is a larger act of magick, which can include a spell or further actions and verbalizations. I can perform a working of embroidering a sigil onto a shirt while singing a prayer-song during a particular phase of the moon; together, this makes a ritual. A ceremony can include several different actions, such as invocations to deities, along with rites, spells, and workings. Sometimes, magick practitioners use the words rite, ritual, and ceremony interchangeably.

Of course, people who practiced common magick in olden times did not say, "Hold my beer, I'm fixin' to do some thaumaturgy." They used phrases like bespelling, bewitching, doing a laying-on, conjuring, enchanting, charming, and "witching" or "hexing." These last two words did not necessarily have any negative connotation. For more passive magick, some terms included *jumping the stile* (wall), *riding the hedge, seeing, divining, soothsaying,* or *taking the spirit road.*

Magickal Principles

English magician Aleister Crowley wrote that magick was a process of using ones' will to effect change.[7] This is sometimes called "bringing force into form." Although they may not define magick in the same manner as ceremonial magicians or witches, folk magick practitioners utilize certain principles, or natural laws, to work with energy for the purpose of causing change. These magickal principles were recognized by Sir James George Frazer in his anthropological work *The Golden Bough.*[8] Author P. E. Isaac Bonewits also wrote about these principles in great detail.[9] These magickal laws, principles, and practices include:

- The Law of Sympathy: This is when a symbolic object or action is used to represent a desired condition. It is also called imitative magick because the condition imitates the object. For example, a person may place a

---

7. Aleister Crowley, Mary Desti, and Leila Waddell, *Magick: Liber ABA, Book 4,* ed. Hymenaeus Beta (Newburyport, Massachusetts: Weiser Books, 1998).

8. Frazer, *Magic Art and the Evolution of Kings.*

9. P. E. Isaac Bonewits, *Real Magic: An Introductory Treatise on the Basic Principles of Yellow Magic* (Newburyport, Massachusetts: Weiser Books, 1972).

rooster spur on a shop's door to repel thieves because roosters drive away predators. The use of the law of sympathy is often called sympathetic magick.

+ Correspondence: This is a type of sympathetic magick in which sigils, planetary signs, colors, or other symbols represent, or correspond to, the desired condition. For instance, the color blue corresponds to a calm sea, and thus I wear blue clothing when embarking on a journey.

+ The Law of Attraction: This term is often used interchangeably with the law of sympathy. For our purposes, it only refers to objects or actions that attract certain conditions. For instance, I will do a ritual dance to summon good weather before I gather my crops.

+ The Law of Repulsion: This is the opposite of attraction magick because it repels a situation. An example of repulsion magick is a person wearing garlic bulbs to scare away malevolent forces. Repulsion magick still uses symbols and thus is a form of sympathetic magick.

+ The Law of Contagion: This means that one object's properties or qualities will rub off on another object or create a similar situation by contact between items. This is also called catching or contact magick. Think of the word "contagious." An example of contagion is placing a toad in someone's pocket so that the toad becomes ill rather than the person.

+ Polarity: This is the notion that opposites cause a magickal charge. Such qualities as male/female, dark/light, and above/below are examples of polarity. Like the positive and negative parts of a battery that cause an electrical charge, polar opposites can create energy. Sacred sexuality such as the Great Rite uses this concept. Common magick users might embrace this practice when arranging for the fertility of animals or crops.

+ Synthesis: This is the process of combining two or more things or conditions, which creates a new whole. The conception of a baby is an example of synthesis. Sunlight, water, soil, and a seed combine to create a plant.

Some magickal practices employed within common magick will be familiar to people of various magico-religious systems. Folkloric traditions may have a different approach, and varying methods, to these praxes. These include:

+ Alchemy: This is the process of transforming one state of being into another. In a popular folktale, straw is spun into gold. Every time someone prepares a cup of tea or mixes garden soil with manure as fertilizer, alchemy is working on a physical level. Alchemy also includes personal transformation, such as turning sadness into joy.

+ Channeling: This includes using the body, will, or emotions to move a force according to one's desire; for example, channeling the power of love toward an infant during midwifery work. Channeling a spirit, also called spirit communication, is relating to energetic beings for the purpose of learning, understanding, and companionship.

+ Divination: This is a magickal praxis that involves viewing past events that are relevant to current situations, using omens to understand certain conditions, or foretelling the future. Divination is considered a more passive type of magick, in which the seeker receives knowledge. In folk magick traditions, ordinary household implements or natural objects are used to divine the future, such as seeing a portent in a flight of birds.

+ Speaking into Being: This utilizes the traditional folk belief in "true-speaking," meaning that whatever words a truthful person speaks will come into manifestation. The individual's breath, as well as their intent, connects them to the verbalization. The words are perceived and understood by a source, such as a deity or the universe, and become true on the material plane. This can also work for emotional truths; try saying, "I am confident."

Other Magickal Conditions

Liminality

Common magick users of the past noticed that certain times and locations were the best for performing magick and used them to their advantage. "Liminal" occasions, places, and conditions are considered as transitional, or said to exist between certain circumstances, especially endings and beginnings. A liminal period is the brief time which occurs between two different events. A liminal place might have two or more boundaries that meet. An example is the beach at midnight, where earth, water, and sky meet while one day is beginning and another is ending. Locations which are liminal can also be man-made, such as a doorway or bridge. These times and spaces are considered "both and neither," fluid, and thus especially powerful for doing works of folkloric magick.

There are two magickal principles within common magick that are not often found in other esoteric systems. These are the concept of an accumulated energy source (available to people of a particular family, ethnicity, country, tribe, or group) and the notion of priordination.

Priordination is one of the most important philosophies of common magick. It means invoking a prior circumstance to bring about a continuance or reoccurrence of a desired situation. The rites or reenactments connected to the past condition may not entirely resemble the anticipated outcome, so it's not quite the same as sympathetic magick. An example is riding a toy horse around a garden to cause healthy growth in the plants. Priordination includes traditional beliefs, like the notion that opening an umbrella will cause rain. It also encompasses ritualized behaviors such as putting on the same pair of socks for every baseball game to help your team to win. An axiom for this process of priordination is "What once was, now shall be again."

Although he did not call it "priordination," Sir James George Frazer theorized that certain symbolic acts represented the death and rebirth of a sacrificial king or god-form, which were used in ceremonies to summon fertility.[10] An example is an enactment of ritualized combat between the Oak King and Holly King, the Summer Lord and Winter Lord, or, in some folkplays, King George versus a villainous knight. Folkloric traditionalists perform these symbolic battles at certain times of the year, usually late spring and around the first day of winter. The purpose is to help one season to end and another to begin.

Magickal Reserves

People engage in rites of priordination in order to tap in to, or to store power within, a magickal container of energetic force. As mentioned in the first chapter, many common magick practitioners believe in a deep reservoir of power that has been created over time. The accumulated energy can be imagined as an immense storehouse or bank. Some of the other metaphors for the energetic reserve include a treasure chest, a fairy mound, a cairn, a stockpile, or a castle. In keep-

10. Frazer, *Magic Art and the Evolution of Kings.*

ing with our electricity metaphor, we can visualize this magickal container as an enormous battery that stores a great deal of power.

My own folk refer to the reservoir of power as a magickal pool of energy. It can be envisioned as a wellspring. Imagery includes drawing water with a bucket, replenishing, quenching, cleansing, and partaking of healing waters. The energetic pool is refilled, supplied, and flooded (in a good way) whenever we consciously perform magickal acts. These metaphors may have come about because my ancestors in the British Isles were surrounded by water and we currently live in the Great Lakes region of the US.

The concept of an energy pool is rather like what Dr. Carl Jung called "the collective unconscious," a repository of combined memories, thought-forms, and emotions of a large group of people.[11] Many folk magick practitioners believe that the power reserve contains not only the shared intelligence of humans, but also energy generated by their actions. The reservoir also contains the forces of nature and energy of unseen beings.

Many of us believe that engaging in magickal rites contributes to our community's magickal pool, but we also believe that positive human emotions raise power and refill our wellspring. This may be why so many folk customs such as dances and folkplays are lighthearted, even silly. Holiday celebrations, with their many delightful rituals, can refill the energy pool for months. Every time we laugh, dance, make love, sing, create something, appreciate beauty, engage in intellectual pursuits, build something, or perform an act of magick, we add to our common energy pool.

Many common magick users believe this magickal reservoir can be used as a source of power to access to bring about change. We may journey to the magickal pool for knowledge and spiritual renewal. We believe that the energy pool is a place we can access in times of trouble or emotional upheaval in order to recharge our own batteries or quench our thirst.

Psychic Abilities and Attunement

Old-line Pagans who practice folk magick recognize that psychic capabilities are perfectly natural. We feel our psychic talents are a great gift, much like the ability

---

11. Jung, *Archetypes and the Collective Unconscious.*

to sing, play basketball, play an instrument, ice skate, or any other art or sport. Practice makes perfect.

Common magick users sometimes call psychic abilities seeing, insight, sooth-saying, channeling, having a sixth sense, kenning, or knowing. Talents include contact with spirits, both those of magickal entities and departed humans, some-times called spiritualism; an ability to use divination to access information that is otherwise hidden; healing touch; and telepathic or intuitive powers, which includes the ability to hear, see, feel, or know things that other people cannot.

In a society that is dependent on documentation and physical evidence, psy-chic ability is sometimes disbelieved by the majority. If people cannot see the stars, they might doubt that any constellations are up there. Unfortunately, in this time and place, having psychic abilities might require taking some precautions so that intuitive people do not "burn out" mentally, emotionally, and spiritually. People who are empathic may need to use techniques such as grounding, centering, anchoring, and shielding before engaging in psychic activities.

While attunement is considered a more passive, receptive type of magick, it still requires energy and focus. Also called alignment, it is the processes of bring-ing one's soul, consciousness, or being into harmony or agreement with other souls, consciousnesses, or entities. Attunement can include striving to under-stand the qualities of animals, plants, landforms, seasons, and the spiritual world. Mostly, this occurs during magickal ceremonies, journeys to the spirit realm, or interactions with nature. Common magick practitioners use techniques to access the spirit world that include lucid dreaming, trance work, and astral projection. Some practitioners also employ meditation. Attunement may or may not include making changes to the physical world once knowledge has been acquired.

three
ETHICS

Over the years, folk traditionalists have developed a system of ethics for the practice of the magickal arts. Practitioners have been entrusted with the ability to direct and utilize powerful forces, which means taking on a great responsibility. Thus, there is a set of religious-based and/or ethical directives around the use of magickal energies, communication with the spirit realm, and interaction with the non-magickal community.

Whenever there is a rule forbidding something, it's because somebody already tried doing it. The action may have been thoughtless, harmful, or even fatal. Think of the signs on large metal trash dumpsters that say something along the lines of "Caution! Do not play on or around." This is probably because someone once climbed on a dumpster, it fell over, and they got squashed. The sign was later put on all dumpsters so that other people could learn to avoid problems.

Folktales as Cautionary Tales

Many of the rules for British folkloric traditions are found, of course, in folktales. These stories may seem to be simple entertainment on the surface, but quite a few of them contain suggestions or proscriptions about human behaviors. This includes recommendations about the use of magick and interaction with the spirit world.

Folktales give a warning to be nice to people with disabilities because they might be a god in disguise. They advise not being greedy when performing a working because everything the spell has attained might vanish in a puff of smoke. Some folktales caution people to revere nature or historic sites because destroying a sacred tree that is home to pixies will cause all manner of bad luck and problems. Folktales about fairies and goblins tell readers to carry an iron nail or a rowan twig to keep people from becoming possessed—which might be a good idea when trying to focus on a goal, preventing distractions and minor annoyances. There are also lots of fictitious witches who worked magick for harm and got their comeuppance.

A fable is a short folk story with an advisory purpose. It contains a moral, or an adage, proverb, maxim, or saying that clearly imparts a lesson about a desired behavior. For example, Aesop's *Tortoise and the Hare* contains the adage "Slow and steady wins the race."[12] The fable "Belling the Cat" is about a group of mice who agreed to place a bell on a cat so they would be aware of danger.[13] However, the mice realized that their idea was impossible, as no one volunteered to put the bell on the cat. The moral is that plans must be evaluated to see if they'll actually work. These homilies can be applied to the practice of magick.

Not all folktales or folkplays have an obvious moral or proverb. More often, the recommended conduct is implied within the body of a story. For example, the Robin Hood legends, which began as poems, ballads, and plays, communicated that gallantry, rebellion against imperialism, working in harmony with nature, and generosity toward the poor are favorable behaviors. Many folktales emphasize honoring the elderly. Often, gods took on the guise of a helpless beggar to test a hero's compassion. If the protagonist acted charitably, they were rewarded. According to Sir James George Frazer, a profound theme of many ritual dramas and folk stories is sacrifice.[14]

Some fairy tales, legends, and stories have multiple layers, and the listener or reader must draw their own conclusions. Over the course of centuries, the folktales' tropes and ethical standards have seeped into the people's collective unconscious.

---

12. Aesop, *Aesop's Fables*, trans. William Caxton (London: 1484).

13. Sybil Marshall, "Belling the Cat," in *The Book of English Folk Tales* (London: Duckworth Overlook, 1981).

14. Frazer, *Magic Art and the Evolution of Kings*.

Honor/Enech, Treading Lightly, and Consent

The Celtic tribes, who inhabited Britain from the Bronze Age onward, had many legends and folktales which contained their codes of ethics. Their values included honesty, fidelity, hospitality, justice, and courage. Stories told of the great valor of warriors, landowners who held generous feasts, people who made good on their debts, and wizards who created change to benefit an entire nation. Lovely inscribed posters with the Celtic values, which can be purchased at esoteric shops or printed from the internet, remind us of our ethical responsibilities. All of these qualities comprised a state of *anrhydedd*, which is the Cymraeg (Welsh) word for "honor."

The concept of *enech*, which translates from Irish Gaelic as "face," relates to putting your best face forward, saving face, facing up to things, and being able to face your family, tribe, and society with a good conscience. Enech was codified into Irish law during the seventh century.[15] The Cymraeg word *wyneb* is a similar construct. Both terms imply honor, pride, not bringing shame upon your family or tribe, and performing actions that ultimately benefitted the community. Enech has connotations of valor, reliability, integrity, and acting with respect. It meant gaining a reputation as an honorable person. This was imparted to British litera-ture in later years as the high concept of chivalry that dominated epic poetry and sagas.

The Matter of Britain, or King Arthur legends, are examples of Welsh folk-tales and poems that later made their way into literature across Europe.[16] They contain examples of honor, bravery, charity, loyalty and noble deportment. These sets of values were used as a guideline for behavior in British society in bygone days; they were not just for magick users, but were applicable to all walks of life. Some of these values made their way into British common law.

Treading Lightly

The honor system for common magick is a bit different from other western eso-teric traditions. For instance, many Wiccans utilize a rede, a poetic law, to codify

---

15. S. J. Connolly, ed., "Enech," in *The Oxford Companion to Irish History* (Oxford: Oxford University Press, 2002).

16. John Jay Parry and Robert Caldwell, "Geoffrey of Monmouth," in *Arthurian Literature in the Middle Ages: A Collaborative History*, ed. Roger Sherman Loomis (Oxford: Oxford University Press, 1959).

their ethical system, summarized as "Do as you will, as it harms none." This means to enact your own free will while attempting to cause no damage. However, to actually harm none is not possible. We harm tiny insects whenever we take a step. For this reason, some practitioners of traditional witchcraft usually do not believe in this rede. Instead they elect to use personal responsibility on a per-case basis during the performance of energetic workings.

Those who practice magick must endeavor to cause as little harm as they can to themselves and others. This concept is expressed in the old-line Pagan adage about "treading lightly on the land." We make a commitment to act responsibly, trying to cause the least amount of harm over the long term. We tread lightly so that we do as little damage as possible not only to the land, but to other people as well.

Another goal is to work and strive for the greater good. This is rather like the Athenian philosopher Plato's concept of *eudaemonia*, or human well-being.[17] The values, virtues, and concepts of anrhydedd and enech are the attitudes and actions needed to attain this state.

Free Will and Consent

Since we believe that all people have free will, it follows that individuals must have control over their own destiny. Interfering with others' free will may inadvertently cause them harm. Informed consent is imperative when doing magickal workings with other people. This includes making them aware of intent, the procedures to be used, and the desired outcome. When directing energy for other people, it is also important to secure their consent. Even when performing a healing rite, a practitioner should ask permission of the person receiving the energy.

If a person is unable to give consent—such as a preverbal child, an unconscious patient, or someone who is so badly injured that they cannot talk—then we can speak aloud the intent that our actions will have only positive results. We might give caveats, as in saying that this working is only for the benefit of those involved or will succeed only with the individual's energetic desire, support, consent, and ultimate true will.

---

17. A. W. Price, *Virtue and Reason in Plato and Aristotle* (Oxford: Oxford University Press, 2011).

The Law of Return

Most common magick practitioners believe there is a universal law that causes a rebound of energy onto a person who enacts any specific behavior, magickal or otherwise. This is called a turnabout, a swingaround, a blowback, or the law of return. The law of return asserts that every action has a reaction; every behavior has a consequence. A similar concept is found in the science of physics, where Newton's Law states that each action results in an equal, opposite reaction.[18] We view the law of return as a law like gravity … or like the natural laws which govern electricity.

Many folk magick users believe that actions done with thought, care, and honor will return good, beneficial results to the sender. Harmful actions done for malefic reasons can cause equal or greater harm to the practitioner. This philosophy is found in most world religions.

The belief in the law of return has been scoffed at by some individuals, yet the philosophy has genuine merit. A principle of magick called the law of attraction, or the law of sympathetic magick, says that "like attracts like." This concept is similar to the law of return in that each condition attracts comparable circumstances. Most common magick practitioners believe that energy used for altruistic purposes will rebound onto the sender as positive feelings or beneficial situations, and energy used for harm will bounce back onto the sender as negative conditions and emotions. Because electricity and magickal energy both have more power at the end of the conduit closest to its source, the sender will receive a greater impact than the receiver.

Historically, harmful rites were labeled "black magick" while helpful rituals done for good purposes were designated "white magick." This may also be called the "left-hand path" versus the "right-hand path." Some of us no longer use those terms (black or white, left or right) because of cultural sensitivity. Instead, these terms can be replaced by the words malevolent, harmful, malicious, and baneful (instead of black or left) and benevolent, altruistic, beneficial, positive, helpful, and good (instead of white or right).

Some occultists believe that any magick done for a selfish purpose is malevolent, but that's not necessarily true for self-actualizing spells as long as positive

---

18. "Newton's Third Law," The Physics Classroom, accessed March 31, 2020, https://www .physicsclassroom.com/class/newtlaws/Lesson-4/Newton-s-Third-Law.

intent and the desire for a mutually beneficial outcome is stressed. For example, a magick user performs a ritual to get a good job based on their skills and merit, stating that no injury will come to the person who currently holds the position. Common magick practitioners must carefully consider their intent, all possible outcomes of their workings, and circumstances surrounding their decisions. We strive to ensure that our actions are beneficial to ourselves and others.

Unfortunately, some magick users adopt no ethical or moral code at all, nor do they take responsibility for their behaviors. They may use "convenience morals," which means doing whatever is convenient for them at the time. This is different from "situational ethics," which means considering a certain situation, then using an ethical code to determine how to proceed.

Some individuals take part in workings and ceremonies that they fully realize are intended for harmful purposes. Some who practice an old-line magico-religion may justify using detrimental practices. They might say, "Our ancestors cursed people," or "A witch who can't hex can't heal." They might rationalize sending negative energies in the name of justice or for personal gain. They might act disdainful toward the idea of applying ethics to the art and praxis of magick. These types of people are to be avoided. Because of the principle of sympathetic magick, they are a magnet for trouble. Since like attracts like, a harmful action can attract further energy that causes injury—to the sender as well as the receiver.

Malicious workings include activities such as cursing, hexing, or using someone else's personal energy without their permission. A curse can strike other people associated with either the magick user or their target, including their minor children. Hexes can bind or attach the magick user to the victim, which is often the exact opposite of the desired result. Curses and hexes can be challenging to undo. The common magick practitioners of Ireland and Wales had a belief that a curse that did not "land" on a target could float around in the ether for seven years, then rebound back on the person that cast the malison in the first place.

Here is an example of how cursing someone can go terribly wrong: During the years of witchcraft persecution in Europe, there were very few witch trials in Wales, and only five people were ever executed for practicing witchcraft. Some anthropologists believe that using divination, spells, herbal potions, talismans, and other folk magick was so ingrained in the Cymric (Welsh) culture that people thought nothing of it. Yet they did not tolerate cursing or using magick for harmful purposes. One woman named Gwen ferch Ellis had performed folk magick for years, healing people and animals, helping with the fertility of crops, and so forth. However, in 1594 her friend became angry at a local gentleman, so Gwen wrote a charm backward for the purpose of casting a *maledythion* (curse) on him. The paper containing the hex was found in the man's home. People accused Gwen of using witchcraft to cause problems, and she became the first person ever in Wales to be hanged as a witch.[19]

The folklore and folk stories of Europe are full of examples of the law of return. In countless fairy tales, those who cast baneful spells or behaved with the intention of harming others usually met a painful demise. In Irish mythology, a baleful witch called Carman blighted the crops and was defeated and imprisoned by the Tuatha Dé Danaan. Carman's three evil sons were banished, and the witch died of grief.[20] In the Scottish version of "Snow White," which is called "Gold-Tree and Silver-Tree," a mother sees her beautiful daughter as a rival and tries to poison her. The wicked mother is outwitted and later, she is poisoned.[21] Shakespeare's Lady Macbeth goaded her husband into regicide, then went insane. In the story of the *Táin Bó Cúailnge* (*The Cattle Raid of Cooley*), soldiers forced a pregnant goddess to run a footrace. The warriors then suffered birth pangs (labor pains) and thus could not fight, afflicting them at their hour of greatest need.[22]

Working with Potentially Destructive Forces

Another consideration for a common magick user is taking precautions when working with certain powers. This is because there is a possibility of damage to the self and others. Some examples include creating energetic beings such as a fetch, using blood in magickal rites, and undertaking necromancy, or summoning the spirits of the departed. Once given power, a fetch or psychopomp can survive for some time, possibly causing difficulties for people and systems unrelated to the original participants. Magick involving blood or the spirits of the dead is

---

19. James McCarthy, *The Story of the First Woman in Wales to be Hanged for Witchcraft*, Wales Online, October 30, 2017, https://www.walesonline.co.uk/news/wales-news/story-first -woman-hanged-wales-13816831.

20. James MacKillop, *A Dictionary of Celtic Mythology* (Oxford: Oxford University Press, 2004).

21. Joseph Jacobs, "Gold-Tree and Silver-Tree," in *Celtic Fairy Tales* (London 1892), https:// www.sacred-texts.com/neu/celt/cft/cft14.htm.

22. Ciaran Carson, trans., *The Táin* (London: Penguin Books, 2007).

viewed as harmful by some cultures, yet many traditions speak to their ancestors. For example, moon (menstrual) blood can be used for fertility of a garden. However, blood is an intrinsically powerful substance and may bind the practitioner to the subject of the rite for an indefinite period of time. It also may attract unwanted beings. Caution is advised.

Necromancy itself is not harmful or bad, but it must be done with care. Some spirits of the dead may just want to rest in peace and will resent being disturbed. Others are happy to help. Of course, demanding that a spirit do something can work as poorly as demanding money from your grandmother. It is better to request aid politely and give sincere thanks.

Some individuals believe that doing certain workings for protection, defense, or returning harmful actions to enact justice are acceptable. This can include binding and hexing. Often, it is easier, more expedient, and better to use magick to create the most beneficial situation possible and to prevent harm or impediments.

Don't Pee in the Magickal Pool

While energy itself is neither good nor bad, the emotional associations of certain energies can have positive or negative connotations. Visitors to sites of great human suffering can sometimes perceive the sorrow, pain, and fear of those who were traumatized at these locations, even if it happened long ago. The "pool" or reservoir of energy associated with these places has a very negative feel.

Common magick practitioners endeavor to tread lightly when doing magick and try to subscribe to an ethical system that emphasizes universal well-being because we believe that using magickal power for harmful purposes can create pools of baneful emotional energy. Cursing someone, hurting an animal to use its pain to fuel workings, or creating a magickal form such as a fetch for the purpose of causing injury can all create a nasty psychic septic tank. It may even pollute the greater magickal pool, contaminating the entire reservoir of communal energy. This can hurt us, our loved ones, and our society.

We also endeavor not to waste power from the energy pool by using magick for what we can accomplish with our own thought or our own physical labor.

Ethics for Interaction with Magickal Beings

Many traditional magick users believe that contact between an individual and certain energetic beings can form a relationship. The connection may be like a benevolent working partnership or an interaction between relatives. Magickal entities are also viewed as sources of power. Therefore, we endeavor to treat these beings with respect.

In British folktales and myths, energy beings are sometimes willing to assist humans with daily activities, like the hob household spirit who helps farmers with threshing grain, or a matron goddess like Dôn, who can lessen the pain of childbirth. In return, there are certain behavioral expectations. Often, the heroes of legend treated the deities and entities as the archetype of a grandmother or the elderly lady next door, a helpful neighbor, a wise consultant, a guild master, or a revered leader. Humans were expected to be courteous and show appreciation. Those who did not were apt to offend their magickal assistants. The entities would no longer provide help.

Many common magick practitioners believe that we should reimburse our sources of energy, similar to how we must pay the electric company that provides our services. Payment can be made by gifts, sacrifices, or reciprocal actions. Tales abound of heroes offering prayers and songs or poetry performed to a deity in exchange for a boon or blessing. At holidays, many folks still leave plates of food out for the ancestor spirits or invite them to join celebrations. Another example is tossing a coin into a well when making a wish or tying a bit of cloth to a tree in exchange for healing. Of course, we thank those who have helped us. Many believe the entities can gain power from human devotion.

Some common magick practitioners believe in appeasing, or propitiating, certain entities. This can mean bribing them to prevent consequences. For example, fairies are given trinkets in order to persuade them to leave humans alone. Spirits of the dead are offered food and things they enjoyed while alive like cigarettes and alcohol, sewing or other hobby tools, poetry and song, and anything that shows appreciation. Many older rites contain sayings and actions to pacify the fairies and spirits.

While some ceremonial magicians see no problem with summoning elementals, spirits, or other magickal beings and giving them orders or commanding them, I do not find this wise. Politeness works much better when interacting with energetic beings.

Of course, politeness and propitiation does not always work with magickal entities. Often historically called evil spirits, demons, imps, or even witches, these malevolent beings can be prevented from doing harm by using spells and ritual objects. Asking for help from an entity with known hostility to humans is also quite unwise. If the being escapes the magick user's temporary control, what is to prevent that entity from turning on its former master? In the most severe cases, the magickal being might need to be banished or removed from the space where it is causing trouble.

Since people who practice nature spirituality have a relationship with natural beings, we honor and respect them by endeavoring to keep their homes clean and by protecting nature. Common magick users try not to waste resources. We strive to reuse things and recycle used items. While some of us are vegetarians, others eat meat. Meat eaters attempt to use every part of the animal and purchase groceries from cruelty-free farms. We thank beings, including animals, who gift us with their energies and physical bodies. We endeavor to "tread lightly" on the physical plane as well as the spiritual realm.

Our Non-Magickal Neighbors

Another consideration magick users must make is how non-magickal people will perceive our community. There is the reason of enech, or face, of course. We have a duty to positively represent ourselves, our families, our folkways, and all folk magico-religions. Yet there are other concerns as well.

People may have a superstitious fear of magickal practitioners because when they think about witches, they think of curses and baneful spells. This is partially the fault of Hollywood and the portrayal of "bad" witches by the media. It is partially the fault of religious orders that associated witchcraft with diabolism or the belief in wizards' contact with entities which were said to prey upon humans. People are sometimes afraid of what they do not understand. Because many individuals cannot perceive the unseen forces that we habitually use, they may be frightened by that energy—and by us. When electricity was introduced as a household tool, some people were afraid of it too.

However, there might be a more concrete reason why non-magickal people fear us: They may have run into a magickal practitioner who had no ethical code. They might have been a victim of malevolent intent. Remember Gwen ferch Ellis. Some people might think, "This happened a long time ago. People aren't afraid of witchcraft these days," yet I often read in the news about discriminatory acts toward magickal people.

Some might think, "If I curse someone, how would anyone know it was me?" They're right, they might not get caught. Instead, people might take out their superstitious fear of the occult on their local esoteric bookshop or on a child whose family is openly Pagan. There's also that law of return to consider.

While some of us may not want to deal with the role of "Pagan ambassador," we might take the opportunity to interact positively with our communities whenever possible.

A Word or Six about Sacrifice

The word "sacrifice" comes from the Latin word *sacer*, meaning "sacred." To sacrifice often involves giving up something, such as part of your meal, energy, a charitable contribution, a material item, effort, and/or an enjoyable pastime such as playing video games. Sacrifices may be permanent or may be done for a set period of time. This is done to show reverence to deities or other entities, to express commitment, and to get the message across that you're willing to do your share to achieve success in a working. In many magico-religious systems, celebrants pour some wine onto the ground in libation to the gods. Some folkloric practitioners and modern Pagans put food out for the ancestors during a holiday. We bury a crystal when we take wood from a tree to make a wand. All of these are rituals of devotion and objects of sacrifice.

Several older recipes for magickal workings include items such as a dove's heart for love, the dried remains of a toad, or another animal body part. Some traditions believe in sacrificing an animal to appease or venerate their deities. This is another gray area of common magick practice. We must weigh the potential with the consequences. Anything used in ritual that comes from an animal who died in pain is likely to carry an emotional charge, usually a negative one. There might be blowback from the law of return. In many locations, it's also against the law of the land.

However, we must weigh the consequence of sacrifice with its benefit. Many of us eat meat from a slaughterhouse, butcher our own food, or go hunting for wild animals such as deer. We thank the spirit of the animal who donated their life for our sustenance. We might give the blood of that animal in sacrifice or use parts of that animal in ritual. This is an area that might require soul-searching, prayer, researching the local laws, and a consideration of one's own ethical code.

The Lens of Truth and True-Speaking

Many folk magick practitioners believe that everything should be examined through a lens of truth. This means assessing situations critically, including our own motivations, and always keeping an eye toward long-term outcome. It means being totally honest with oneself. Using the lens of truth also means comprehending the natural state of any entity. Snakes can bite, spiders can be venomous, and some fairies can act like a pack of mean teenage girls. Some deities are not benevolent or kind. This does not mean you should squash each spider and banish all energy beings. Instead, it means understanding—and thus respecting—an entity's true nature. Remember: while snakes may bite, they also eat the mice and rats that destroy human food sources and spread diseases. A deity that is related to death, pain, storms, cold weather, or justice has their place in the legends and mythology of a people.

Common magick practitioners must learn to examine not only our own conscience, but also the motivations of those around us. This includes coming to understand forces that may seem brutal or damaging like storms, aging, or death. We must comprehend the "nature of the beast" when it comes to human greed, violence, and stupidity. Considering long-term consequences is necessary; for example, in the event that a person is doing harm, whether it is beneficial to use magickal strategies such as binding. While we do not tolerate abuse toward ourselves or our loved ones, nor do we send love and light toward criminals, we do our level best to solve problems without using magickal powers for the purpose of causing long-term damage.

We also endeavor to use truth when speaking words aloud. Many common magick users endeavor to practice a way of communication called truth-speaking, also called true-speaking. When verbalizing words of power, folk magick practitioners should strive to be as accurate as possible, which works hand-in-hand with the magickal principle of speaking one's word into being. However, true-speaking goes one step further.

We believe that when a person speaks only words of truth, their magickal spells are more easily manifested. This relies on an *ad hominem* concept of truth, like the Egyptian concept of *Maa Kheru* or "truth of voice." When a practitioner says something like "We need rain," the deities or universal consciousness will hear them and respond appropriately. All of the truthful person's spoken words will thus come true.

True-speaking also includes making oaths. Swearing an oath or pledging a troth means making a declaration before one's family, society, and energetic beings. It has the connotation that a person's word equals their bond. An oath may include an intent to act in a certain manner. It may mean stating that a specific condition is true. Oaths in folklore and literature were sometimes made in the name of god-forms, elementals such as "earth, sea, and sky," or by the health of the individual or their loved ones. The implication was that if the oath was broken, the bond or surety was forfeit. I speculate that this concept may be behind the saying "His word is his bond." Breaking an oath could mean consequences, such as a compromise in health, or that the elements or god-forms would enact justice.

In true-speaking, intent must be verbalized mindfully. For instance, if I note "We need rain," I must also think about how much rain, for how long, and ensure that other locations are not deprived of rain. Another example is a person who requests "abundance." Do they want an abundance of zucchini, or an abundance of kittens, or an abundance of money in their bank account?

Caution: Do Not Play On or Around

These are activities that most common magick users believe are harmful. They should be avoided.

+ Performing magick that goes against someone's free will
+ Magick done with the intent to manipulate someone. Example: a spell enacted to compel a specific individual to do something
+ Using someone else's energy without their knowledge or consent, such as "stealing luck." This also includes using energetic beings' life forces
+ Doing an act of deliberate harm. This includes cursing, hexing, or otherwise performing a malevolent rite for the purpose of causing damage
+ Doing any magickal act out of anger, jealousy, or hatred
+ Performing love spells or rites that deliberately bind or enslave a specific person

The following are considered gray areas.

+ Doing magick to help someone to heal or positively improve their lives without their full consent
+ Performing magick which will protect oneself and loved ones by intentionally harming someone who is deliberately trying to hurt you. Can they be stopped without doing them harm?
+ "Rebounding" energies onto someone who has caused harm. It may backfire between them and the magick user or bounce onto another person
+ Binding a person and preventing them from doing something harmful to others
+ Magickally preventing someone from doing something that is viewed as self-harm. They may need a life lesson. Can they be helped in other ways?
+ Blood sacrifices

These gray areas require thought, mindfulness, prayer, meditation, and/or use of the lens of truth. Any magickal act must be done with serious consideration of its long-term effects.

The main concern of ethics is to not intentionally create victims. That about sums it up.

four
RITUAL TOOLS OF COMMON MAGICK

Practitioners of folk magick traditions often use physical objects during the course of enacting workings and rites. Ritual tools are the material items used in common magick to raise and direct energetic forces, as a place to store power, or to represent a certain condition, like a rose quartz stone that symbolizes love. Magickal tools can be used to move energy from a source to a receptacle, such as extending a wand to capture power from a thunderstorm and pointing the wand to send healing to a person. Venerated items are used to symbolize a deity or other spiritual entity. Ritual tools can also be used to store energy, such as a chalice that is believed to contain good luck. Some objects are said to have an intrinsic magickal quality, such as a magnetic lodestone, certain types of wood, crystals, or metals such as copper or iron. These are usually items found in nature. Other ritual items are crafted specially for use in a folkloric rite.

Tools are not required for the practice of magick, but using power objects can certainly help. They can be considered as mere stage props, used to convince ourselves and others that something is really happening, or to get us in the proper state of mind to perform energetic workings. Ritual objects can be viewed as the magick user's connection between themselves, a source of power, and the desired outcome of their ritual. Some consider their tools as energetic weapons against malevolent beings. Others view them as we would any other implement, from a butter knife to a chainsaw to a motor vehicle.

Some tools, like those found in Wicca, correspond with elements/elementals or other beings. Some common magick users use these objects in their rituals, including the wand, chalice, ceremonial knife, and incense burner. Other items are found in nature and the symbolism is what the practitioner makes of it: a bird's nest to represent home, a fossil to emblemize stability, etc. Power objects need not be fancy or ornamental, but if having tools that are aesthetically pleasing is important to you, there are many magickal items that are richly decorated. Magickal tools can also be common, ordinary, and plain; those everyday utilitarian objects found in the home, workplace, or farm. As in all things, common magick users are adaptable and practical in our use of ceremonial items and ritual tools.

Dual-Purpose Tools

Different traditions have varying outlooks on using tools exclusively for ritual or magickal purposes. Some say that a power object should only be used for rites and spells, which helps it to retain energy for a specific objective. These items may be dedicated in a ceremony to a particular entity or for a unique purpose. Others use their implements every day for mundane reasons, such as cutting vegetables with a knife in the kitchen and also using the knife to direct energy in a ritual.

In the past, tools were usually employed in practical matters as well as esoteric rites. Farm tools were used for work as well as for ritual. A pitchfork was good for tossing hay to animals and also used as a symbolic warding item. Home tools, such as a besom (broom) were used to sweep the floor and to banish harmful influences.

Working and crafting tools like the spindle, wood saw, and grinding mill were used for repetitive movement to raise energy. One of the songs of traditional witchcraft has the words "Make the mill of magick turn," which refers to using a hand mill or grain-grinding wheel to generate magickal power. This also has the effect of allowing the practitioner to enter a trance state through repetitive movement.

Some groups will not allow any metal implements within the working area, as they believe it disrupts the energy. Others are just fine with metals in ritual. Tools are often "charmed" to render them more effective; for example, a butter churn with sigils and a verbal enchantment will make the process of churning butter easier.

Acquiring Tools

Besides employing household or workplace implements, folkloric traditionalists can purchase or craft their own ritual tools. Magickal objects can be bought at a metaphysical shop, online, at hobby suppliers, at thrift shops, or even your local big-box store. The advantage of purchasing something new is that no one else has ever used the item for an energetic working. Often, an object will "speak" to us and we will know that the item is right for our practice. It feels perfect in our hand, it exhibits a quality that we like, and we have sensory input that tells us the item is good for us.

If a magickal item is purchased, no haggling or arguing over price should take place. The tool should be thoroughly cleansed to remove any energies or past attachments, including from the workers who manufactured it. Magickal tools can also be created by a craftsperson or by the magick user. In this instance, no cleansing is likely to be required.

If taking an item from nature, one should use ethics in obtaining it: leave some to regenerate or for the next person. Politeness and appreciation is required. Thank the nest of rocks in a crystal mine; thank a tree for removing its branch to make a wand. An offering of a song, poem, gemstone, coin, piece of biodegradable cloth, art, food, or drink is appreciated.

Cleansing Magickal Tools

Cleansing new-to-you tools means not only a physical cleaning but also removing any lingering energies. After continued use, it is a good idea to cleanse tools and perhaps rededicate them to deities or to a specific purpose. Some common magick practitioners do this periodically, for instance at the time of the new moon, during seasonal holidays, or on Fridays. Others cleanse their tools before performing a rite.

Cleansing can be done in the course of a ceremony or just as any other act of ordinary housekeeping. This can be enacted by smudging with smoke, sprinkling with water, immersing the tools in water, salt, sand, or earth, or leaving the tool in sunlight or moonlight for a period of time. Metal objects can be shined with commercial products.

Some people spray their tools with essential oils. Others clean objects with rubbing alcohol or vinegar. All of these methods can remove any lingering energies. The reason is that an implement used for banishing in one rite and healing in the next ritual might retain certain qualities that cross over from one ceremony to the next. This could bring about confusion or even a conflict of purposes. Caution must be taken to not ruin the physical object when cleansing: for example, some crystals do not react well to salt, and feathers or animal hides can be spoiled by water.

Customizing and Caring for Tools

Magickal items can be customized by the user by inscribing them with sigils, words of power, or designs; adding extra items like crystals, metal wire wrapping, paint, and animal products like leather or feathers; or anointing with perfume or essential oils. In other words, anything that makes the tool your own. Some practitioners consecrate their power objects for their magickal use, asking energetic beings for help in their works. A ceremony can be enacted to dedicate the item to the users, to consecrate it to an entity, or to connect it to its purpose. Some magick users do rites to focus intent for each tool. The more one adds to and handles your magickal objects, the more they become *yours*, and the better they work.

Ritual tools must be cared for and stored properly, not only to keep them physically functional but also to preserve their magickal qualities. Many magick users store their tools in an altar, trunk, or cupboard kept specifically for that purpose. This might have wards or other containment systems designed to protect the ritual objects from acquiring unpleasant energies. Other people leave their tools on display; others keep them in the home, barn, garage, or workplace. They might serve a dual purpose as everyday working apparatus as well as being magickally charged implements.

When ritual tools break, they should be discarded, burned in a ceremonial fire, or buried. Please do not give away magickal objects to a charitable organization, as they might cause problems for non-magickal people. Some things can be repurposed, but many should not; for example, some people believe that candlewax used for a ritual that was not thoroughly consumed should be cast into a fire and burned away without reusing it for a second magickal rite.

Magickal Objects Used in Common Magick

Alraun

An alraun is a talismanic image created from a piece of wood or root, usually in the shape of a human, and is often used as a symbolic stand-in for a person.

Figure 2: Alraun

Sometimes English mandrake or American mayapple roots are used, but anything will do, including a turnip or carrot. An alraun to represent a small child or person for healing can be fashioned from a peony root.

Anointing Oils

These substances, which include oils, flower essences, or tinctures, are used to ritually sanctify a person or item, to bless or consecrate for a specific purpose, or for veneration. Ritual symbols can be drawn using the anointing substance as "ink." Some common magick practitioners use plain apple cider vinegar. (Note: Please ensure that no one in the household, including kids and pets, has an allergic reaction to essential oils before using them.)

Antlers, Horns

Made from the hard organic material found growing on the head of a deer (cervid), goat, or bull (bovine), antlers and horns embody the male principle as well as wild magick of the woodlands, mountains, and meadows. Horns and antlers represent deities associated with hunting, herding, agriculture, warriors, the underworld, and male fertility.

Antlers and horns can be used on a helmet or mask in ritual theater dramatizations (see "mask"). They can be cut into thin pieces to make runes or other divinatory tools with carved, burnt, or painted symbols. Antlers can be used for protection emblems, used to top a staff to make a "moonrake" (see "staff"), used as a wand (see "wand"), made into candleholders, or used in place of a ritual knife. Horns can also be used as a drinking vessel or to make a musical instrument called a sounding horn, which is used to summon people and entities to rites.

A symbol of the horn can dispel the evil eye. A horn hung in the home can be a symbol of hunting, fertility, and safety.

Apotropaic Objects

Talismans, amulets, charms, and other ritual items are designed to remove or repel evil and banish harmful entities. They can prevent the influence of negative emotions or energies, avert bad luck, or cast off baneful intentions. The word "apotropaic" comes from the Greek *apotrepein*, to turn away from, and *apotropaios*, averting evil. These are sometimes created within a working.

Arrowheads

Used in protective magick, arrowheads can frighten away maleficent energies and can direct power. The old stone ones, created by Native Americans or the aboriginal people of the British Isles, were sometimes called elf darts and carried earthy force as well as the quality of the stone, usually flint. They represent strength, cleverness, skill, and stoicism.

Baling Hook

Originally used to grab bales of hay, this tool is a long, curved, sharply pointed metal spike with a handle. Some traditional witches and common magick users from farming communities use these to "bend the wind" or change the weather. The hook is raised to the sky or twirled around in the interest of causing a strong wind to calm or change direction.

Baskets

Baskets, made from straw, woven wicker twigs, reeds, and other fibers, symbolize bending, weaving, and shaping. This is said to be duplicated by acts of magick, which bend and shape reality. As containers, baskets represent the female principle and the womb. They can be used for gathering herbs and storing magickal supplies. Baskets may be stuffed with offerings of fruit and vegetables or burned as a sacrifice on an open fire. The famous Wicker Man was likely just a basket on steroids ... the same principle of making an offering is employed.

Bells

A single bell is used to summon people or entities to ritual. A sharp, clanking sound is used to drive away fairies and other spirits while the pleasant, tinkling music of tiny bells, chimes, or musical instruments can invoke positive entities. Bells on animals such as cattle protect them from malevolent beings as well as helping the owner locate the herd. Bells on the doors can protect the home from harmful entities. Some folk dancers and performers in ritual dramas wear bells to summon or banish certain spirits, or just to be noisy.

Bellows

The fireplace bellows, an implement used to "breathe" air into a stove or fireplace to increase the flame, symbolizes the elements of fire and air. It can be used ritually to bring air into a room or to banish disquieting energies.

Besom, Broomstick, Baculum

Many sources have loads of information about the witch's traditional broomstick and its supposed history and purposes. The familiar image of a witch flying on a broom may have come from folktales about the Germanic Frau Holda, although she actually rode a distaff. An image of a woman riding a besom first appeared in 1451 in Martin Le Franc's *Le Champion des Dames*, or *The Defender of Ladies*.[23]

The handle of a besom is called a stale. For magickal purposes, it is usually made of wood with a folkloric significance such as rowan, oak, hazel, birch, ash, or a tree called broom. The straw part is constructed of birch twigs or a plant called broomstraw, then attached to the stale with willow withes, which symbolize bending and shaping. The besom handle can be inscribed with sigils or symbols to increase its power.

A broom can represent male energy (the phallus-shaped handle), which meets female energy in the triangle shape of the straw. The besom also represents domesticity and female power. The two energies conjoining can cause a reaction according to the law of polarity.

The besom was traditionally used for cleansing baneful feelings or energies from a room or ritual area, sweeping negative emotions or beings from the air, and chasing evil out the door. To prevent negative entities such as evil spirits or the devil from entering a home at night, a broom is placed by the door, bristles up, and the malevolent creature has to count every straw before coming indoors. Usually the sun will rise before all the straws can be counted, driving away the evil spirit.

---

23. Allison Meier, "The First Known Depiction of a Witch on a Broomstick," Hyperallergic, October 24, 2016, https://hyperallergic.com/332222/first-known-depiction-witch -broomstick/.

"Jumping the broom" as a wedding rite, found in both European and African American cultures, likely came from travelling Romani people.[24] Decorated brooms are sometimes used as a gift for newly married couples. Spinning a broom on the floor or in the hands, like twirling a baton, can generate power. Some traditions require stepping over a broom that is flat on the floor in order to enter a ritual space.

Bones
Bones can be used to replace wands or ritual knives. The bones of a toad were often used in old-line witchcraft and crafts guilds for multiple purposes. The wishbone or breastbone of a bird or fowl is used for making wishes come true. Bones that are cut into the size of coins and then painted or carved with sigils or symbols can be cast for divination. Remember, the bones of any animal that died in pain can carry a very negative energy, subject to the law of return.

Bottles, Jars, Containers
Mostly, bottles are used as containers for herbal powders, ink, potions, herbal tinctures, and alcoholic beverages. In past days they were made of clay; in modern times, glass or plastic. The substance, color, shape, any inscribed symbols, and the label can affect the bottles' contents. Sometimes pure energy without a physical substance was contained; think of the story about the "genie in a bottle." Energy or a potion can also "marinate" or gain strength and power within a bottle. Bottles might be used to symbolize pregnancy or incubation.

In the American South, bottle trees are used to scare away baneful energies, which is a common magick practice. The bottles are placed onto tree limbs or a specially constructed frame, and the wind blowing through them creates a sound and vibration.

A container can be used to trap, hold, or dispose of negative energies, as in a witch's bottle. Bottles are also put into windows to collect sunlight, moonlight, and to cast pretty colors of light into the room.

---

24. Alan Dundes, "'Jumping the Broom': On the Origin and Meaning of an African American Wedding Custom," *The Journal of American Folklore* 109, no. 433 (Summer 1996): 324–29.

Bowls, Plates

Bowls and plates are used for offerings of food to deities and other entities. A bowl mostly symbolizes something being kept or used, while a plate represents something being offered. Bowls filled with salt are for protection, while bowls containing bread, acorns, or other natural items attract prosperity and an abundance of sustenance.

Like bottles, bowls are also used to catch the energies of sun and moon, or used to "marinate" magickal energies. Bowls can also symbolize the female principle.

A bowl filled with water can be used as a tool for descrying, or viewing images for divination purposes.

Bread

Bread represents the harvest, the sacred loaf in Paganism, bounty and plentitude in Earth religions, the god and male principle, or the goddess and female principle. Sharing bread is seen as a sacred act, said to ensure hospitality, seal deals between two or more individuals, and to encourage kinship.

At Lammas (also known as Lughnassadh, Calan Awst, and Harvesttide), celebrants eat bread containing trinkets symbolizing prophetic conditions. A sixpence baked into bread pudding at Yule has the connotation of wealth and good luck. Bread is baked into various shapes to symbolize different states of being; for example, a sun shape at Lammas, hot cross buns for Alban Eilir/Oestara, or dark rye in a round shape for Hallowe'en.

Brooch, Pin, Kilt Pin, Cloak Pin

A brooch is an implement used for keeping clothing pinned together or an ornament worn on clothing which can have a ritual significance. The pin may have sigils or symbols inscribed on it for good luck, protection, and to repel negative entities. The pointy end was used for pricking the fingers to draw blood, which was then used for ceremonial purposes. The pin could also be used to "prick" or drive away harmful spirits. Some pins had significant designs so that members of secret societies or magickal groups could recognize one another.

Bullroarer

A bullroarer is a flat stone or piece of wood with a hole at one end attached to a string. It is then whirled in the air to produce vibrations and sound. It is used to sanctify a space, to call to air spirits, and to change air temperature. This tool is also called a coldmaker, rumbler, or turndun.

Candles, Candleholders
There are dozens of books and websites dedicated to the magick of candles, color correspondences, and ritual use. Candles carved with sigils or inscriptions can create a certain magickal condition as they are burned. Candles can also "fuel" magickal workings by creating energy from the flame. Divination can be performed while staring at the movement of the fire. If a candle of the right color can't be found, use white.

Carpenter's Square
One of the tools used by Masons, the carpenter's square is used for drawing perfectly straight lines in magickal rituals, especially in making sigils. It is also said to keep positive energies and entities within the lines while keeping harmful or negative conditions out.

Cask
A cask is a wooden barrel used to hold wine or whiskey and also nail kegs. Casks are usually made from oak wood and bound with iron, both of which represent strength. Put something inside that needs to be "toughened up." Casks can trap, hold, and contain magickal energies.

Some communities in Britain and Scotland still fill a cask with flammable items and oil, tar, or pitch, then light them on fire to commemorate one of the solar holidays. This is extremely dangerous but fun.

The metal hoop on the exterior of the cask was removed and used by small boys as a rolling toy, which also had the magickal significance of generating power and symbolized continuity.

Cauldron
Also called a caudle, kettle, or stewpot, the cauldron is used for containing a substance and heating it over a fire. It was also a symbol of goddesses and the female principle. Many sources tell of legends and uses for this traditional witchcraft tool. While associated with witches due to folklore and movies, in past days a cauldron was found in every home and was used for making soap, cooking stews,

boiling laundry, and creating beverages, so no one noticed the cauldron or suspected its magickal associations.

A cauldron can be used for brewing together substances such as potions, imbuing them with magickal powers, or used as a container for energy. Stirring a cauldron clockwise invokes a particular condition or entity; counterclockwise dismisses them. The famous cauldrons of the goddess Cerridwen and the god the Dagda, called a *coirc* in Welsh, inspired many legends, but also symbolized the sacred powers of the Celtic nations contained in a body of lore. (Note: If a cauldron is intended for cooking food or drinks, ensure that it is safe for that purpose. Cast iron is usually okay, while copper and other metals may have lead solder on the seams which, when heated, can seep into food and become dangerous.)

Chain, Rope

Used for bindings, a chain symbolically means attaching one condition to another. The chain can be used for counting spells like cords formed into a "witch's ladder."

Lay a chain or rope on the ground to delineate a safe ritual space. Snakes will not crawl across a rope, so encircle one outside your tent when camping (see "cord").

Chalice, Cup, or Other Drinking Vessel

This is another tool which symbolizes the female principle and a container or repository for magick. Chalices can be used for offerings to deities and entities and to share a drink with a group, thereby serving a purpose of contagion magick. All participants are bound together by drinking from the same cup. Sharing a cup is also said to seal deals made between people, including the ritualized swearing of oaths. Sacred vessels contain energy drawn into the cup from a magickal source, and drinking of it infuses a person with power. Drinking water that came from a wellspring symbolizes becoming involved with the fairy or deity associated with that particular location and also promotes healing. The beverage in the chalice may take on a magickal purpose, said to transform through alchemy into another substance, as in the Cup of Wisdom of Celtic legend. The chalice can symbolize the Holy Grail, which is a Christianized version of a Welsh legend about a magickal cup that represents the divine feminine.

Sprinkling water from a cup, also called asperging or aspergating, removes negative energies or entities from a person or location and represents cleansing.

Tossing water from a cup onto the ground or into the air can summon rain. Pouring a beverage from a cup onto the ground, an outdoor altar, or statue shares the drink with ancestors, deities, and spirits. This is called making an offering or a libation. A cup, glass, vase, or other vessel can serve as a "trap" for negative energies or evil spirits.

Clothing, Costumes

Costumes and clothing have many significant uses in magick. Robes, national or ethnic dress, and cloaks are often worn only for sacred rites to discern between everyday activities and ceremonies. Colors of clothing can correspond with particular conditions, such as wearing red for power and creativity or green to signify fertility and abundance. In some locations, wedding or funeral garb has a particular color: Celts often wore fertile green to marry and unbleached cloth (pale beige) for a death or to perform magick.

A shawl is piece of clothing worn around the shoulders or over the head as a hood, which can symbolize the wings of a butterfly or bird, the energetic sensation of floating, or be used as a disguise, cover, or protective device, usually by elderly ladies. Many shawls are shaped as a triangle and can be used as a magickal implement when lain on the ground as a safe space in which to perform a ritual or cast bones or stones.

In folkplays or ritual dramas, costumes are worn to identify with a particular character or archetype. The players and audience recognize the character by their clothing. This is part of the magick of aspecting or avataring. Costumes in common magick may include everyday clothing; tattered, ragged jackets festooned with ribbons; an outfit worn in many different ceremonies, but only during rituals, not every day; or a costume worn exclusively for a particular rite. Costumes can include the motley or patchwork clothing of a sacred fool; the animal skins, masks, hoods, antlers, horns, skulls, or animal heads worn by hooded animal figures; old-fashioned outfits worn in past days to signify a particular role; body paint, wigs, bundles of straw, and leafy branches; and/or clothing that represents a particular image such as a witch, a king, or a maiden (see "mask").

Costumes often become infused with magickal energy over time. For example, a ritualistic stag outfit can take on the powers of Cernunnos /Herne /the Buca or another hunt and woodland deity. In some cultures the costumes are treated with reverence, as they represent the character, entity, or archetype. In Britain some of the folkplay costumes are housed in museums or churches. Some have been used for many years, while others used in current performances are replicas.

Coins

Coins can represent prosperity, material goods, abundance, and commerce. Offering a coin to a fountain to make a wish is well documented, and many sacred wells in the British Isles are full of coins from the Roman era onward. A buried coin can be used as a gift to a spirit being in exchange for cutting a wand from a tree or taking a stone from a location. Coins placed on an altar or used during a rite can bring material success and prosperity, although some practitioners frown on this because coins have been handled by many people and carry residual energies. Some traditions require removing coins from the pockets before entering ritual space. The properties of the metal of a coin can also influence magick.

Compass

As in the tool for finding directions, a compass can be used to aid in outlining a circular or spherical ritual space (or magickal circle) and/or finding and delineating the location of the cardinal points or directions. Some traditional witchcraft practitioners call drawing a ritual circle "making the compass." As in the tool for drawing circles in carpentry or other skilled trades, the compass is one of the symbols of Masons. It was often used in Britain to draw a symbolic "daisy wheel" sigil, used for protection of a building.

Cord, Singulum, Cingulum, Girdle, Ligature, Measure, Rig

Cords, yarn, string, or leather strips can be used for binding, tying knots for counting spells and prayers, and holding items such as beads. Tying a cord in knots is also a magickal device for raising energy or for inducing trance work. A red cord can anchor a person's spirit to their body during astral travel. A cingulum is a cord tied around one's waist to hold a robe closed. Wrapping cords around the waist is said to prevent fertility, so use caution. Tying a cord to an object, or between two items, establishes a magickal connection. A cord or rig is used for measuring a ritual circle. A peg is inserted into the ground and a cord of nine feet attached, then the other end is held while walking around the perimeter, creating a circular ritual area (see "chain").

Crystals, Stones, Gems, Minerals

There are hundreds of books and websites devoted to the use, energies, symbolism, and care of crystals. Crystals can be used in divination, as a repository of energy, as a symbol during sympathetic magick, for healing, for protection, and for qualities intrinsic to the stone. Crystals are believed to have particular vibrations that aid in magickal practice. Stones are said to have a type of memory or record that allows them to transmit information, emotion, or abilities such as healing. Colors of crystals can symbolize their purpose, such as blue for tranquility and yellow for energy. Plain clear quartz can augment other stones' abilities. Wearing crystals, gemstones, and minerals as jewelry not only looks pretty but can also store energy to draw from for personal use and aid in healing and protection.

Stones that are found in the British Isles can align with magick users who are working with those ethnic currents; for example, black British jet can be used to repel a baneful entity like a bogey or *cythraul* (harmful energy creature). There are and were huge reserves of gold and silver found in the British Isles, which has been used for jewelry since at least the Bronze Age.[3] Minerals and gemstones were and are also used to ornament weaponry, symbols of authority, and ceremonial implements.

Divination Tools

Divination is based on images and symbols found in objects. Common magick practitioners sometimes utilize natural objects, like sticks or bones carved with sigils or "tell-stones" painted with representational art, which are cast onto a surface or cloth. Folk magick traditionalists sometimes practice divination by gazing into a bowl of water or a crystal ball, also called a shew stone, show stone, or seeing stone. This is called descrying. Common household tools were also used for divinatory purposes. For example, the sieve and shears are referenced in many older books on augury (see "sieve").

Dowsing Rods, Divining Rods

These are used for finding lost items or water or other precious minerals underground. A dowsing rod might be a long, forked stick of a wood with magickal significance such as rowan, hickory, willow, or birch, which have a connection to the element of water. Divining rods can be two sticks made of wood or metal wire which are the length of a practitioner's arm from middle fingertip to elbow. They might have a handle on one end. The magick user holds the rod or rods with both hands, palms up or down, wrists sometimes crossed, and points the long part(s) of the wand(s) level with the ground. The rod may quiver and dip, or the two rods may point or cross, when the desired item or object is located.

Fan

A hand fan is a tool that represents the element of air. It can be used to "blow away" disquieting energy and baneful spirits. It can also "stir up" positive energy through a ritualized, repetitive gesture and can be used to summon beings associated with air such as fairies and other spiritual entities, birds, and beneficial insects. Fans are often made of feathers, folded paper inscribed with symbols, or natural implements such as thinly sliced horn, wood, or turtle shells. A communication symbology is based on the positioning of a fan.

Feathers

Often used to make fans, feathers are also used to make quills for writing, drawing, and inscribing magickal sigils; as ornaments; and as a symbol to invoke qualities such as communication, truth, and fairness. A feather worn upright in the hat can prevent black flies or horse flies from landing and stinging. Finding a feather can symbolize acquiring knowledge or a message from the spirit world. Different colored feathers, or the feathers of various birds found in the wild, can be an omen or portent.

Fire, Bonfire, Balefire, Hearth Fire, Need-Fire

A fire can be used for scrying or divination by seeing shapes in the flames or as the focal point for a drum circle, ritual, or ceremony. Old-line Pagans jump over the fire to increase fertility. Dancing, skipping, or pacing around a fire clockwise can raise magickal power. Storytelling around the fire was and is prevalent in many cultures. The hearth fire was considered the center of the home and related to household magick. Old, worn-out talismans and offerings can be burned in a ceremonial fire.

Hardwoods such as oak, elm, maple, and beech are preferred for bonfires. Only dead wood is used, and the spirit of the tree is thanked for its life. Pine causes a quick, hot flame, while "wet" trees like sycamore and box elder might not burn well at all. A need-fire is used to make wishes or do workings and must be kindled with two sticks or flint and steel. Then it must burn throughout the night. Nine woods were traditionally used, including holly, rowan, alder, and hawthorn.

Fishing Tools, Seaside Implements, Boating Tools

Much of the British Isles is located close to the sea, rivers, and bodies of water. Magickal tools were and are used to keep ships and boats safe, to protect homes from storms, and to aid in commercial ventures associated with seafaring. Fishing nets are used to trap and bind energies or as a magickal barrier to keep harmful entities out. Fishing floats are round glass spheres filled with air that kept nets afloat and could symbolize the element of air or be used as a gazing crystal for divination or trance work. Fishhooks are used, along with pins, to guard windows and doorframes from being breached by negative beings and are sometimes placed in witch's bottles. An oar symbolizes hard work for a purpose and staying on course. A kayak paddle can be substituted. A fishing creel made of woven wicker served the same purpose as a basket (see "baskets"). The nautical star, a five-pointed symbol similar to the pentacle, is used to protect buildings near the water.

Grimoire, Spell Book, Recipe or Receipt Book, Missal, Grammarye, Granary, Grammar

The word "grimoire" likely comes from "grammar" or textbook. Literate practitioners inscribed magickal sigils, symbols, alphabets, diagrams, recipes, spells, rites, images, and so forth in their grimoires and also used these books as a type of journal or diary. Although many old-line Pagans were functionally illiterate, some of their lore may have been written down by scholars. If you have a recipe book from an older relative, treasure it. It might contain instructions for cooking foods, household hints, making soaps and cleaning supplies, and herbal healing as well as lore related to the weather. All of this is powerful magick.

Guns, Bullets, Gunpowder

Used mostly by magickal practitioners in the US, gunpowder is added to some talismans and magickal recipes to bring about protection and boost energy. Old-fashioned gunpowder (black powder) is made of sulfur, charcoal, and potassium nitrate, which forms saltpeter. This was used in older spells as a substance for cleansing and to repel negative energy. It can be sprinkled across the doorway or windowsill to keep out harmful entities. Some older potions called for salt-peter, and recipes suggest that it can be ingested (eaten); do NOT do that, as saltpeter is toxic. It's also flammable. Bullets are placed in talismans for warding purposes. Firing a gun into the air was said to drive away malevolent spirits. (In modern times, this is not recommended. What goes up must come down and also, aircraft can be hit.)

Hagstone, Fairy Stone, Peep Stone, Seer Stone, Show Stone, Holey Stone

Used in common magick to represent the female principle, a hagstone is a rock that has a hole going all the way through it. It has magickal powers but only if the hole occurs naturally, worn through the stone by water or geological compression. Looking through the hole in the stone is said to enable people to see fairies and other energetic beings and to reveal people's true nature as a "lens of truth." It can also be used as a divination device. Talismans made from hagstones can protect people, livestock, ships, and the home. Tying a holey stone with feathers, beads of wood or bone, and colored yarn or thread can increase its magickal properties of healing, protection from spirits, and fertility. This device can be hung above the bed or near the chimney. It is not recommended to paint the stone or inscribe it with sigils. In legend, the rocks are called adder stones, said to protect from snakebite, which may work; however, it does not cure a person once they have been bitten by a venomous snake.

Hairbrush, Comb, Hairpins

Anything connected to hair can use contagion magick to bind or attach a particular object or condition to an individual's energy. Ornaments in the hair can be used as amulets or talismans for health, protection, eloquence, prosperity, and well-being. Brushing the hair can induce a trance state. A chant or words of power can be spoken while combing hair to bring about magickal situations and effect change. Hairpins made of metal can be used as binding objects to connect a working to a person or situation. Individuals must be cautious in disposing of hair because negative beings can use it for mischief. Hair taken from the brush should be put into the garden or released outside rather than burned or thrown into the trash. Burying it is fine too.

Hammer

In Britain during the Norse occupations, symbolic representations of Mjölnir, or Thor's hammer, were used as protective talismans or invocation tools for deities. Besides Thor, deities who used a hammer include Weyland the Smith, the Welsh Govannon, the Irish Brigid and Goibniu, Jesus the Carpenter, and those who represented skilled trades. They were also one of the sacred tools of Masons. Hammers can be used as magickal tools to pound something into manifestation or out of existence. Magick users can speak word into reality while pounding a nail. Hammers also have the intrinsic quality of strength and physical capability.

Incense

Sweet-smelling incense, made from herbs, plant resin, and other natural substances, is a symbol of the element of air. Smoke is used to "smudge," or smoke-cleanse, which removes baneful energies and spirits from an area. The incense clouds fill a room and protect the space, preventing any negative energies from returning. Smoke can also attract beneficial entities including fairies and angelic beings. Incense can work upon the emotions, bringing about calmness or ambition, depending on its ingredients. Smoke that spreads outward indicates a peaceful environment, free from strife, while tight spirals of smoke can warn of harmful qualities or problems. Incense can also be used for summoning thought, memory, intelligence, communication, and the breath of life. Incense can be placed in a special burner, on a burning piece of wood or charcoal, or cast into a fire.

Keppen

A keppen is a short magick wand and also a tool for measuring. The root word is "kep," which has the same connotation as catch or capture. The keppen is usually used for catching energy and redirecting it into a talisman or toward a specific purpose. It also symbolizes the male principle. The keppen is often carved from wood that has a specific magickal significance, such as rowan for power or oak for strength. It should be taken from a living tree, and the spirit of the tree should be thanked for its donation. Keppens created from downed or fallen wood are believed to have less magickal power. Stones, crystals, metal, carven sigils, attached feathers, and/or colored yarn may add specific symbolism or magickal energy to the keppen (see "staff" and "wand").

Keys

Keys can bring harmony and peace to the home, especially old-fashioned iron or brass "skeleton" keys. In ritual, keys symbolize unlocking mysteries and secrets. Keys represent knowledge, power, wisdom, understanding, the heart, and "the key to dreams." It can symbolize being locked in or conversely, freedom. Hang a group of keys on a chain from a window or mantle for home security, both physical and magickal. A key on a string can be used as a pendulum for divination.

Knives

These include the athamé, Scottish dirk, other ceremonial edged weapons, and household or workplace tools with a blade, such as a paring knife, axe, or scythe. They can be used for directing or banishing magickal energy. Some people use a ceremonial blade for delineating sacred space, drawing protective sigils in the air, invoking and dismissing spiritual beings, casting a spell or a magickal circle, and/ or fighting harmful entities. Old-line Pagans use a ritual blade more for cutting off negative energies, chopping through symbolic cords used for binding spells, and for tasks related to performing magick such as whittling wood, carving symbols, cutting herbs, and slicing ritual foods. Scissors can also be used for symbolically cutting ties and for a divination rite. Placing edged tools with their blades facing up or out can repel harmful entities.

Ritual blades can be crafted of various metals like iron, steel, bronze, and copper or stones such as flint or obsidian. A black-handled knife is used in some witchcraft traditions for performing esoteric workings while a white-handled knife is used for the mundane tasks associated with creating magickal items such as cutting a sigil onto a candle. The white-handled knife is also called a kerfane, kerfan, or kervane. Cornish pellars and Manx witches use a red-handled knife, called a *shelg*, for blood magick. The Scots awl, called a *burrin*, can serve the same purpose. Druids used a sickle-shaped bronze ritual blade called a *bauline* or *boline* for cutting magickal herbs and plants such as mistletoe, and some common magick users still do.

Some traditions maintain that inscribing the knife blade or handle with sigils or representational art increases a ritual knife's magickal properties.

Lantern

A lit lantern can be used as a symbolic beacon, representing the element of fire and the magickal conditions of truth, light, illumination, and positive energy. A lantern can be used for home protection, blessing, and to symbolize deities and entities associated with light or the sun. Nothing should be burned in a magick lantern fire for the purpose of banishing or dismissing. The custom of gathering fireflies or lightning bugs in a fruit jar to use as a lantern began as a magickal practice. The bugs represent illumination and fertility. Be sure to punch holes in the lid and let them go before daylight.

Lightning Rod

Of old, some folks used a lightning rod to charge magickal implements made of metal or to direct lightning. This is highly dangerous and I don't recommend it. It can be used symbolically instead.

Lodestone, Magnet

A natural lodestone has the intrinsic magickal powers of attraction, bringing force into form, and summoning beings. A lodestone on a string will turn toward true north. Magnets and lodestones also have the qualities of polarity magick.

Mask

A mask represents a character, hero, animal, deity, or concept. They can be made from animal skins, fur or bones, leather, feathers, wood, paper, papier mâché, very thin ceramic clay, or fabric. Masks are a bit more personal than costumes or face paint and can change the mind, psyche, personality, emotions, and demeanor of the person wearing it. Like the costume, a sacred mask can take on the quality of the being it represents or serve as a home for a particular entity or archetype. A mask or costume can be used for sympathetic or contagion magick, and they are a primary source for doing priordination rituals (see "clothing").

Mazy Stone

A mazy stone is a carven stone or a tablet made of clay or carved wood with a twisting maze design. It represents mysteries, the route to the otherworld, or the path to a magickal working. The practitioner traces the maze with their fingers in order to attain a trance state through repetitive motion. A verbalization may be recited to further alter consciousness. Mazes carved onto a rock are called Troy stones, which came from the Greek. In the British Isles, mazes are carved into several ancient stone monuments.

Mill

A mill is a handheld device to grind substances into a powder, such as wheat or coffee beans. Sausage grinders, egg beaters, hand-powered drills, or food mills can also be used for the rhythmic circular motion of turning the handle. In past times, large mills were worked using human or animal power by pushing a hand-grip and walking around in circles as grain was pulverized between large grind-stones; thus, the old-line Pagan rite of "treading the mill." This is exhausting, repetitive work which can be used to fuel a spell with energy or to induce a trance state. This can symbolize transformation from one state to another.

Mirror

A mirror is a reflective surface that can be plain glass over a silver backing, black, smoked glass, or polished metal. It may be considered a portal to other dimensions or realms such as the spirit lands. A mirror may be used for descrying, using the reflective surface to view images that represent the past, future, and alternative states of being. A mirror can also be used to view spirits of the departed or magickal beings. Holding a mirror so it faces over the left shoulder and gazing into it may show a potential lover or the spirits. The reflective quality of the "magick mirror" can project energy, send negativity back to the sender, examine the self to discover truths, and be used for contemplation and reflection. In older books a mirror is sometimes called a speculum.

Mortar and Pestle

A mortar is a cup with a rough surface on the inside that is used with a grinding tool, the pestle, which crushes herbs, smashes seeds or nuts, and grinds things into a powder. The cup symbolizes the female principle and the pestle represents the male principle. Some use their mortar and pestle exclusively for workings; others grind food items too. Be sure to thoroughly wash the tools after grinding herbs that should not be ingested, or use two different mortars and pestles.

Musical Instruments

Items used to make music, especially drums, can attune people to the rhythms and vibrations of nature. A four-count drumbeat is symbolic of the heartbeat of the earth. Fast, staccato rhythms can increase energy, while slow, even beats can be calming, soothing, and prepare a person for interaction with spirits of the land and deified nature. Sometimes the drum is said to be talking and may take on a spiritual energy of its own. Drumming and dancing around a fire can induce trance, or it can be used to "tread the mill," meaning to use energetic movement to bring force into form. A drumhead can be painted with symbolic images, the body can be painted or carved, and other things can be attached to the drum, such as wooden beads, leather cords, seashells, feathers, and any other organic things. The drum's beater or drumsticks can be similarly decorated. Rattles, tambourines, a squeezebox, and wind instruments such as a flute, panpipe, hornpipe, and other musical devices can also be used for ritual purposes.

Needle, Pins, Knitting Needles

The needle as a tool has the connotation of industriousness, prickling, repelling, and binding together. Needles can be used to place sigils or symbolic art onto cloth items. A needle hung from a piece of thread can serve as a pendulum. Bent pins can be placed on or in things to repel negative energy, especially window frames and the witch's bottle. A pin, needle, or *burrin* (awl) can prick a wart, wound, or affliction, then be bent and cast into a hole or well in order to remove the problem through the principle of contagion. The process of using tools for sewing or knitting can induce a trance. The repetitive action of needlework can also raise energy.

Pentacle, Paten

While this item may be associated primarily with Wicca, it can also be a common magick implement. Pentacles are often made from copper, silver, wax, clay, or carved into the wood of a round section of a branch. It is usually inscribed with a pentagram sigil. Pentacles or coins may also represent the element of earth and the qualities of stability and wealth.

Pitchfork, Trident

Think of the trident of Poseidon or the pitchfork used by the Abrahamic religions' depiction of the devil. A pitchfork in common magick is used to direct or repel negative energies, scare away baneful entities, and prevent evil from entering the barn or stable. The combination of iron and wood had an intrinsic property said to affect potentially baneful energetic beings. It can also be used to draw or conjure power.

Potions

Potions are mixtures of herbs, liquids, and other substances, edible or not. They may be ingested if safe, applied topically if not poisonous, or used purely for symbolic purposes. Potions utilize principles of sympathy or contagion to draw and direct power. They were also called philtres.

Pouch

A pouch is a purse or storage place made of leather or sturdy cloth that is used to hold other ritual tools or magickal items. Pouches embody the female principle. The purse can be stamped, painted, or embroidered with designs and symbols. Smaller cloth bags may be used for talismans and amulets. Some believe putting symbolic objects into a bag and then performing a ceremony lets the items "percolate" or "marinate" together, gaining magickal power. A pouch can also be called a mojo bag, medicine bag, talisman, amulet, or fetish.

Scourge, Whip

Old-line Pagans used a whip, such as that used to direct horses or other beasts of burden, for cracking, making a noise to scare away malign influences. Whips were also used to direct power by pointing one or swirling it in the air. A fly whisk could be made from the hair of a horse's tail and serve the same purpose.

Scythe, Sickle

A scythe is a curved-blade tool used for harvesting grain or cutting grass. Think of the Grim Reaper's tool. It's much larger than the Druids' traditional *boline*. Scythes are made from iron. Like the athamé, a scythe or sickle can be used for directing power, but it's more for cutting something down as a sacrifice, removing or banishing energy, and eliminating or dismissing a particular condition. A scythe was used in folkplays and ritual dances by a death character to harvest grain, ritually sacrifice an autumnal deity, or shepherd the dead. The sickle can represent the waxing, waning, new, and dark phases of the moon. The curved blade, facing up or out, can protect a location from harmful energies and malign beings.

Sieve

Also called a strainer, a sieve can symbolically separate undesirable qualities from beneficial conditions. The sieve represents the element of water and can be used to attract rain. It can also be used with scissors for divination.[25]

Shield

A shield, often painted with heraldic devices or symbols, can be used as a magickal shield for deflecting harmful energies.

Shovel

Like other farming tools with a wooden handle and metal end, shovels are used to represent strength. They can connect the ground to the magick user or the sky. Shovels were also used for banishing rites. They are one of the sacred tools of the Masons.

Skulls

A skull can represent intelligence, symbolize mortality and death, and contain spirits and energies. The type of energy depends on the type of skull; for example, a feline skull can bring cleverness or a homey atmosphere and can scare away rodents. The skulls of horses, rams, goats, and cervids (deer family) were used to top a stang or staff called an *ermula*. Skulls are used for a ritual crown, mask, or headgear in British folkplays, folk dances, and hunting rituals. Some of these bone helmets were found in Star Carr in North Yorkshire, England, dating back to the Mesolithic era.[26] Several areas in rural Britain, Wales, and Cornwall had or

---

25. Peter Muise, "Conjuring by Sieve and Scissors," *New England Folklore* (blog), November 30, 2014, http://newenglandfolklore.blogspot.com/2014/11/conjuring-by-sieve-and-scissors.html.

26. Nicky Milner, Chantal Conneller, Barry Taylor, and R. T. Schadla-Hall, *The Story of Star Carr* (York: Council for British Archaeology, 2012).

have processional rituals using a skull attached to a pole, such as the *Mari Lwyd* or Derby Tup. A ram or goat skull can symbolize male fertility. Skulls were sometimes hidden in walls or in rafters or buried under a threshold to protect a barn. The skull of an animal could also be painted or inscribed with sigils and used as an altar piece, possibly as a symbol of mortality, but also to represent the bounty of the hunt.

Staff, Rod, Stang, Ermula, Gwelan, Bacculum, Galdarstaf

A staff is usually the size of a cane, or a walking stick that reaches from one's shoulder to the ground. It can be made of wood, metal, resin, or another substance. In Britain, they were often constructed of yew, ash, or blackthorn wood. The type of substance can affect the staff's magickal properties. A staff can be carved, painted, or otherwise inscribed with magickal sigils or designs. Stones, crystals, metal, wire, feathers, animal parts such as hide or bones, strings, or yarn can be attached to add specific symbolism to the staff.

The main purpose of a staff is to magickally extend the practitioner's "reach." Some staves (plural of staff) are used to connect sky or air energies to the magick user or to the earth for the purpose of grounding or bringing force into form. Some farmers used a garden rake, shovel, or pitchfork for the same purpose, while fisherfolk employed a trident. A staff could also be used as a representation of the male principle, a magickal weapon against baneful forces, or a literal weapon for self-protection against physical threats. It is often used as a walking stick as well.

A stang is a staff with a set of antlers or horns attached to the top of a wooden shaft or a long bough that is forked at the top, with two or three branches. A stang is sometimes called a "moon rake," used for attracting and capturing lunar energies. A candle can be set in the tines of the stang, representing the sun or moon. A stang can also be used for attracting or repelling wild energies such as the forest, meadow, desert, or those of animals. Some use the stang for delineating magickal boundaries.

An *ermula* is a staff with an animal skull attached to the top. It was used as a boundary marker during Saxon times in Britain, but also as a tool for protection. A croomstick is the traditional shepherd's hook, which can serve as a staff or be used to capture magickal energies. The *gwelan* is a Cornish staff, forked at the top or with an antler attached and an iron nail driven into the bottom for the purpose of grounding energies.

Star Plate

A piece of flat metal, usually tin or copper, with holes punched in it, used to represent particular constellations.

Sword

The larger, fancier version of an athamé or ritual knife. In past times, the only common people who could afford a sword were soldiers or professional guardians. A sword was used for protection against malevolent spirits as well as human enemies. Some soldiers used the polished blade as a reflective surface for scrying, the same as a crystal ball or magick mirror. The sword can be used to direct energy, banish harmful beings, summon entities, and represent the elements of fire or air. When used as a device for grounding, the sword tip must touch the earth or a tree, and excess energy is sent from the handle into the ground.

Thurible, Censer

A thurible is a metal container for burning incense. It is often on a chain so it can be swung about to send the smoke further.

Wand

Wands are usually the length of a magick user's arm, from the person's elbow to the end of the middle finger. The wand can be made of wood, metal, a crystal rod, bone, antler or horn, resin, or another substance. The type of material can affect the wand's magickal properties. For example, an applewood wand can be used for attracting love, while a wand made from a single large selenite crystal can attract lunar energies. Twisty, crooked wooden wands are said to have serpent powers, while straight ones are used for conjuring. The wand can be carved, painted, or otherwise inscribed with magickal sigils or designs. Stones, crystals, metal, feathers, beads, animal parts such as hide or bones, strings, or yarn can be attached to add specific symbolism to the wand. The more personalization the magick user adds to the wand, the more magickal qualities it will embody and the more personal connection the individual will have to the tool.

A wand is used to direct magickal energy from one location to another, usually from a power source to a ritual area, person, talisman, or other receptacle. Wands can also be used as the "rapper stick" in ritual folk dances. The clacking sound of two wands connecting drives away negativity. Priappic wands are topped with a pinecone or acorn and represent male fertility.[27] Other wands can also symbolize the male principle. The wand of a sacred fool is often topped with a doll's head or pig's bladder as a balloon and is decorated with ribbons and bells. In some traditions, a wand made of rowan wood was wrapped with ribbons and decorated with flowers, called a Maypole or gam. Wands are also called magick wands, batons, gams, gands, keppens, rappers, rods, and sticks (see "keppen" and "staff").

Wheel

In past days, a broken or discarded wagon or cart wheel was used to represent the changing seasons. A wooden wheel was covered in a flammable substance such as oil or tar, lit on fire, and thrown into water or rolled downhill at the advent of summer or during a summer holiday. The flaming wheel represented the sun. This is dangerous as heck because burning pieces and sparks fly everywhere, but it looks really cool. A wooden or metal wheel is used in a type of circle dance where the participants grasp the outer part of the wheel, each person grabbing between a spoke, and dancing "sunwise," or clockwise, to bring about fair weather and a bountiful harvest. Ribbons or colored yarn could be attached to represent seasons or individuals. People who want to try this can use a bicycle wheel if an old wagon wheel is not readily available. This working can also be used in "treading the mill" to raise energy.

Whetstone

Used for sharpening edged tools, a whetstone can be handheld or a grindstone wheel. Pumping or turning the grindstone is another repetitive action used for generating power, as is the circular or long swiping motion used during sharpening a blade. The whetstone itself has magickal powers associated with honing or creating sharpness. It may also take on the ritual significance of a blade through contagion magick.

---

27. Frazer, *Magic Art and the Evolution of Kings.*

With or Without?

Now that I've gone into detail about all of these tools, it must be restated that none of these things are absolutely necessary in the praxis of common magick. Energy can be directed by the hands or the force of the mind. The bottle or cup used to hold a beverage can serve as a chalice. Words of power can dispel harmful entities and attract beneficial conditions. A sigil can be visualized or inscribed with a finger in the air. Some people can pick up a stick or a rock and use them as a wand or a pentacle, then replace them in nature.

Yet some of us feel that tools are necessary and that using a substitute is like trying to unfasten a screw with a butter knife. The proper tool merely makes things easier for some magickal practitioners. If I had to pick some tools that I consider the most essential, I would choose a few objects to attract energy, something to direct energy, a couple items to repel various entities, and something to contain magick. Everything else can be obtained from my garage or from nature. Here's my personal emergency magickal toolkit:

- Knife
- Mason jar
- Besom
- Something to make fire
- Rope or cord
- Keppen (this mini-wand can go anywhere; a multipurpose wood like oak is best)
- Antler (can replace both knife and wand)
- Cauldron (because I like food as well as magick)

five

GODS, FAIRIES, ANCESTORS, AND ENERGY BEINGS

Many common magick practitioners believe in, attune to, and work with certain energetic beings that have special powers. These entities include fairies, the spirits of nature, the spirits of the departed/ancestors, deities, and psychopomps or fetches. Most of the folk who practice nature spirituality personify these beings, meaning we view them as having human characteristics, talents, emotions, and foibles. Some are seen as divine, immortal, and as more powerful than humans. Many supernatural beings were mentioned in folklore and folk literature. Some folkloric traditionalists believe in entities that are associated with an Abrahamic faith, including deities, demons and angels, and associated figures such as the apostles, saints, and the Virgin Mary. Others revere nature as a holy being with a consciousness.

Belief in an entity means accepting that the being is real and capable of action, although that entity may not be actually proven to exist within consensus reality. The magick user feels the presence of the being or sees the result of the entity's work. People sometimes have a psychic encounter with a spirit. Contact between a human and a magickal being can establish a relationship.

Attuning with an entity means developing a connection to them. This can include appreciating the being's qualities, endeavoring to communicate with or interact with the spirit, cultivating an emotional relationship with them, gaining knowledge from an entity, and striving to understand them. It can mean changing oneself to become more like the magickal being or taking on their aspects. It sometimes includes aspecting them or serving as an avatar. Energetic beings can be contacted through journeying or astral travel.

Working with a being means asking them for emotional support or help during a magickal rite. Some people request changes in the natural world, like bringing fair weather or rain. Healing, divination, and seeking wisdom from entities are examples of working with them.

Deities can assist their worshippers (and ancestors help their kinfolk) because they delight in their offspring's joy and appreciate our veneration. However, some entities operate under their own laws; they may not seem favorable to people. Deities can test humans to find the limits of our capabilities or to encourage qualities such as strength and fortitude. Spirits may have their own set of behaviors that are considered acceptable. Some fairies are mischievous and play pranks on humans. Spirits of the departed can have their own agenda, like finding a reason for their death. Nature spirits and elementals are sometimes indifferent to the needs of humans; the wind will blow whether it inconveniences us or not. Truths that we hear from magickal beings can feel emotionally unpleasant. Some entities desire something from us, such as safety of their home, a dwelling place like a spirit house, tributes, or a certain behavior. Some are actually malevolent, intending to cause harm—in the same manner as fleas, who view us as a tasty snack. Others merely want to be left alone.

Common magick practitioners can request help or a material item, sometimes called a boon, in return for something, often called a sacrifice. Some beings can be propitiated, or appeased, with words of power, songs, rituals, movement such as dance, or material gifts (or bribes). However, some magickal beings require a bit more consideration.

A "spirit pact" is like a contract made between a magick user and an entity with the mutual consent of both. The spirit and the human are both expected to keep their side of the bargain. It is in our best interest to clearly think through any contracts made with magickal beings. Do not make promises in haste. Consider every possible eventuality. Folklore has many examples of spirit pacts. For instance, some Welsh fairies gave an old farmer a bag of gold with the stipulation that he not tell anyone about its source. His wife accused him of gaining the money illegally, so he told her that it had come from the fairies. Of course, the gold then turned into useless rocks. Some pacts are simple: Set out bread and ale for the leprechaun and he will cheerfully fix your shoes. Don't steal his gold. Don't stomp on his house.

Other spirit pacts are more complex, with many clauses and contingencies. Some of these things are impossible for a human to carry through. Certain magickal entities want things of us that we would be wise to carefully ponder. Giving them a drop of our blood might bind them to us indefinitely. Particular situations can nullify the contract, but these are uncertain at best. Recall the tale of Rumpelstiltskin, who offered to help a young lady spin straw into gold so that her master, the king, would not have her killed. In return, she had to give the elderly fairy her firstborn child. But the lady overheard Rumpelstiltskin saying his name, so she claimed she could guess it. She guessed correctly, which rendered the contract void…but that was a lucky chance. Breaking a contract with a magickal entity can result in dire consequences, including illness, madness, and bad luck.

Some beings may want to cause us harm for their own reasons, or may unintentionally bring problems. For example, a wind can fill a ship's sails, or it can knock the ship over and wreck it. The wind doesn't really understand the difference. Some entities, such as those considered demonic or malevolent, may not honor any contract, instead doing what they want—usually, nothing good for people.

Therefore, we banish certain energies or beings. We also do protection rituals so that malevolent energies can't harm us in the first place, or we use talismans to repel negative beings.

Practitioners of folkloric traditions often use sigils, ritual tools, costumes and masks, and other physical objects to contact magickal entities. The idea is that the symbol is connected to the entity and thus has an influence over them. Words of power, ritual gestures, and magick circles can also be used to invite, contain, and dismiss certain entities. Some magick users try to use these implements to help control spiritual beings, summon angels, invoke elementals, and so forth. While the emblem might represent the magickal being, and the ritual or items might help restrain it, these types of rites must be used with caution. It is better to politely request aid from an entity—and even make a pact with them—rather than try to control or enslave them.

The ethical considerations of free will and consent apply to energetic beings as much as they do to humans. We must always treat magickal beings with respect, acknowledging their aid as well as thanking them for their assistance.

Deities

Also known as gods, these are energetic beings who possess great power. Some consider them immortal and divine. These entities might have a connection to "the ether" or the universe, allowing them to have profound energetic abilities. In Cymraeg, they are sometimes called *Awenyddion*, or the inspired ones. Deities can embody the qualities of a natural force such as winter, the sun, or the sea. They might be related to a human interaction with nature such as hunting or agriculture.

God-forms are often personified as humans and viewed as having human genders. Deities can take on other human attributes such as appearance, emotion, and intelligence; be subject to human foibles; and participate in the activities of humans. They might possess the qualities of certain traits or conditions, such as wisdom, or a profession like healing or smithcraft. Some people experience deities as pure energy; others experience deities as a force such as love or amazing wonder. Deities may be considered archetypes, or representations of situations that are common to all humans, such as motherhood or death.

Those of us involved in folkloric magico-religions usually do not believe our deities are omnipotent or omnipresent. We mostly feel that one deity has one capability, like controlling storms, or several talents and influences, like Dôn (also known as Danu, Donia, Danann, Anu, Ana, and Annan): the goddess of motherhood, the household, bodies of water, mountains, and childbirth. However, even the gods or powers of nature have limitations. For instance, most deities must obey the laws of physics.

Some folk magick traditionalists practice a form of monotheism, believing that all spirits combine to create a deity, sometimes represented by Gaia, a collective intelligence, or an anthropomorphized Mother Nature. This concept is rather like the neoplatonic principle of the *anima mundi*, animated world, or *spiritus mundi*, world spirit.[28] Other common magick practitioners, such as Wiccans,

---

28. Donald Zeyl and Barbara Sattler, "Plato's *Timaeus*," *The Stanford Encyclopedia of Philosophy* (Summer 2019), ed. Edward N. Zalta, https://plato.stanford.edu/archives/sum2019/entries/plato-timaeus/.

believe in the duality of God and Goddess. Some old-line Pagans practice a type of polytheism. They may believe in a pantheon, or family of god-forms, who come from a particular ethnic background or culture. Some of us deify our ancestors, embodying them with godlike qualities. Likewise, some believe that people with psychic abilities have descended from the gods.

Folkloric traditionalists might combine deities, syncretize two or more pantheons, or choose several patrons or matrons from several different societies and families of gods. This is called eclectic devotion. Of course, some common magick practitioners do not believe in any deities at all.

People who practice a magico-religion that originated in the British Isles often choose deities (or are chosen by gods) that derive from this location. They may interact with entities from one or more cultures who dwelled in or occupied Britain throughout history, such as Celtic, Roman, and Norse. Some folkloric religions believe that all deities representing a certain concept are the same. For example, they may honor the Celtic Ogmios, the Roman Minerva, and the Norse Odin, all of whom represent wisdom, intelligence, and study. That said, some people find that different god-forms from different backgrounds and nations are not the same being at all. The Irish Goibniu, the Roman Vulcan, and the Saxon Weyland are all gods of smithcraft and metalworking, but they have very different personalities and behaviors. Some deities, such as Brigantia, for whom Britain was likely named,[29] have dual or triplicate aspects. A seeker might call upon Brigantia hoping for her motherhood virtues, or for protection and security, and instead feel aggressive ... because she is also a warrior goddess.

We must remember that the numerous societies who've inhabited the British Isles over time may have waged war with each other—Irish and Norse, for example. Practitioners must be careful to make sure everyone on the guest list gets along, so there are no fights during the party. Folktales, myths and legends tell us which deities formed alliances with one another, and with which groups of humans.

A relationship with the divine may happen organically. A person may notice a symbol that represents a deity recurring in their everyday life or during ritual. Sometimes deities can seek us out, appearing to us and giving us an omen, psychic

---

29. George, "Brigantia," *Brigantes Nation* (blog), accessed April 2, 2020, https://brigantesnation
.com/sites/brigantia.

visions, or verbal messages. People may also contact a god-form for whom they feel an affinity, call upon a deity for a specific condition or working, or meditate or enact a journey to find a deity that works for them.

Not all deities of myth and folktales are kind and munificent. Some have their own agenda. A few of the gods seem indifferent to humans' needs, emotions, or suffering. For example, a deity that represents winter may not have an awareness of the physical pain caused by freezing weather. Other gods operate outside of the realm of human understanding. While a deity such as the personification of death can seem adversarial, this god-form has a specific role to play in the cycle of life. Gods may be supplicated, or entreated for mercy, or even bribed with material goods or promises of dedication. Not honoring a pact or contract with a deity can have repercussions. Folk tales describe humans who angered the gods and were subject to a terrible fate.

The gods might test an individual's fortitude by issuing challenges, quests, or trials. This is usually meant to strengthen a person or improve their moral character. Adversity is viewed as bringing wisdom, understanding, and tolerance. Folktales and myths also tell us about deities who disguised themselves as swineherds or elderly women to see how a person would behave.

However, most god-forms are viewed as benevolent and concerned for human well-being. They are believed to interact with mortals as elders do with children. They might impart inspiration and wisdom. They can intercede on a mortal's behalf. Many common magick users feel that our deities provide comfort, support, love, education, security, creativity, and guidance. Some practitioners think that our gods are the source of our magickal power.

Folkloric traditionalists often honor our deities, showing devotion and reverence. Some people perform acts of veneration for their gods, which can include offering tributes and gifts or creating a shrine just for them. Some practitioners make sacrifices of time, material items, personal talents, or perform charitable acts in the deities' names. Declarations of favor are made by the gods in British folktales and myths; they rewarded honorable, noble, hardworking humans with special abilities, loving relationships, fame, and contentment.

Some common magick users believe that the deities receive as much from our veneration as we do from their intercession. A few old-line Pagan legends tell of gods who withered and died from lack of belief in them. This might be in keeping with the idea of the magickal pool, or wellspring of energy. Performing rites and devotional actions can help to replenish the deities' power as much as it can renew humans' spiritual strength.

Fairies

The Fae and similar energetic beings are prevalent in the lore, images, songs, and the fairy tales of the British Isles. The *Creideamh Sí*, or Fairy-Faith, of Ireland and the belief in *Tylwyth Teg* in Wales [30] have survived to the present day, including in locations where Irish and Welsh emigrants settled. Folk magick practitioners may consider fairies to be personified spirits of nature, connected to the earth and naturally occurring phenomena. Others believe fairies are supernatural beings composed of pure energy, ancient races, or spirits of the dead.

While Victorian artists and modern cartoon movies portrayed fairies as tiny, lithe, humanlike beings with gossamer wings, they can appear in various guises. Some look like protohumans, such as the hobs that resemble miniature Neanderthals. Others can appear as a glitter of light, a swirl of air, a pool of water, or a mossy, green, leafy figure. Some fairies actually have wings, usually those of a butterfly. Fairies can be shining and lovely or ugly and scary. Folkloric beings' appearance does not necessarily equate with their true nature. A pretty, sparkly entity can be nasty, while a hunchbacked, leathery, wrinkled brownie can be kindhearted and helpful. Sometimes, fairies simply remain unseen. In England the fairy folk were said to have material bodies at some times and be invisible at other times. Intuitive people might perceive them as a drift of energy or a feeling of awe. When a cat seems to be chasing nothing, she might be after a fairy.

Unlike gods or other spirits, fairies are not often summoned. They may simply show up. People encounter the Fae when visiting sacred sites, circles of standing stones, or human tombs. Fairies might inhabit natural places such as wellsprings, a thorn tree, or "fairy rings," which are a circle of toadstools where the wee folk are said to dance and cavort. They might live within the dwellings of humans. Other legends say that fairies exist in an alternative dimension, sometimes called Fairyland, Faerie, Elfhame, or *Caer Sidi*.

Most fairies seem much closer to the common folk than deities do because they can inhabit the land and our homes. They may appear as quasi-human, or

---

30. W. Y. Evans-Wentz, *The Fairy-Faith in Celtic Countries* (Mineola, NY: Dover Publications, 2002).

at least as a recognizable being, so we might anthropomorphize them. However, these entities might not show human behaviors and feelings. Fairies can take on aspects of wild magick or untamed nature that we may find discomfiting. Sometimes they prefer to wear no clothing. They can exhibit hedonistic tendencies. These spirit people often do not acknowledge time, aging, pain, or language. Nor might they be susceptible to human needs. Conversely, fairies can display human-like characteristics, act playful and mischievous, or guard their natural homes.

Sometimes fairies choose to interact with humans, sharing lore and wisdom, especially about herbalism. They might act benevolent, generous, and helpful. Many fairy tales tell of energetic beings who help people to do tasks around the home, farm, and workplace. The *Ghillie Dhu* was known for finding children lost in the woods in Scotland. Cornish pyskies (also known as piskies or pixies) can lead lost children to a familiar landmark. Water sprites who live in holy wells or in the sea can aid in healing. Other fairies sometimes invite humans to join them in dancing and partying.

Some fairies like to play mean pranks like hiding keys and tools, pinching people, riding horses to exhaustion, or tangling people's hair. Since they don't always have any real sense of individual possessions, the Fae might borrow or take small items. There are folk stories of fairies who steal children and take hostages in Fairyland. Some "evil spirits" or malevolent fairies are viewed as the cause of illness or bad luck. Fairies may cast a glamour or spell onto a human, causing confusion and disorientation. Being "pixie-led" meant spinning in circles, losing one's way, dancing to the point of exhaustion, or becoming otherwise befuddled.

Certain fairies are believed to do harmful acts to frighten humans away from their natural homes. Some, like the yarthkin, are baneful nature entities. A few spirit beings are fairly dreadful, such as the Welsh morwen, who purposefully causes shipwrecks. Others are just too big for their britches, like the puka (also known as pooka or pwca), sometimes seen as a large horselike creature, which might be a precursor of the nightmare legend. In one story, the puka was said to recklessly cavort around a farmstead, knocking down fences, chasing livestock, damaging tools, and wreaking havoc. The puka could be appeased or distracted by leaving the last dregs of the harvest out over the winter for the spirit to eat. People sometimes call the Fae by other names like "the Gentry" or "the Wee Folk" in order to avoid specifically invoking a baleful entity.

Fairies can be propitiated by giving them gifts of coins, food, beverages, and shiny trinkets. Magick users can make offerings to the Fae of music, poetry, and art. Malevolent fairies must be repelled by apotropaic objects, spells, gestures, and other acts of common magick. In fact, there is much more folklore about trying to prevent contact with fairies than there is to initiate it. If you want to get on the good side of the fairies, try displaying "fairy lights," hanging tinkling windchimes, putting "fairy houses" in your yard or on your apartment balcony, and leaving out offerings such as strawberries and milk on spirit nights like Beltane eve, Midsummer, and Hallowe'en. If the Fae have hidden keys or stolen a hairbrush, folks should laugh at their prank instead of getting angry and yelling, then politely ask for the return of belongings. We can and must coexist with natural entities.

Elementals or Nature Spirits

The spirits of nature are energetic creatures that correspond to a specific element or state of being found within our natural environment. Some folkloric practitioners may not differentiate between elementals, the spirits of nature, fairies, or deities. Elementals and nature spirits often take an actual, physical form such as pure water. These spiritual forces may also have anthropomorphic qualities or be seen as personifying or controlling a certain element like air or fire. Nature spirits and elementals in common magick can also include the energetic beings who are related to the weather or a particular location.

The Romans and Romano-Britains who occupied the British Isles for several hundred years recognized four elements and their respective elementals. According to the philosophy of Paracelsus, a sixteenth-century alchemist, these include Gnomes of Earth, Sylphs of Air, Salamanders of Fire, and Undines of Water.[31] These creatures are associated with the cardinal directions of north, east, south, and west. Other British ethnic groups recognized different directions or other beings like firedrakes or dragons, earth spirits, a living flame, the four winds, the sacred wellspring, or various god-forms.

Some nature spirituality practitioners acknowledge spirit beings that represent conditions and places such as a bog or fen, snow, moonlight, a lake, sunshine, a mountain, a river, or a woodland. They might not have any relation to a cardinal

---

31. Paracelsus, *Four Treatises of Theophrastus Von Hohenheim Called Paracelsus*, ed. Henry Sigerest (Baltimore, MD: Johns Hopkins University Press, 1996).

direction. Spirit beings and elementals sometimes appear only in one single location, such as a hot spring, or during one specific occasion, such as a thunderstorm. Nature spirits can also be guardians of a holy place, like a forest or waterfall.

Many folkloric traditionalists endeavor to cooperate with the spirit people in everyday life. Elementals can be allies during rituals and workings. They may be invoked, invited, or summoned. Then one can interact with the specific powers they represent. They might guard a ritual space. Many magic-workers use the forces of lightning or the bubbly moving spirit of a brook to help charge a magickal implement or to fuel a spell. Some locations and their attendant spirits offer tranquility, the revitalizing of the human spirit, or creative energy.

Nature spirits are not usually dismissed. Instead, when working natural magick outdoors, they can be invited to participate and asked to lend their qualities, then told that the rite is finished and requested to leave the space if they wish. Elementals should be treated politely, as they can hold great power. For example, an air elemental can manifest as one of the Merry Little Breezes, cheerfully stirring wind chimes and playfully tugging at your skirt.[32] An air elemental can also become a gale, hurricane, or tornado. For this reason, the spirits of nature should be treated with respect. As with deities, elementals and nature spirits should be appreciated and thanked.

Spirits of the Deceased

For my purposes, I will define this type of spirit as the disembodied, energetic remains of a human who has departed the physical plane; in other words, a person whose physical body is dead. A spirit of the deceased can also be called a shade, phantom, phantasm, poltergeist, ghost, specter, apparition, haunt, glimmer, wight, wraith, or soul.

Spirits can resemble the person they were while alive or a younger version of themselves. Some are transparent, or composed of light, while others are opaque. Some spirits appear as a bird or animal with human consciousness. Some have no visible materialization. Intuitive people can hear the spirit whispering or perceive a ghostly manifestation. A magick user may smell flowers, food cooking, or brimstone (like burnt fireworks) in the presence of a spirit. People might feel as if someone is standing close behind them, then turn to see nobody there. Some

---

32. Thornton W. Burgess, *Old Mother West Wind* (New York: Grosset & Dunlap, 1910).

ghosts are said to rap or knock on hard surfaces. Poltergeists can physically materialize, move or throw physical objects, turn water faucets on (seldom off), cause temperature fluctuations in an enclosed room, or cause flickers of electric lights and electronic implements.

Some ghosts can have a consciousness but not be sentient, or they possess awareness, even keen intelligence. Some may be confused or befuddled; they may not be oriented to time and place. Some spirits have benevolent intentions or behaviors while others may be hostile. If a person was a grouch while alive, their demeanor probably has not changed after death. Others are jealous that living humans can still enjoy the physical qualities of life. Some ghostly entities desire to be a guardian spirit and may protect their relatives, watch over an individual they were close to while alive, or serve as a guide and counselor to people who have moved into the spirit's former dwelling. A few spirits are attached to objects like an item of clothing, piece of jewelry, a tool used for work, or a piece of furniture. Others are connected to a place or a family.

Many common magick users share a similar approach to ghosts. Folk magick practitioners seek to communicate with the departed for the purposes of augury, knowledge, or just good conversation. Goals include comforting the relatives or friends of the spirit and passing information on to them. Some spirits want something; for example, news about their families or a reason why they died. Most are just lonely and, delighted that someone can hear them, they have a desire to chat.

Rituals for viewing a spirit include holding a mirror over the left shoulder with the glass facing behind the person. Ghosts can sometimes be seen when descrying in a bowl of water, crystal ball, or other reflective surface. A spirit can be invoked by speaking their name, by using one of their possessions such as a piece of jewelry or a work tool, as a touchstone for contact, or with a photograph.

As with deities, fairies, and other entities, there are several different types of ghosts. There are, of course, random phantoms that just happen to show up. A tutelary spirit is one who wants to help teach mortal humans. "The Beloved Company" are spirits of magick users who have chosen to stay on this plane to be of help to living practitioners. Ancestors are our forebears, which can include anyone with whom we share genetics or with whom we had an affinity while they were alive. Some ancestors are not physically or genetically related to us, but we hold them in esteem for their past deeds or their connection to our family, profession, or ethnic group.

In folkloric traditions, ancestors are vitally important. Many of us deify our ancestors, assigning them powerful qualities. Ritually, we often request the presence of spirit beings, asking for "our beloved dead" or "those who preceded us" to join us during a rite. Many old-line Pagans communicate with ancestors, perform acts of devotion, share food with them, display their pictures or personal items in our homes, show them love, and honor them during ritual. An ancestor can help us magickally by protecting us from harm, sharing wisdom, and offering emotional support. Many folkloric traditionalists with a Celtic background celebrate Hallowe'en, Samhain, or *Nos Calan Gaeaf* as the holiday to commune with and give reverence to our ancestors.

Most ancestors are benevolent and want us to be happy and successful. However, a few may be spiteful or nasty. In fact, we may not feel comfortable working with our biological ancestors—just because someone is our relative does not mean they have our best interests at heart. However, most of us feel that our ancestors are closer to us, and therefore more accessible, than deities. They can serve as intermediaries between humans and the otherworld. Sometimes we try in vain to contact our ancestors. We must accept when they have chosen to move on to the afterlife that they believe in, such as heaven, Summerland, Valhalla, or reincarnation. We still treasure our beloved memories with them.

Angels

Angels may be seen as energetic beings, supernatural entities, or semi-deified humans and are sometimes called holy guardians, augoeides, or the higher genius. The word "angel" derives from Old English.[33] These entities were brought to Britain by the Romans and Christianized Normans, then incorporated into folk magick practice.

Angels may or may not appear human, have a halo or visible light or aura, or have wings—some legends say they receive them after performing good works. Angels can possess divine qualities such as the ability to heal or foretell the future. Some are viewed as messengers from a deity. Angels are believed to be guides and protectors, but they could also be judgmental. Some people believe that the deceased who lived a righteous life become angels or similar spirit beings.

---

33. *Oxford English Dictionary*, s.v. "angel," accessed April 2, 2020, https://www.lexico.com/en /definition/angel.

Some view angels as a race of powerful magickal beings with no particular connection to religion.

Those who practice a spirituality that is syncretized with an Abrahamic faith may believe in and call upon angels. Christian practitioners might say that angels dwell in the celestial realm or the afterlife called heaven, yet do workings on earth. Some may believe in a personal "guardian angel" who watches over and protects them and their loved ones. Some people of the British Isles revere similar angelic beings, such as the Valkyries of the Norse paths, devas, nature spirits, fairies, watchers, and the spirits of the departed. Others think this is a false equivalent and feel that Christianity imposed its beliefs on native British faiths.

Demons and Related Beings

The word "demon" comes from the Greek *daemon*, which simply means "a spirit." I define demons as malevolent energy beings that have characteristics or behaviors considered to have a detrimental impact on humans. This is a different concept than the diabolism of Abrahamic faiths, which views demons as evil beings connected to the god-form of the devil or Satan. Some common magick users do not distinguish between demons and other potentially dangerous entities such as malicious fairies, disgruntled nature spirits, or baneful ghosts.

British Isles folktales and folklore are full of terrifying demons who seem to serve no purpose other than causing damage. Demons were blamed for bad luck, illness, financial problems, difficulties relating to nature, troubles within the home or workplace, malfunctioning tools, and other negative situations. "Black magic," or deliberately harmful energetic workings, were attributed to these entities.

Demons can appear as the classic Abrahamic image of a nasty creature with horns, leathery bat wings, and a tail, depicted in many drawings of witchcraft trials. Malicious beings can assume the form of an animal, most often a cat, bat, toad, carrion fly, black dog, goat, or hornet. Demons can appear as a dense cloud of energy, lightning bolts, a miasma of swampy discolored goo, a dead human or animal, darkness, or have no physical form at all. They can also present themselves as a living human with strange characteristics, like being partly obscured by fog. Often, they manifest as a perception or emotion of dismay, anxiety, fear, or sadness.

In native British languages or dialects, several negative entities had specific names and behaviors. The bogey, bogeyman, or boggin, called a *bwgi* in Cymraeg, might try to frighten a person to feed off the human's fear response. The Scottish *kelpie* and the Welsh *ceffyldŵr* were nasty monsters in the shape of a horse who liked to drown people. The will-o'-the-wisp led travelers into unstable, boggy ground. One tale that comes from Welsh Americans tells of a malicious being associated with winter who appears as a bobbing lantern light or a young maiden crying for help in an effort to lure would-be rescuers onto thin ice, with the intention of drowning or freezing them.

Much of folklore is devoted to methods of preventing demonic activity, and folktales abound with heroic figures who fought or thwarted fiendish entities. In past days, many magickal workings, spells, and rites were devoted to repelling, containing, or banishing malicious energetic beings. Apotropaic objects such as talismans and amulets were used to repel demons and their effects. Charms, prayers, chants, and spells were said aloud to protect humans from harmful situations. Rites were enacted to banish demons or to shield people from demonic powers.

Familiar Spirits

These are disembodied entities or energetic beings who aid humans in magickal endeavors. They are also called a *magistellus*, guide, or puckeril. Some are referred to simply as a "friend" or, here in the US, a buddy or pal. These beings may or may not take the form of an animal, a human, or another life form. The witch trial transcripts described creatures like toads, rats, mice, cats, bats, black dogs, black roosters and hares, or even the conventional horned, pointy-tailed demon of Christian literature. Familiar spirits may or may not be nature spirits, spirits of the departed, angels, or fairies. They can resemble a composite animal, such as a gryphon, or a mythological creature like a dragon; they can look like twinkling lights or a ball of darkness; or they might not take any material shape at all. My tradition also has the belief that real animals can serve as a familiar spirit, including pets, farm animals, or wild animals.

Familiar spirits may demand a contractual agreement or a pact, and they might request some type of a sacrifice or reward. The witch trial victims told of creatures that fed from a witch's "teat," which could be a mole or skin tag, but that is not actually true. Some familiar spirits will request a bit of human energy or a material thing, including drops of blood, food, or trinkets, or an emotional response, such as love. As with any magickal being, caution should be used when making any promise of rewards, especially your body fluids. Some guides assist people out of a desire to see humanity evolve or because of affection. Others simply want to use human energy.

Journeying or astral travel can be utilized to find and form a bond with a familiar spirit, just as it is used to discover a deity. Being deprived of sleep for two nights can cause a person to see their familiar on the third night, especially if it is the full moon. Familiar spirits can enter this realm through a wardrobe, cupboard, mirror, or the bubbles in a boiling cauldron. They can arise when a "toom," meaning an empty cradle or rocking chair, is rocked. Leaving laundry outside in the rain or failing to put work tools away can bring a spirit which claims these items. If an animal approaches a campfire at midnight, it's very likely a familiar spirit.

Here is a funny story about a familiar spirit: Our family and friends were at a bonfire on Hallowe'en. A large black dog approached the fire, scaring everyone out of their wits. The dog did not belong to any neighbors. It had never been seen in the area before. The black hound walked clockwise around the fire once, its eyes glowing in the eldritch light. Joking nervously, we said it was one of the *Cwn Annwn*, the hounds of the otherworld. The black dog approached my eight-year-old son, wagging its tail, nosing his hand, and slobbering all over him. It accepted a hamburger, wolfing it down. The hound then vanished into the night, never to be seen again. The next day, my son got an important message. We believed we'd been visited by a familiar spirit.

Fetches

A fetch is an energetic being that is a temporary creation, made or invoked by people exclusively for the purposes of magick. These human-made energy creatures may inhabit a clay or wax figure, a cloth doll or poppet, or a drawing. A fetish is a power object which contains a fetch. These beings are also called a psychopomp, bid, bidewell, bud-will, spirit baby, ergregore, eidolon, fylgja, imp, servitor, or fith-fath. Some call them familiar spirits, an elementary (elemental), demons, or angels, but for my purposes, these are separate, distinct beings.

Energy creatures may be constructed of a magickal force which is raised for that specific purpose. The fetch may be formed from a portion of a human's psyche or consciousness that was deliberately cut off or set aside for the reason of movement independent of the person. The energies of lovemaking that do not result in physical conception can be used to create a fetch. A group of practitioners can each lend personal energy to produce a fetch. The magick user's breath may be used to bring the fetch to life, to imbue the fetish object with power, or to connect the energetic being to the practitioner. A fetch can be attached to the fetish. The fetch can also roam freely and be unseen by most humans.

The energy creature can be used to gather knowledge, bring luck, avert harmful situations, or perform a certain action, like changing the weather. Sometimes a fetch was used to spy on other people. It can be set as a watcher or ward, issuing an alarm when disquieting entities are afoot, or alerting people to opportunity. Documents from the witch trials were full of descriptions of fetches, familiar spirits, and other temporary energetic beings, often with accusations of using them for harmful purposes.

Another definition of "fetch" is the part of the human spirit which ranges afield when the person is undertaking trance work or journeying, which will be addressed in a subsequent chapter.

Heroes

Heroes are humans who were imbued with special powers and qualities or who performed valiant feats as outlined in folktales and legends. Not quite deities, heroes may be descended from gods or magickal beings or may have supernatural abilities. They can be summoned, as can deities or ancestors, for the purpose of lending their unique qualities to a practitioner.

Heroes can take on the energy attributed to them by a society. They can represent a certain capability such as wisdom, strength, or fortitude. They may become an archetype. Because heroic figures have human characteristics and emotions, they may be more relatable than deities or the spirits of nature. They may be more approachable and be invited to attend rites or everyday activities. Heroes may be used as a "sounding board" for human difficulties, such as unrequited love or a particularly thorny problem at work. They may serve as intermediaries between people and deities. They can also be requested to fight against malevolent forces.

Some of the heroes of Britain, Ireland, the other Celtic lands, and Saxon sagas are well-documented and renowned, such as King Arthur, Morgan le

Fey, the Knights of the Round Table (who may have been minor deities at one time), Cu Cullain, Robin Hood, Beowulf, and various Shakespearean protagonists. Heroes may be fictional characters, real historic figures, or a composite. For example, Queen Boudicca was a real person whose army defeated the Romans,[34] yet she has become somewhat of a demi-goddess. Other heroes may be Catholic saints or other religious figures associated with British or Celtic deities, such as the goddess Brigid, also known as Saint Brigit.

Common magick practitioners sometimes choose a patron god and matron goddess as spiritual parents. We might develop a personal relationship with a fairy, elemental, or spirit. We may feel we have a guardian angel. These entities are called upon during religious rites and magickal workings. We believe our spiritual assistants can do many things; they can help create beneficial conditions, offer guidance, impart wisdom, and support us emotionally. However, energetic beings cannot (or will not) make all our troubles vanish, give us everything we desire, tell us every last detail about future events, or carry us when we are capable of doing things ourselves. The gods are loving parents, but it can sometimes be tough love.

My own heritage has a set of deities, heroes, and deified ancestors with magickal qualities. We believe they were living people at one point in time, yet they are now aligned with natural forces. They come from Wales but may not share names or legends with known characters of Welsh literature like the *Mabiongion*. These are considered "folk deities," which means they are spiritual beings that common people believe in. One example is Arawn (also known as the Angau or L'Ankou), an entity related to death. Images of him appear in graveyards all over Wales, Cornwall, and Brittany, and stories are told about his wagon with one creaky wheel, drawn by a pale horse, which collects the souls of the departed.[35]

---

34. Joshua J. Mark, "Boudicca," *Ancient History Encyclopedia*, November 8, 2013, https://www.ancient.eu/Boudicca/.

35. Nicole Corbin, "Facing Death: Representations of the Ankou," *Celtic Breizh*, March 20, 2018, http://www.celticbreizh.com/facing-death-representations-of-the-ankou.

Of course, our forebearers did not say, "I am interacting with a spiritual entity who personifies the state of beneficence." Instead, it would be "Reckon I'll talk with the Old Ones and ask them to help me conjure up some good luck." The gods were also called the Blessed Ones, the Shining Ones, the Mighty Ones, the Mothers and Fathers, the Keepers, and by family names such as the Children of Dôn.

six
PREPARING TO
DO MAGICK

Folk magick traditionalists often have ways of performing rituals that are different than modern, Western esoteric systems. Common magick may incorporate older rites into more current ceremonies or vice versa. We might syncretize our ways with the practices and beliefs of other cultures. Folkloric nature spirituality and magick are truly eclectic. There are some conditions that no longer apply to us, like needing a talisman to ward against smallpox or a charm for butter churning. There are new things to consider, like how magickal energies can affect devices such as a cell phone or a motor vehicle.

Some old rituals are timeless and can be applied to new situations. People still need help for success at their workplace. A deity related to childbirth or crop fertility can aid us in current situations. Many of us long for a connection to our natural world. This is why common magick is still relevant today. In this chapter, I'll go over some of the basics that can apply to any energetic rite, then discuss some of the particulars of common magick.

Some traditional witches tell me they don't need all the rigmarole of ceremonies, calling magickal helpers, and protection from harmful beings. They simply walk outdoors into the electrically charged air before a thunderstorm, grab some moss and a granite rock, and use it for healing. However, those actions still involve a type of rite. They utilize natural tools, a particular time and event, and a ritual space. The principle of sympathetic magick is employed. There is an objective. There is a focus of magickal energy. There is an outcome. Although they might not acknowledge it, the witch has created some type of shielding for protection from harmful energies. Not every step is necessary to do a magickal working... but many of them truly *are*.

Until people have practiced magick for a while (longer than five years of continuous working), I strongly suggest that they go through certain steps when enacting a ritual. While they may not call upon deities for help or buy a long list of fancy ritual tools, there is still a procedure to successfully use common magick. Going through all of the following steps helps to attain the desired result.

After this checklist for performing magickal workings or rituals, I will go over some of the steps for getting ready and actually performing the rites.

Magickal Checklist

1. Thought and intent
2. Shopping list
3. Preparing oneself
4. Engaging
   + Preparing a space
   + Shielding
   + Calling for help
5. Declaring intent
   + Visualization
6. Directing power or attuning
   + Raising and directing energy
   + Receptive magick and attunement
7. Sharing
8. Disengaging
9. Acting in accord

The checklist is a guideline, not an absolute. Not every single prayer, spell, working, or rite must utilize every single step. For example, if someone is greeting the dawn, they might think about intent, which is showing appreciation for a natural event. They don't need any particular tools. They might briefly prepare themselves as they would for any social encounter. They will engage by putting their feet firmly on the ground and raising their arms toward the rising sun. The sacred space is wherever they are; most common magick users will not need to create a protective place, other than ordinary personal shields, for this type of rite. Curious spirits may just show up, or the practitioner may want to call upon a goddess of the dawn such as the Roman deity Aurora or the Celtic Anu, the dawn mother. The magick user might simply wish to acknowledge the natural event. Intent is declared when the person says, "Hello, beautiful sunrise. I greet you!" The person is attuning with the natural world as the sky turns pink and gold, they are immersed in the sun's first radiant glow, and they feel a sense of awe and contentment. The person disengages when they lower their arms and go about their business. Analysis includes noting how this rite makes them feel. It really is that simple.

Other workings and rituals are, of course, much more complex. First I'll give an example, then I will go through all of the steps one by one. Things will be explained in more detail during subsequent entries and chapters.

Ritual Example Containing the Checklist Steps

Say that my bank account could use a little boost. I want to pick up more overtime hours at work; maybe even get a raise in pay. How to go about it?

I've read in tables of correspondence that Saturday and Wednesday are aligned with deities and energies that represent commerce. I check my personal calendar and an almanac, and I find out that next Wednesday will be during the waxing moon, the time of increase and continuing projects. The optimal planetary hour is morning, but I must go to my job, so I settle for doing the rite in the evening right after I get home. I choose a liminal place that represents new opportunities opening: a windowsill.

My intent is to gain more money through my hard work without causing harm or distress to others. It would be bad if a coworker got sick and had to take time off just so I can be given their scheduled hours. Better situations include gaining new clients, performing more services, or attracting more customers. I also must consider a limit to the amount of overtime I can handle. Writing all this down helps me to focus my intent.

Next is considering any tools and ingredients I may want to use. This is the "shopping list" part, although I needn't purchase everything. Some items I have on hand; others are found in nature. Things that symbolize money are coins, the color green, the abundant dandelions growing in the yard, a malachite stone, a paid bill, and a beautiful coin purse that I got on sale. These ritual ingredients will use the principles of sympathy and contagion. The coins and the paid bill might contain residual energies of other people and situations, so I blow smoke at them for cleansing. Then I dab them with "money oil" that I purchased at a metaphysical shop, visualizing what these objects represent to me: income, commerce, security. I don't have a green candle so I use white. I inscribe it with sigils that represent dollars or euros. I often work with fairies, so I avoid things they dislike, including iron. I remember a nice reward for my magickal assistants: a shiny new penny and a bowl of milk. Finally, I choose a garden rake, a tool that symbolizes work and is used for drawing and directing power. It has aluminum tines, which should not adversely affect the fairies.

Wednesday evening comes and I prepare myself by taking a shower, putting on a loose-fitting green bathrobe, eating a protein bar, grounding and centering, and thinking about my intent. I voice aloud my goals and use visualization to "see" myself working hard, helping customers, and getting a fat paycheck deposited in my bank account. I do *not* focus on unpaid bills or my need for money. I want to envision positive results.

I prepare my ritual space by opening the window and arranging the tools on the windowsill, including the bowl of milk and the penny for the fairies. I shield myself from unwanted energetic situations or beings by visualizing a spinning three-pointed daisy wheel sigil around myself. I set a ward to watch over me. The ritual area is left open for free-flowing energy. The open window acts as a symbolic portal from my home to other realms—a "window of opportunity," so to speak.

Summoning help for my working includes calling upon beings known for labor and industriousness. In folktales, brownies, leprechauns, and hobs perform tasks around the home and workplace, and they are compatible with one another. I politely invite them to join me and ask them for their assistance in exchange for the milk and the penny.

Voicing intent is the next step. I read aloud from my written statement, saying that I wish to gain more income from my efforts. I will be able to handle ten extra hours of overtime per week at my job, and I'd like that to be derived from new customer accounts with my company. I'd appreciate if the payment manifests as money rather than stock options or free products. Declaring that no injury will occur as a result of my actions is crucial.

Now it's time to connect my ritual tools to my intent. I light the candle, then hold the wooden handle of the rake with my dominant hand and place its end onto the floor, visualizing the wood connecting with the bountiful, abundant earth. The tines face the ceiling, and I envision it drawing power from the sky, the sun, and the waxing moon. Through the open window, I consciously, deliberately accrue energy. This can feel like a tingling sensation, the exhilaration felt on an amusement park ride, or a sense of "rightness." It may sound like wind, radio static, a ringing noise, or it may be silent. With my receptive hand, I touch the items which symbolize money—the purse filled with coins, the malachite stone, the paid bill, the dandelions. While doing these actions, I again think about my purpose and intent. I can verbalize the wish, sing a song, or be silent and recall the reason I'm performing this rite.

When it feels right, I taper off on drawing power. As an intuitive, I can perceive the power that I've accumulated. It can feel like a crackling ball of electricity or seem like the presence of a mighty being. I can feel it flow into some of the ritual objects, creating a repository for energy. Hopefully, I will be infused with a sense of strength, accomplishment, and success. Now is the time to release the energy for my goal. Focusing on intent, I throw the ball of energy back out of the window, picturing it landing on my target (or I could envision shimmering light, a flash of color, or a swift animal running). It might feel like waves flowing toward my goal. Sometimes, I perceive a sound like a slingshot snapping or a bird's wings in flight. Others may not see or hear anything, but that's all right. Again, I focus on intent.

I declare my commitment to share the milk and penny with the fairies and speak aloud my reasons for performing the rite. This is the sharing portion of the working. "I will be very happy with my raise in pay." This uses the magickal principle of "speaking into being." Now is also a good time to thank the entities that were present.

Disengaging includes grounding and centering again, if needed. It may mean telling the energetic beings that they are free to go home if they want. The penny is put outdoors and the bowl of milk is set on the kitchen counter. The candle is placed in a safe spot and left to burn down or is extinguished. Any wards or guards can be taken down. Ritual tools are stored away.

After the ritual, I might feel that one or more of the objects took on power, so I may want to keep them on a nearby shelf, the headboard of a bed, or a table used for work. I may want to carry the objects around for a period of time. I also may wish to do a cleansing on the room, such as waving a besom to dissipate extra energies.

Now is the time for analysis. What went well? Do I feel confident and empowered? Did I think the tools and ingredients were right for this working? What could use improvement? This step may be revisited after the results are in. Must a similar rite be enacted again at another time? I might think that once is enough and patiently wait for the outcome, or I may consider that the ritual should be repeated, perhaps at the next new moon, or until I get the desired result.

The most important part of a ceremony takes place afterward. People must act in accord with their workings. My husband has a saying: "In order to win the raffle, you've gotta buy a ticket." In order for a rite to achieve goals, a practitioner must perform behaviors in "accord," which means in agreement or in harmony. This means taking action toward the objectives. I will have to show up at my job on time and work extra hard. I'll mention to my supervisor that I am willing to take on some overtime hours. I will endeavor to treat customers well and be nice to my coworkers, even the grumpy ones. I will also carry my power objects with me to work.

This probably sounds like a lot of effort, but the results can be amazing. Things might not happen the way that people originally envisioned it, either. Rather than overtime, they could receive a promotion. They might get a new job offer in a better location. Magick can be limitless.

Below are more suggestions regarding each step for a magickal working or ritual.

Thought and Intent

This is one of the most crucial parts of performing any magickal act. Everything else follows one's intent; follows as in chronological order, but also meaning that intent leads the rite and everything else lines up behind it.

Some questions to consider include: Why is this rite or working being done? Is it to celebrate a holiday? Does a goal need to be accomplished, such as creating an object to store power or directing energy to a person or cause? Is the working intended to continue a situation that already exists or bring about a condition that previously happened? Is it a brand-new circumstance? All reasons should be considered using the lens of truth.

Magick workers must think carefully about their desired outcome and any bonuses or side effects. A proscription should be included against any possible negative result, including how the working might affect oneself and others. People should leave themselves open in order to accept positive forces, which achieve objectives that they may not have thought of. Conversely, they might wish to make some specific requests. Again, I'll use the example of abundance, a term that can be interpreted in multiple ways. Do I want an abundance of weeds in my garden or an abundance of food in my cupboards? Some other words to carefully consider include wealth, opportunity, fertility, plentitude or plenty, fame, fortune, success, attract, repel, know, be aware of, understand, perceive, justice, revenge, bind or binding, restrict, impair, control, influence, manage or rule. I must define what constitutes "plenty," and in regard to what. Material objects? Time? It's suggested that the words positive, beneficial, good, helpful, and favorable be added to the verbalization of intent.

It's a good idea to write down and analyze the reason for a rite as well as every consideration or contingency related to it. Written intent can add to the magick, aid as a memory device, and help to focus one's will. Some people write out an entire ritual; others find one online or in a book. Some magick users improvise, but the steps outlined above are still utilized.

Next is planning the rite itself and its time, date, and location. What is available? What lines up the best with the goal? Is an altar required? Is the location of the rite practical, legal, and safe? The nearest crossroads at midnight might be the most magickal place and time but could garner unwanted attention. Outdoor spaces are wonderful but can take some extra preparation. Here in Michigan, when we have four feet of snow on the ground, the wind is high, and the temperature is below zero, hardy people can stand outside for about fifteen minutes … while wearing winter coats and huddling around a bonfire. It's best to have the outdoor winter rite last for a few moments, then go indoors. Liminal periods can be considered as well. Day and time correspondences are based on natural occurrences, such as fertile periods of the year and moon phases. Some are absolutes—like the dark of the moon, which lasts for a brief time—while others are merely a guideline. For instance, the common magick practitioners of old celebrated the harvest season anytime during the months of autumn.

Shopping List

Before making a shopping list, consider the steps outlined at the beginning of this chapter and the purpose of the rite. Will a talisman need to be crafted to store magickal power? Will specific tools be needed to direct energy? Magick users should think about the laws of sympathy and contagion when choosing material objects needed for a rite. What is on hand? Can items be found in nature? What needs to be purchased? Facsimiles may suffice; if a crown of real holly leaves for the Winter King can't be found at Midsummer, a headdress can be made out of paper or cloth. Do any items need to be cleansed or consecrated? Are tools legal and appropriate for the setting? Some locations do not allow blades, food, open beverages, or open burning.

How about food and beverages to share? Certain magickal treats or ethnic dishes correspond to specific gatherings. Some rites include passing a chalice or horn. A gift for magickal helpers should be considered as well. This can be food, a trinket, a beverage, or another item that represents the entity. The object should be buried in the earth, cast into a fire, left outside for the spirit, dropped into moving water, put in a place that holds importance, or discarded after a certain number of days.

Preparing Oneself

As a person physically prepares for a rite, it is important to mentally focus, think about the intent of the rite, and get in a proper emotional state to participate in a working. Cleansing and purification may be needed. This might mean taking a soothing herbal bath beforehand, symbolically cleaning the spirit as the physical body is washed. Some people use a sauna or sweat lodge to remove toxins from the body. These impurities are considered to be both physical and spiritual. (Yes, the ancient Celts actually did build sweat lodges. Archeologists have discovered stone structures used for purification rituals.[36]) Ceremonially anointing oneself with essential oils, water blessed for that purpose, vinegar, and/or smudging may be undertaken. (Note: Before using any oils or bath additives, people should do a "patch test" on the inside of the wrist in order to check for a possible allergic reaction.)

---

36. Ronan Foley, *Healing Waters: Therapeutic Landscapes in Historic and Contemporary Ireland* (Farnham, UK: Ashgate Publishing, 2010).

Preparation can include fasting to empty and purify the physical body. If there is a medical issue such as hypoglycemia, fasting is not recommended. Some people may want to beef up with protein or carbs for physical energy. Hydration is important as well.

The energetic body should also be purified. This includes intuitively checking for unwanted attachments, such as bindings or symbolic cords fastening one to other people. Check for "psychic leeches," which might appear like the animal, bloated with discolored energy. They may also appear as a demonic being, a cloud of gray polluted energy, an infestation of fleas, or a strange feeling of disquiet and worry. Folk magick practitioners can use a ritual tool, such as a ceremonial knife, to remove bindings that are no longer functional. The saying about "cutting ties" is applicable here. Visualization is also effective—imagining a sizzling energetic weapon to "cauterize" unwanted bonds, or water to wash away undesirable conditions. A sigil can be used to remove a binding, such as a daisy wheel or pentagram acting like a lawnmower blade to chop through restraints.

Grounding and centering may be necessary before beginning a rite. Grounding means connecting the physical body to the mind, emotions, and spirit and touching base with consensus reality. It is orientating to time, place, and physical surroundings. Some common magick users say "rooted," which carries the image of a plant sending roots into the ground. Others call it "earthing." Grounding may involve keeping a stone, amulet, or statue as a physical connection to this material plane. It can include placing the feet flat on the ground and emphasizing a connection to the earth and one's surroundings. Being "anchored" means connected to the physical realm. "Centering" means finding one's inner being and ensuring safety and confidence. Some folkloric traditionalists simply call this "getting right."

Grounding and centering are important so that a person does not retain excess energy, which can make them agitated, anxious, "spacey," or "airheaded." Conversely, grounding and centering help to ensure that an individual's personal energy reserves are not drained or depleted, which can make them feel exhausted and depressed. (Note: This is different than the medical conditions of clinical depression or an anxiety disorder, which may require treatment by a professional.) Meditation, breathing exercises, connection to the earth, affirmations, speaking one's name and lineage, or simply closing the eyes and finding one's inner spiritual core can work. Grounding and centering may need to be redone after a rite as well.

Words of power can be verbalized, stating readiness for a folkloric magick rite to begin. Many folkplays begin with "In comes I…" Even a simple starter like "Ready, set, GO!" can work.

I further suggest securing children and pets before a working, although small kids and animals can wander in and out of a ritual space, folkplay, procession, or other ceremonial location without adversely affecting the energy. Children may benefit from attending a holiday celebration or other religious occasion, and familiar animals can actually help by enhancing the power. However, much as we love them, kids can be a distraction when trying to focus the will and intent. Some pets may be overwhelmed by the energy and flee or act uncomfortable. This fact may have led to the cliché about witches holding their mysterious rites at midnight. While it can be an auspicious time for a ritual, it's also the hour when the kids and doggies are asleep. At the very least, children and pets will need shielding, which we'll get to in a moment.

It is also recommended that electronic devices are turned off, or left outside of the ritual space, since they can interrupt one's focus, or worse, get "zapped" by the energy and stop functioning. Besides, they're annoying.

Engaging
Preparing a Space

The purpose of this step is to clear a spot in order to raise and move energy or secure a location for doing more passive rites, like taking a spiritual journey. The ritual space is often considered holy ground. It can be used to keep out negative energies and to contain and strengthen magickal power that is conjured by the rite's participants.

Casting a circle is one tried-and-true method of creating a sacred place. This is an area surrounded by magickal energy. A tool such as a ceremonial knife or wand is used to draw power from the surrounding area or another realm. The force is then shaped into a sphere, which may resemble a shining globe of light or feel like an enclosed place of safety. Cardinal directions may or may not be included in this rite. This widely practiced method might be familiar to anyone who has been involved with Western esoteric traditions, but common magick has many other ways of protecting a ritual space. Of course, some folk traditionalists don't use any ceremonial place at all.

Folk magick users of Cornwall, called pellars, use a staff or stang placed in the center of an area to create an energy circle or dome. The power unfolds from the instrument like an umbrella. A string or cord can be attached to the stang in the middle of the space to ensure that the ritual circle is a certain distance from the center, usually a precise nine feet across. Another method is using a cord called a rig, anchored with a peg called a dod or doth, which is driven into the ground at the center of the ritual place. The other end of the rig is grasped in one hand and the practitioner walks clockwise to create a circle. This is sometimes called "making the compass." Some people use a blanket or tarp with a circle called a compass painted on it, which is placed on the ground. A round ceremonial area might also be called a mill, a sphere, and a bought.

Other methods of enclosing a ritual area include passing a skein of yarn around to participants, winding energy and connecting people. The yarn may also be placed on the floor or around trees and bushes at the perimeter of the rite. Putting rope down in a circular shape is believed to keep negative energies and snakes out of a ceremonial space. Drawing a chalk outline around an area can work to outline a sacred space. Different shapes can be used to delineate a ritual location, including a square, a spiral, or a maze. A triangular shape is sometimes used to enclose power and energetic beings while standing outside of the triangle. Other shapes work as well, including the stereotypical pentagram, marked by paint or chalk with lit candles at each point, which genuinely works.

Some common magick practitioners do not isolate ritual areas from other spaces. We might prepare a certain location by "hallowing" it, which means declaring that it is especially holy. We may also cleanse and/or protect our ceremonial space without separating it from the outside world. A ritual location can be sprinkled with droplets of water, vinegar, or salt water, which is called saining or aspergating. Other substances can be scattered about the ceremonial place, including cornmeal, salt, flower petals, glitter, or sand. When purifying or hallowing an indoor ceremonial area with a fine-grained material like salt or sand, it's best to have hardwood floors or linoleum, as it's not fun to remove these substances from the carpet. Only natural, organic materials should be used outdoors. Sigils can be chalked at the perimeters of the ritual space for hallowing and protection. Moonstones or feathers can be tossed onto the ground to catch the attention of magickal entities.

"Smudging," or cleansing a ritual area with smoke, is often done for purification and protection. While associated with Native Americans, the word "smudge," meaning a smoldering fire, is actually from Middle English.[37] The rite was and is practiced in Britain, using herbs such as mint, burning heather stalks or dried raspberry canes, or hazel twigs. "Enhazeling" a ritual area is done by encircling it with hazel wands, or hazelwood crosses, bound with red string. Liquid witch hazel, found at grocery stores or pharmacies, has the same result. Sweeping around the perimeter of a ritual space with a besom or feather fan also works.

Magick practitioners can perform a ritualized movement in order to protect an area, like making the sign to repel the evil eye. This gesture resembles the forked fingers that represent the Texas Longhorn sports team, or the sign used by fans of heavy metal music. However, the ward against the evil eye is unique. The thumb is placed on the palm of the dominant hand and the middle two fingers are folded over it while the pointer and pinky fingers make horns. This may represent a horned deity such as Herne, the Buca, or Cernunnos, and is used to protect a specific area. The thumb can also be placed between the pointer and middle finger, and the ritual area is delineated by pointing. Another gesture, done with the dominant hand, palm out, can be used push away unwanted energies. Common magick users can whirl in place, arms extended, either to delineate a ritual space or to raise energy. Walking clockwise around a specified area, usually three times, can sanctify and protect a sacred area.

Another method of creating a safe place for a working is to bang a drum with a staccato beat, which is said to scare away negative energies. The drum can be played in a heartbeat rhythm to bring participants in sync with Mother Earth. Additional musical instruments both frighten harmful spirits and summon pleasant, helpful beings. A handbell is often used for creating sacred space as well as summoning entities. Whirling a bullroarer can purify an area. The location in which the sound travels is considered as being within the ritual place. Folk magick users can stomp the ground with their feet around a circular area in order to delineate the circumference and frighten malevolent spirits. Songs, chants, and the spoken word can accompany any of the above ritual actions. Intent may be

---

37. *Merriam-Webster*, s.v. "smudge," accessed April 2, 2020, https://www.merriam-webster.com/dictionary/smudge.

verbalized, such as "I consecrate this space to my deities and my working" or simply saying, "Here and now."

Moving clockwise (also called sunwise, southwise, or deosil) is preferred in many folkloric traditions. This is because moving in sync with the earth's rotation "winds up" magickal energies, like winding thread on a bobbin or spindle. There is nothing harmful about going counterclockwise (also called northwise, wraingates, or widdershins), but it does unwind energy. Moving counterclockwise is best used for dispelling, or when something is banished or repelled. Tornadoes in the Northern Hemisphere usually spin counterclockwise, while water going down a drain moves clockwise. Most British ritual dances and ceremonies use a clockwise movement.

Common magick users often envision or set wards or guardians around the exterior of a ritual space. We call to friendly spirits, a familiar, animal helpers, or ancestors to protect us during the rite. We may invoke a watcher, a spiritual being who will cry an alarm if the perimeter is breached, or even repel harmful entities. The wards can be physical objects, sometimes made of natural materials such as eggs, which are said to absorb negative energies. They can be certain magickally charged items, such as crystals, prisms, hollow glass balls, iron nails, or sharp blades, edge facing outward, believed to repel harmful beings and conditions. The wards can be sigils drawn in the air or symbols inscribed with chalk around the perimeter or onto objects. Wards or guardians might not encircle the rite; some are placed at the four corners or at entrances to a home like chimneys and windows. Warding or protecting the working space utilizes the magickal principle of repulsion. In addition, some wards, guardians, and related beings can help summon, contain, and send magickal energy.

Some rituals, such as folkplays, processions, or ceremonial dances, are not held in a singular location, and thus do not have a designated sacred space. They still might require cleansing and/or protection. These rites may use talismans, wards, guardians, or personal shields for magickal safety. Folk dancers can wear bells, which jingle as they dance down the streets to repel baneful energies. The folkplay character of the fool usually carries a staff or baton, which rids an area of harmful beings.

Of course, many common magick practitioners do not use any type of ritual space for protection or containment. They prefer to let the energy flow freely in and out of the location where they are performing their rite. For some, using personal shields are enough.

Shielding

Folk magick users who do not contain a sacred place or set wards for a ritual depend solely on personal protection rituals. Most of us use a technique called shielding, which can defend a person and their loved ones. Rather than being attached to the ritual space, shields protect the spirit and physical body of the individual.

Shielding is wise if a person is participating in a rite where they are not familiar with everyone who is present. It is also a good idea to shield when performing a folkplay or dance in public. Any alternative state of consciousness can leave one open to unwanted energetic attachments. Thus, shielding must definitely be performed in times when a person is most vulnerable; for example, while journeying. Protection rites should also be done before enacting a solitary ritual that involves working with spirits of the dead, unknown spirits of nature, or performing any type of banishing.

A person may use a magickally charged item, such as a talisman or amulet, to shield themselves from psychic harm. Sigils can also be used for shielding. Protective words of power are intoned, such as prayers or blessings. A practitioner can envision a sphere of light around themselves, a crackling electric fence that keeps negative critters from invading, or a guardian spirit designed to prevent a psychic attack. When shielding with an image or visualization, be sure to protect the unseen parts of the body such as the bottoms of the feet, private parts, armpits, and the back of the head. Remember to protect any vulnerable attendees at rituals, such as small children, as well.

Calling for Help

This is the portion of the ritual in which energetic beings are requested to attend and lend their powers and qualities to the ceremony. This can be done verbally, by speaking the entity's sacred name or a phrase that invokes them, by singing a song, and/or requesting help. Summoning aid can be done by writing to the entities, drawing a picture, or using something that represents them, including a statue, photo, or a ceremonial object. Visualize how they look and remember or imagine how they feel, smell, and *are*.

Another way to attract an energetic being is to use ritualized movement. A gesture such as crossing your arms over your chest, representing an embrace, might be used, or a beckoning "come here" motion. Standing with the feet firmly planted on the ground and hands raised above the head, palm-up or palms facing out away from the body, connects a person to the earth and sky. The placement of the hands depends on whether the magick user believes that spiritual beings dwell in the sky, in an underworld location, or in an alternative dimension on the same level as the material realm, such as Fairyland or the otherworld. The idea is to reach out to the entity and to connect with the beings' location.

Common magick users who perform folkplays and ritual dances may avatar, or ritualistically "become" an entity, which brings them to life within the ceremony. Performers can put on the mask and/or costume that represents the being before or during the actual ceremony, which serves to invoke them. More about this will be explored in a subsequent chapter.

As previously mentioned, some magickal practitioners are nontheistic. Thus, calling for assistance is not a required part of a ritual. Remember: If you do call for aid, a warm greeting is advised.

Declaring Intent

Intent should have been considered during the very first step. Now it is time to bring the will into manifestation. Some folk magick users choose to make verbal statements about intent, sometimes using song, verse, or a strongly voiced proclamation, as if they were giving a speech before an audience. Others use imagery or movement. Words and images have power under the law of sympathetic magick, the law of contagion, and speaking into being.

Caution is advised because anything requested during a magickal rite within a sacred space can be spoken into reality. Many folkloric magick users believe in the axiom "from your lips to the gods' ears." Gossiping, complaining about a boss, and hating on a former partner can be considered as a curse. Negative emotions and verbalizations can also divert the energies from the actual purpose of the rite. At worst, it can pollute the magickal pool. Instead, concentrate on desired conditions. During a ritual is not the time for self-doubt or mistrust. Stating things such as "I sure hope this works" might cast aspersion on one's words, which can undermine the positive verbalizations and weaken the will. Act confident, be optimistic, and stay focused on goals. Determination goes hand-in-hand with intent.

The step of declaring intent is also a good time to make requests of magickal beings. Some folks believe that an entity must be politely asked for a boon using very direct words. Others think that saying something like, "I would like good health for my daughter" is enough; the deity or entity will offer help on their own terms.

To avoid intruding on another's free will, it's best to not speak or write their name unless granted permission. "I would like to have a better relationship with my neighbors" is a truthful phrase, and also does not infringe on their rights.

Making positive statements to invoke beneficial conditions is much more effective than trying to abate the negative. For instance "I would like more income" is more powerful than "I want to stop being poor." Attraction magick means that positive statements attract positive outcomes.

Strong verbs like manifest, invoke, invite, call forth, bring, create, enchant, empower, summon, embody, and determine are helpful to cause or bring about a condition, and words such as banish, remove, cleanse, change, and cast forth are used to get rid of something.

Some folkloric practitioners may believe in proclaiming something as if it has already happened. Affirmations such as "I feel strong" or "My neighbors are always nice" are believed to bring about the positive circumstance which has been declared. Others feel this is not in keeping with the concept of true-speaking. "I feel strong when I carry my crystal" or "I attain newfound prosperity with each paycheck" are modified affirmations that include a time frame or condition.

Of course, some ceremonies have no verbalization or sound—the rites are totally silent. Some rituals, such as folkplays, do not verbally declare intent. Priordination rites do not require a statement of purpose, as it is implicit in the working. A performer might want to declare intent and purpose anyway to inform any non-Pagan onlookers of what's occurring. Other peoples' skepticism or disbelief is unlikely to affect the rite as long as the participants are fully invested.

Visualization

This magickal technique is used to see with the mind's eye, to imagine, and to create a desired situation. Visualization can be done in conjunction with statements of intent or during the energy-raising portion of the ritual. This can also be called conceptualizing, picturing, evoking, conceiving, envisioning, or conjuring.

Common magick utilizes visualization, but all of our other senses are involved as well. Practitioners endeavor to see, taste, sense, smell, emotionally feel, tactilely feel, and intellectually understand each requested condition as if it had already occurred. This helps to focus the will and bring about a positive outcome. Engaging all the senses, emotion, and intellect can help increase the probability that a desired situation will transpire. Magick users also use visualization and involving the senses during passive rites like astral projection.

Directing Power or Attuning

These are two different situations that can take place during the next step: active magick or passive magick. Folkloric practitioners believe it's best to choose one or the other for a single ritual.

Both active and passive magick use power. The energy needs to be accumulated before it can be employed. This can be done by raising or generating a force or by drawing power from one's surroundings. This energy is said to be used to "fuel" a magickal rite.

Raising and Directing Energy

To raise energy, a participant can dance, sing, burn a candle or bonfire, spin yarn from fiber, knit or do needlework, grind a mill or perform other repetitive movement, walk in a clockwise direction, drum or play an instrument, use gestures, rotate a staff around like a baton twirler, or whirl around in circles. Skipping, setting off fireworks, making love, and creating sound can all produce energy. Nearly any activity can raise power.

Magick users can also draw or summon energy from their surroundings. Force can be accessed from the consciousness of a deity or the sentience of the earth. It can be acquired during natural events like the sunrise or a lightning storm. Power can be channeled from an energetic pool. The practitioner must use care to not deplete any one source of power, including their own reserves.

To tap in to the power, a folkloric magick user can visualize or sense it. An energetic force can appear as a bright beam of sunshine or moonlight, a mighty river with rolling waves, or a lightning bolt. It can be sensed as static electricity, a rush of air, a vibration, sound waves, the force that gathers before a storm, wind, the sensation of moving at a high speed, or a strong emotion.

Power can be accrued into one's own being or within a ritual tool. Power can be stored in a talisman or other magickal implement until its release. Energy can also flow freely from a person or a receptacle, like a stream. It can be emitted like a sound wave or pushed into an object or person. It might "zap" from the witch's fingertips or wand like a bolt of lightning, as seen in so many movies and television programs about magick, or it might waft slowly and deliberately like a scent. It is subjective; unique to each practitioner.

One way of channeling power is called an "onlay" or "laying on of hands." One's hands are held up, palms out, attracting and absorbing the power. Then the hands are placed onto the intended receptacle, releasing the energy. It might feel like an electric current, like water flowing from oneself into the target, or like blood moving from the heart to an extension of the body. It might feel as if all of the senses are heightened with everything looking especially bright, causing hyperawareness. Conversely, it might feel soothing, like a fantastic hug. Channeling power through oneself requires excellent grounding and centering skills.

Energy can also be directed right from the source of power to the intended recipient without any intermediary. Some healing rites or workings to bring a desire into manifestation send energy from its supply to its target. A wand, athamé, staff or stang, farm tool with a long wooden handle, broomstick, or large crystal point can also be used to direct energy. Catching and tossing the power can seem like throwing a ball or hitting a puck into the goal, which might be why it's called "casting" a spell. A chalice or other container, physical or imagined, can be filled with power and the energy can then be poured out onto the recipient.

It is a good idea to restate intent while directing power. A simple statement like "I release this energy into this stone for healing my friend" works. So can a word of power like "Go!" This is to ensure that the energy is aimed at its intended recipient, and this makes it more likely that the energy will land successfully. Energy that is unfocused can scatter and affect other beings, persons, or situations. Scattered energy can also have no effect at all. Regardless, this is wasteful of all the time, effort, and resources that have been mustered for the ritual.

Directing power is one of the most wonderful, magickal feelings. Energy can seem very dynamic and vivacious, full of the life force. The magick user might feel exhilaration, strength, an adrenaline rush, or (of course) empowered.

Speaking of which…Another essential thing to do is consciously replenish the common magick pool. Remember to retain some energy for oneself. One's own personal life force and energetic body or spirit is important and may need a boost. This is called recharging, drawing power, renewing, propagating, or revitalizing. It works like recharging a battery, a power storage device that can accept energy from another source. The same process is used as sending power toward any other receptacle.

Receptive Magick and Attunement

Divination, astral travel, alignment with a spiritual being, and using one's own natural psychic abilities are passive, receptive forms of magick. Attunement can mean coming into balance with nature, the spirit world, and/or oneself. Folkloric practitioners use certain techniques and rituals to attain the change in consciousness or heightened awareness required for attunement, or to help them navigate the otherworld.

Attunement and other psychic work can require some type of distraction for the physical body so that the mind can open. While the material body is occupied and the senses are being engaged, the mind will quiet or empty, and the spirit comes into awareness. More about this topic will appear in a subsequent chapter.

Once the mind has been distracted and the mind and spirit opened, energy is raised or channeled in the same manner as for an active rite. The forces can be used for the purpose of divination, attunement, or journeying. Power is also used for personal protection during the process of the rite. This requires sending energy inward, to the self, as well as reaching outward, toward the ether or universe, in an attempt to connect with the being or with a source of knowledge.

While not every folkloric magick user performs augury or uses their psychic abilities within a ritual setting, a ceremony can help with summoning power and granting protection. Doing a deliberate magickal working for attunement rites can also help to prevent the draining, tiring depletion of energy that sometimes accompanies an intense spiritual encounter. A magick user who undertakes astral travel can have difficulty orienting themselves in a place where there is no "down" or "up," or where time is meaningless, and thus must work on processing their experience. This leads us to…

Sharing

Sharing can mean talking to others about involvement in a magickal rite, the effectiveness of a ritual, and emotional reaction. It can mean journaling or creating art. These actions help a person to comprehend what just occurred during the ceremony. Sharing can help to process an event that might seem fantastical or unreal. After a ritual, it can assist the practitioner with evaluating what things went well and what needs improvement. Sharing can also help a person to interpret and calm emotions that may be difficult to experience, to readjust to consensus reality, and to analyze any information that is not quite clear.

Sharing can also mean giving gifts or food to the entities who helped during the ritual. This may be part of a magickal pact and also embodies the virtue of hospitality. Sharing food and material goods with spiritual helpers must be done before fully disengaging from the rite. This might be accomplished by pouring a libation from a cup onto the ground, placing food in a special location for the spirits, putting an item onto an altar, tossing an object into water or the bonfire, or burying it in the ground.

Sharing information and food with other celebrants can be done after the ceremony is over, if preferred. Sharing connects the individuals who just participated in a ritual. "Breaking bread" is symbolic in many cultures of getting along and being peaceful. Nutrients can help to ground and stabilize a person after a rite. Eating connects the spirit and emotions to the material body. It may help replenish physical energies. Certain foods may have symbolism to an ethnic group or holiday ceremony. As a bonus, food is yummy, and many Pagans are really good cooks.

Disengaging

These activities take place to conclude a rite or working. A magickal practitioner can verbalize that the rite is at an end by saying, "So be it," "What's done is done," "It is good," or "Thus, it has become." These phrases affirm that the ritual is finished. It works like the period at the end of a sentence. In Welsh, a practitioner might say "*Bendythion*" or "*Bithdedwydd*," which are blessings.

Actions including tying a final knot in a magickal cord, stomping one's foot or the end of a walking staff three times, clapping hands, ringing a bell, or making some other gesture that tells people and magickal beings that the working is complete.

After a working or ritual is completed, a magick user may want to ground and center again. Some practitioners physically touch an object stuck into the ground like a stang, pitchfork, or sword. Excess energies from the body are believed to dissipate into the earth, using the tool as a conduit. Other techniques include sitting down on the floor, or touching one's bare feet or hands to the ground while visualizing the surplus power trickling out into the earth. Some folk magick users work to reclaim themselves, verbally affirming identity or stating, "I am here. This is now." This is also the appropriate time to retract any anchors and to "cut ties" with any magickal tethers. A ritual blade may be used for this purpose. Some people visualize reeling in a cord or having the energetic ties simply unravel or disintegrate.

If someone feels particularly disoriented, spacey, hyperactive, or "out of it" after a magickal working, they may need special attention. The person can lie down on their back, fully in contact with the ground. Other participants can "lay on hands" in the attempt to siphon off extra energy. They draw surplus power from the affected person into their palms, then shake off the force, like shaking water from their fingers. Participants can also direct excess power to a ritual object or the ground. The affected person can orient themselves to time and place by stating their name, names of loved ones, their profession, address, the date, and several qualities about themselves that are part of their consensus reality. They can name a few things they notice through each of their five senses. They may wish to become "rooted," or attached to the earth and the material realm. A magick user can take deep, cleansing breaths, counting to ten with each breath. Cooling the body with a sponge bath or warming with a blanket might be required. Eating plain, bland foods and drinking water can also help.

During the time of disengaging, it is also appropriate to thank and release any entities that helped during the ritual. Offerings or rewards can be given at this time. Personal shields may be retracted into the spiritual body, put away in a place like a cabinet or trunk of the imagination, or let go into the ether. Some magick users retain their shields in everyday life.

Sacred space may be "devoked," let go, retracted, or taken down. Some of us leave things as they are to dissipate on their own. If you wish to release a magickal circle by moving counterclockwise, I suggest you don't, as that can banish energy that has just been raised, undo one's efforts, and work against the desired outcome of a rite. Moving counterclockwise can be effective if banishing or removing certain conditions is the intent.

A besom or feather fan can be used to sweep excess energies out of the room. Verbalizations can be spoken: "This rite is ended" or "Now we end and begin again." Some rites end by a natural event, like birds singing as the sun rises. Others simply finish when the song, folkplay, or dance is completed. The words "Merry meet and merry part" are a genuinely older way to signify that a ritual is complete and were spoken after the conclusion of ceremonial dances and folkplays.

Acting in Accord

Now comes the time for analysis and acting in accord. Analysis is looking at the ritual with the lens of truth. What worked? What did not? Was it too long, or not long enough? Was energy raised and directed according to plan? Should anything be added to the rite to make it more efficient next time? Other subjects to consider include the effectiveness of tools, the contribution of magickal beings, and whether or not power flowed smoothly. Divination can help ascertain if the rite was successful and if goals were achieved.

Some common magick users feel that a magickal rite done for a specific purpose should be performed only once, then left to manifest on its own terms. The reason is that doing a ritual multiple times is pestering the deities, similar to the way you may feel if a child repeatedly called your name. It can also show a lack of faith that requests will be heard and honored. Others believe that a working must be performed repeatedly until the desired result has been attained. They feel that the squeaky wheel will get the grease, and so a rite must be repeated as often as is needed. Of course, seasonal rites are performed on a yearly basis, while full moon ceremonies occur monthly. Rituals for priordination can reoccur often. Attunements may have to be refreshed once in a while.

"Acting in accord" is vitally important to any active working. While magick works by using energy to create change, the conditions must be present in the physical, material world for it to function. A magick user must act in accord with a magickal ritual in order to fulfill their desires and cause their endeavors to have a positive result. In other words, doing a rite to gain employment is great, but a practitioner must also send out resumes, network with others, brush up their skills, and go to interviews wearing appropriate clothing. Just performing a ritual and then sitting back and waiting does not always accomplish the goal. Common magick, like any other magick, increases the probabilities that the desired condition will occur. So does putting physical and mental effort into the undertaking.

seven
SIGNIFICANT TIMES
FOR MAGICK

Folk magick practitioners, who studied the cause and effect of energetic workings for generations, discovered that particular hours and days were best for performing certain esoteric rites. These times include the phases of the moon, various astronomical events, and solar occasions. Additionally, our forebearers celebrated important life events and used them as an opportunity for blessing loved ones.

Some readers might be wondering about the reason for discussing these traditions, and whether these customs have any relevance in the present day. For the ancestors, each magickal act had a purpose, such as calling for good health and prosperity during a particular moon phase or holding a feast on a sacred day. Helpful beings were summoned and negative influences were banished. This is still necessary in current times. Of course, we also dance, create art, and celebrate holidays because it's fun. These observances can create a bond between humankind and deities, ancestors, or nature. The rituals can also assist in building a community.

Yet common magick practitioners have another good reason for holiday gatherings: enacting rites for the purpose of priordination. Celebrating during certain times is a way to "pay it forward" using magickal power. Every dance performed, each artistic object that is created, the satisfaction of a delightful feast, and the laughter and joy of an audience watching a folkplay recharge the energetic battery and refill the magickal pool. These forces can be drawn upon later in times of need or difficulty. The reserves of energy sustain each individual and create a support network amongst a family, tribe, ethnic group, or people with a common purpose.

We might not be able to climb a mountain on Lughnassadh or cut fresh greenery in the woodlands on Beltane. However, many rites and workings can be replicated with whatever is available or by using facsimiles. This utilizes the principles of sympathetic magick. Visiting a farmer's market and buying gourds and squash for Hallowe'en is as legitimate of a celebration as selecting the perfect jack-o'-lantern from the pumpkin patch. Bonfires can be replaced with candles. Blossoms from the florist or sprigs of holly from a greenhouse can replace the May basket or Yuletide greenery. Taking a hike on a nature trail on Beltane replicates a woodland jaunt. Groups can gather to enjoy the spirit of the rite, thinking about the past and ancestral customs as well as reveling in the moment together.

Solitaries can read about group ceremonies in books or watch videos online. A celebrant might create a harvest feast for one or share their bounty at a shelter or care facility. Those with an artistic flair can draw symbolic pictures or create an item that represents the holiday. Solitary magick users can create beautiful rituals for one person and connect to deities and nature. Local, regional, and national events for Pagans can replicate age-old traditions during the holidays, and sometimes, unique celebrations are invented and new friends are made.

Liminality

When we enact rituals during special times, such as a solar holiday or particular moon phase, it causes the magick to be especially potent. A liminal period is an ending of one era or phase and the beginning of another, and thus carries the significance of both time periods. An example is twilight, when daytime is ended but night has not completely begun. Liminal times combined with places that are between two locations might have a dual or triplicate nature, taking on the qualities or characteristics of both, all, or neither of the circumstances. Liminal periods have their own particular fluid energy. Folkloric practitioners call liminality betwixt and between, thresholds, straddling the hedge, the borderland, an edge, or a cusp. A metaphor of traditional witchcraft is "jumping the stile," a stone boundary wall, which connotes a demarcation that ends one situation and begins another.

The esoteric significance of liminal times and events is ambiguity. These natural states are seen as being in fluctuation. Liminal periods are optimal for performing magick because they have fewer limitations and restrictions between what is and what could be. When a rite is undertaken at these borderline times and places, it uses the powers of each feature and of all qualities, which amplifies the forces exponentially. For example, if a ceremony is enacted on Hallowe'en, it takes advantage of the end of high season of summer and beginning of winter as well as the end of the harvest and the beginning of a fallow period, when days are becoming shorter and nights becoming longer. This creates an incredibly powerful experience.

Quarters and Cross-Quarters

The "big eight" holidays celebrated by modern neo-Pagans were often called quarter days, also known as cross-quarters in England and Scotland in the past. These dates align with agricultural holidays as well as Catholic saint's days.[38] In old Welsh, a cross-quarter was sometimes called a *Ysbrednos*, or a spirit night, due to a belief that energetic beings were more active at these times. Quarter days mark the borders between seasons, while cross-quarters or spirit nights have profound magickal energies because the boundaries between endings and beginnings are blurred. These holidays, as well as the phases of the moon, are optimal times to perform rites and workings, to reconnect with the cycle of the seasons, and to celebrate life.

I have been asked if it is crucial to celebrate a holiday on the actual date of an equinox or solstice, or if it is essential to perform a rite at the exact moment the moon enters a different phase. While it is not absolutely necessary to use the precise hour and planetary sign to execute a magickal rite or to enact a ritual on the date of a holiday, it surely can help. Timing can influence a working. Specific dates and times, such as the sun being situated in a particular constellation or the moon in its waxing phase, can increase or decrease certain forces or encourage certain conditions.

Days are named for deities and thus may carry the aspects of that god-form. For example, Tuesday was named for the Norse god Tyr, who was known for

---

38. *Encyclopaedia Britannica Online*, s.v. "quarter days," accessed April 2, 2020, https://www.britannica.com/topic/Quarter-Day.

strength and prowess as a warrior. He is associated with the Roman god Mars and the Welsh war god Nuada, and thus Tuesday may carry those martial qualities. Rites performed on this day will have an added potency.

It is easier to do abundance magick during a period associated with harvest, to initiate a project in the spring, and to perform a banishing rite during the winter or the dark of the moon. Anything that decreases resistance, overcomes inertia, and optimizes probability is beneficial in magick.

Magickal energies are strongest when it's closest to the actual time of the height of power, or zenith. Doing a ritual after the designated day is more effective than performing a rite beforehand. The day after the vernal equinox contains new springtime energies, while the day before the equinox still carries the old, tired winter energies. Because we must work, attend school, and/or care for our kinfolk, we sometimes must wait to celebrate a holiday until the weekend. When the summer solstice falls on a Tuesday, it's better to hold your celebration on the following Saturday rather than the preceding weekend. The energy zenith might occur at 2:00 a.m. on Tuesday, June 21, but the time leading up to that hour contains the waning energy of the previous season. The same holds true for moon phases; observing the day after the moon turns full takes advantage of the full lunar energies.

Almanacs can help when determining the exact hour of a planetary occurrence and the location of the moon and sun in the zodiac. This also has an influence on magickal powers. Some signs of the zodiac are viewed as more fertile. For example, Taurus and Cancer are seen as more fruitful than Gemini and Leo. (No, the zodiac did not originate in the British Isles. However, common magick users still find it helpful.)

It is possible to set up a spell or rite beforehand, leave it to "charge" or gain power, then resume the ceremony afterward. A person who works nights can set a crystal on a western windowsill to absorb energy under the light of the setting full moon, perform a brief ritual, leave to complete their shift, and return to find the crystal full of moonlit power. Common magick, by its very nature, can be flexible. Adaptations may cause the loss of a portion of energy … but a little power is better than none. However, there are some events that will not happen twice in our lifetime, like a full solar eclipse during Lammas or an alignment of all the planets with Earth. If we miss these once-in-a-lifetime events, well, it's over.

Not every nature spirituality tradition goes by the calendar, as our ancestors surely didn't. Instead, they used intuition about optimal times for magick or calculated time by a particular natural event to mark the seasons. This was done in place of observing days based on positions of the sun. Folk magick users might consider the first frost to mark the first day of autumn and spring's onset as the day a certain flower blooms. Others mark the seasons on the first full moon after the solstice or equinox. Still others go by the time that the sun enters a particular constellation. And some common magick workers still go by the old Julian calendar, celebrating the solar holidays from seven to eleven days after their current calendar dates. In that case, Hallowe'en is observed on or around November 7.

The Moon

Sailors are aware that the tides of the ocean and large lakes are affected by the gravitational pull of the moon. Lunar transitions also influence certain types of rites. The point when the moon "turns," the minute and hour when the lunar phase changes from waxing to full to waning, are considered liminal times. Common magick practitioners use the moon phases as an influence for our spells and divination. Each moon phase lasts for approximately a week.

Here is how to recognize the moon phases and when they are visible in the Northern Hemisphere:

> **Dark of the moon.** Probably not visible in the sky. Rises and sets with the sun, or rises at dawn and sets at sunset. A very brief period before the new moon. Time for banishing.
>
> **New moon.** Resembles a thin crescent or U shape. Rises and sets with the sun. Time to initiate new projects.
>
> **Waxing moon.** Also known as first quarter. Resembles a D. Rises at noon and sets at midnight. Time for working on projects.
>
> **Full moon.** Rises at sunset, sets at dawn. Time for asking for boons, celebrating, performing magickal rites, and the culmination of endeavors.
>
> **Waning moon.** Also known as third quarter. Resembles a C. Rises at midnight and sets at noon. Time for banishing or removing undesirable conditions.

| Dark | New | Waxing | Full | Waning |
| Moon | Moon | Moon | Moon | Moon |

Figure 3: Shapes of the moon

Dark of the Moon

The dark of the moon occurs for only a short time, between one-and-a-half to three days. This is the last visible crescent of the waning moon or a time when the moon is not visible in the sky at all. The dark of the moon, or the phase just prior to the new moon, is the best time to end something that no longer serves us, such as a relationship, or to permanently banish a condition. The color associated with the dark of the moon is black.

New Moon

The new moon is a time of beginnings, optimal for initiating new projects and starting new relationships. Magickally, it is time to do rites to ensure a project will be successful or to optimize changes. The color of the new moon is silver or pale blue.

Waxing Moon

Waxing moons are perfect for continuing projects that have already been initiated. Almanacs suggest planting above-ground crops during the waxing moon, during periods when the moon is in a fertile zodiac sign, or aligning with constellations representing watery, fruitful energies, such as Cancer. Magickally, it is a good time to do rituals for increase in material things, to bring about positivity in personal relationships, and to count blessings and thank deities. The associated color of the waxing moon is white.

Full Moon

A large body of folklore is devoted to occurrences at full moons. Madness used to be called "lunacy," and the werewolves of folktales transmogrify during the bright moon. The behavior of animals and plants seems to be affected by a full moon. In modern times, the full moon is considered a time of fruition and completion. Full moons are equated with mother goddesses and pregnancy.

Some believe that magickal workings are best performed when the moon is full and that participants should ask for a boon from the gods at these occasions. Other practitioners believe the full moon should be reserved exclusively for celebrations or used to give thanks. Full moons are great for rites that involve the revealing of secrets, cleansing magickal tools, and charging talismans and amulets. They are also a good time for working on projects. Divination seems to be especially accurate when done beneath a full moon. Magickal tools can be charged in the moonlight, absorbing the lunar energies. Many shamanic practitioners host full moon drumming circles. Folk magick users set cups of water out at moonrise to capture the essence of the moon, taking the cup indoors before dawn. The water can be later used in spell work. Colors associated with the full moon are silver, pale blue, and bright white. The full moon is also associated with pink in spring and yellow in autumn.

The planting moon is a bright full moon in springtime, while the harvest moon and hunter's moon are when the moon is full and bright during autumn months, making it easier for farmers and hunters to see and to complete their tasks after sundown. Seeing the full moon through the leaves of an oak tree means good luck. People can wish on the full moon, asking that the same moon that shines on them also shine benevolently onto their loved ones.

At the full moon in springtime and during the harvest, young ladies work this divinatory incantation: "Luna, every woman's friend, now to me your good descend. Let me in this night visions see, emblems of my destiny." The young woman would then fall asleep and dream images that foretold the following conditions. Flowers could mean trouble or a job; a ring meant marriage; a storm meant getting the bad things out of the way and having a good future; bread equated plentitude while cake meant prosperity; a shovel meant death; diamonds, jewelry, or money signified wealth; a flock of birds symbolized having many children; geese meant marrying more than once; a willow tree represented treachery; and keys meant property and power.

Full Moon Names

Nature spirituality traditionalists of both British and Native American cultures had names for each full moon that designated specific times or events that usually occur during that month. These are:

January: moon after Yule, cold moon, snow moon, old moon, ice moon

February: wolf moon, cold moon, hunger moon, storm moon

March: worm moon, egg moon, sap moon, chaste moon, moon of sprouting grass, plowing moon, hare moon

April: Lenten moon, pink moon, milk moon, hare moon, fish moon, paschal moon

May: flower moon, mead moon, rose moon, planting moon, merry moon

June: hay moon, lovers' moon, strawberry moon

July: grain moon, buck moon, thunder moon, hay moon

August: fruit moon, grain moon, sturgeon moon, green corn moon, barley moon

September: corn moon, barley moon

October: hunter's moon, blood moon, harvest moon

November: beaver moon, oak moon, fog moon

December: Yule moon, cold moon

Waning Moon

Banishing rites take place during the waning moon. The waning phase is good for "cleaning up" and for finishing projects. Almanacs suggest planting root crops during the waning moon as well as harvesting during dry or barren zodiac signs, such as Virgo or Gemini. The waning moon is a good time to cleanse the home and one's magickal tools. Colors associated with the waning moon are white, blue, and gray.

More Moon Lore

+ A gibbous moon is at more than a quarter, yet less than full.

+ Blue moons are the second of two full moons that occur during one month or zodiac period, while black moons are the second new moon in one month.

+ A black moon can also be a February with no full moon, which occurs roughly every three years.

+ The second full or new moon in a month can add strength to rites of creation and banishment, possibly because of participants' beliefs rather than any actual power of a moon phase.

+ A super moon is a full moon that is close to the earth and appears very large in the sky.

+ A red moon could mean a bloody year, either in terms of slaughtering many animals or a terrible war.

+ Rain on the harvest moon is a bad omen.

+ A bright full moon that is close to the earth foretells blessings.

+ Witches and fairies were said to dance in the moonlight.

Lunar Deities

British Isles moon deities include the Roman Luna as well as Diana and her daughter Aradia; the Greek Hecate; the Greco-Roman Selene; the Welsh goddesses Arianrhod, Rhiannon, and Nimuë or Vivienne, who represent the waxing and full moons, and Cerridwen, who represents the waning moon; the Irish Áine, who is said to light up the night; and the Gaulish and Breton horse goddess Epona, said to ride at night. Those common magick users who work within Norse traditions honor the moon god, Máni, who may be the precursor of the folktales about the man in the moon.

Natural Liminal Times

Other liminal periods are related to the position of the sun, stars, and moon, relative to the earth. These include dawn, the time when the morning star first appears in the sky, the time when the evening star rises, dusk (also called twilight, the gloaming, shotsele, and owl light), sunset, and, of course, midnight. Midnight does not necessarily occur at 12:00 a.m.—it occurs at the exact midpoint between the sun slipping under the horizon and the first rays of dawn. True midnight can be calculated with the help of an almanac that shows the exact times of sunset and sunrise. Midnight is also called bull's noon, the fairy hour, the small hour, dead of night, and the bewitching hour.

Nighttime is special for esoteric beings, who seem to be most active in the darkness. The Celts reckoned time by the setting of the sun, which was viewed as the start of a new day. Moonrise and moonset are liminal periods, as are a meteor shower, the appearance of a comet, and a display of the northern lights, also called aurora borealis or the merry dancers. Wishing upon the first star seen in the darkening sky is said to manifest our desires. All of these cosmic occasions are optimal for performing magick appropriate to the time, such as cleansing rites and the inception or completion of a project.

Solar and lunar eclipses also hold significance in nature spirituality. Often, the moon will turn red just prior to a total eclipse because of particles in the atmosphere. This is called a blood moon and can also be used for magickal rites. The change in energy during an eclipse can affect animals, humans, and the weather. Birds stop singing, nocturnal creatures emerge, and there are an abundance of natural portents and signs. Eclipses foretold an alteration of personal fortune or meant that an era was coming to an end. The magick of a lunar eclipse is an abrupt ending and beginning. In the old days, bad rulers could be deposed during an eclipse. An eclipse of the moon could be used to remove a baneful female ruler, while an eclipse of the sun could be used to banish an unjust king. A solar eclipse is a good time to make a sacrifice of something precious to us in order to completely end a condition that no longer serves us and to begin a new phase of life. Banishing rituals are quite effective during an eclipse.

Conjunctions are when heavenly bodies appear to line up in the sky. Two planets in conjunction mean that their powers are doubled or aligned. The conjunction of the sun, moon, and earth can lend the energies of all three heavenly bodies. The magickal significance of a conjunction depends on the symbolism corresponding to the planets; for example, Venus often represents love, while Jupiter symbolizes stability. Therefore, if Venus and Jupiter appear to align, it can augur stability in love or be an opportune time to do a working to bring about that condition. Venus and Mars together in the sky foretells harmony between the genders.

Omens such meteor showers and comets were used to foretell events. Comets were and are a strong omen related to drastic change. Halley's Comet passing the earth in 1066 CE was said to have presaged the Norman Conquest. The Christian legend of the star in the east could have been this comet, which also passed the earth in 11 BCE. It also may have been a supernova or a conjunction of two or more bright stars or planets. The Perseid, Orionid, and Draconid meteor showers are used for wishing on falling stars.

The Stars

Liminal times can also be based on the positions of constellations and planets in relation to the earth and sun. Celtic people studied the science of astronomy,[39] or the location of planets, stars, the sun, and the moon relative to the earth during particular times of the year. Pliny the Elder of Rome noted that the Druids used astronomy and other natural sciences.[40] Qualifications for becoming an astronomer are outlined in Brehon Law.[41] This shows us that our predecessors considered the positions of the planets to be useful. Many of the ancient stone megaliths located in Britain, including passage tombs and standing stones, have astronomical significance. Tomb doorways and the architectural design of various sacred sites align with the sunrise, sunset, moonrise, and moonset during a certain event such as a solstice.

Common magick users sometimes formed a type of star chart out of a flat piece of metal, used to predict the onset of the seasons and times related to agriculture. Usually made of copper or tin, these "star plates" had holes punched in them to represent particular constellations. The practitioner would hold the metal plate up to measure against a natural feature, like a tree or rock formation, or a man-made structure, like a dolmen, at certain times of the year. When the stars of the

---

39. A. Gaspani, *Astronomy in the Celtic Culture*, Osservatorio Astronomico di Brerea, accessed April 2, 2020, http://www.brera.mi.astro.it/~adriano.gaspani/celtcab.txt.

40. J. A. MacCulloch, *The Religion of the Ancient Celts* (Edinburgh: T. & T. Clark, 1911; Project Gutenberg, 2005), https://www.gutenberg.org/files/14672/14672-h/14672-h.htm.

41. Laurence Ginnell, *The Brehon Laws: A Legal Handbook* (London: T. Fisher Unwin, 1894; Internet Archive, 2009), https://archive.org/details/brehonlawsalega00ginngoog/page/n5/mode/2up.

constellation shined through the holes in the plate, the tribe would know that it was time to plant, harvest, or gather firewood for winter.

Speaking of astronomy, the Celts of Britain recognized some different groupings of stars than the constellations we've accepted today.[42] Some of these celestial designs are based on Welsh myth and legend, especially the body of literature found in the *Mabinogion* and the King Arthur tales. The name Arthur is associated with bears, so the Great Bear and Little Bear constellations have that symbolism. These two formations are what we now call the Big and Little Dipper. Lyra, the constellation of the harp, was called *Telyn Arthan,* or Arthur's Harp. The Milky Way was *Caer Gwydion,* named after the deity that represented communication and astronomy. The northern circle was named *Caer Arianrhod* for the goddess of the stars and beauty.

Life Events

Common magick practitioners recognize that life stages such as birth, coming of age, learning a profession, marriage, elderhood, and death also constitute liminal periods. One period of being comes to an end while another begins. This is all part of an endless cycle. Yet these events are also very personal for each individual and their loved ones. Rituals are performed to educate, prepare, and help the person adjust to the change, as well as to give well-wishes, aid, and comfort. Magickal rites can be enacted at these powerful times of change, which carry the "betwixt and between" energy of conclusion and initiation. Blessings and rites of protection are the most common. Suggestions for these appear in chapter 10.

The Celts used certain omens to forecast potential occurrences during a person's life; for example, seeing a dog on one's naming day might mean the individual would be loyal. Augury was often performed before the birth of a baby or during a rite of passage to predict how things might go for that person in the future. A person born during the "chime hours" from midnight until dawn was said to be able to view the spirit world.

---

42. Bryn Jones, "Names of Astronomical Objects Connected with Wales," *A History of Astronomy in Wales,* last modified March 3, 2009, http://www.jonesbryn.plus.com/wastronhist /namesobjects.html.

Solar Holidays

Those who practice folkloric magico-religions celebrate holidays and do magickal workings related to solar events, which mark the four seasons. These dates are usually considered as the beginning of each season: winter around December 21, spring on or near March 21, summer circa June 21, and fall around September 21. However, it must be noted that Celtic people often reckoned the beginning of the summer high season as May Day and the beginning of the winter high season as Hallowe'en. While Wiccans call the quarter days, or onset of each season, the "Lower Holidays" or "Lesser Sabbats," many common magick users recognize these days as the "big four" in magickal significance. The sun also enters different zodiac signs and constellations during these times, such as Libra around the autumnal equinox.

There are also sacred days that fall at the midpoint between these occasions. These are called cross-quarters, half-quarters, quarter days, or off-quarters. These include the days of April 30–May 1, August 1, October 31–November 1, and February 1 or 2. They are the center between the beginning and ending of each season, about six weeks after the season has turned. These days are considered liminal times and carry a special magickal significance.

Modern-day Pagans often celebrate these eight seasonal holidays, which they call Sabbats or the "Wheel of the Year." In the Cymraeg language, they are called *Ysbrednos*, or spirit nights. In old Irish Gaelic, *raitheanna*, quarters and cross-quarters, are headed by *raithe*, the beginning day of each period. For common magick users, these days and nights are sacred. They are considered as liminal times optimal for performing certain rites related to weather patterns and to the agricultural cycle. Some of us believe the holiday starts at sundown the night before the quarter or cross-quarter.

The solar holidays are based on the position of the earth relative to the sun. The summer solstice is the longest day and shortest night of the year, and the winter solstice is the shortest day and longest night. *Sol* means sun, while *stice* refers to stillness and stasis; thus, solstice is when the sun was perceived to stand still. The vernal (or spring) equinox and the autumnal (or fall) equinox mark dates that are equally balanced between night and day, darkness and light. *Equi* refers to equality, while *nox* is a word for night; hence an equinox is an equally long night and day.

When Catholicism became widely practiced in Britain, many of the old-line Pagan solar holidays were syncretized with saint's days, and customs were attributed to the particular saint. For instance, St. Michael's Day in late September was celebrated with harvest feasts and agricultural games. Sometimes a new day was used for older activities, and some magico-religious traditions were moved to the new day. For example, many merry May Day festivities were transferred to Whitsunday, a Catholic observation.

Some of these days were not observed by certain British-based cultures at all. For example, harvests lasted for several weeks, with hard work all day and feasting and partying every weekend. Rather than recognizing Lammas and Mabon, the harvest season began when vegetables and grains were ripe and ended at Halloween time, or when the crop was all picked. For most of my life, I never did anything for February 2, Imbolc, because not many Welsh folkloric practitioners celebrate this holiday. However, it's a really big deal in the Irish traditions. I only began participating in Imbolc rites when I encountered neo-Pagans. Other days are majorly important to us, like the calendar new year and the opening day of hunting season.

The next chapter will go over some celebrations, rites, and workings for the solar holidays.

eight
THE SUN AND
SOLAR HOLIDAYS

In past days in the British Isles, many celebrations, spell workings, magickal rituals, and feasting took place during the solar holidays. Rites and workings include the practice of divination, fertility rituals, protection ceremonies, honoring deities and appeasing fairies, journeying, and ancestor worship. They also included folk dances and folkplays for the purposes of raising energy and implementing priordination rites.

We usually think of trick-or-treating, wearing costumes, and parading through the streets as associated with Hallowe'en whereas singing carols is a Yuletide activity, but the common people of the British Isles performed these rituals much more frequently. Nearly all Brythonic traditional solar holidays involved wearing a disguise or ritual garb and going from house to house, singing songs or performing a skit. Participants asked for treats, drinks, or coins as a reward. This was and is called guising or guizing, masking, masquerading, mumming, souling, hodening, hoodening, going *galoshans* in Scotland, and *skeckling* in the Orkney Islands, or wearing "fancy dress."

Nowadays, the solar holidays are good for connecting to the cycle of the sun, the dance of the seasons, and doing magick appropriate for each time period. Winter is an occasion for introspection, spring for beginning projects, summer for growth, and fall for gathering and finishing endeavors. We can relate the seasonal events and their cultural significance to our own activities. For example, many people of Celtic descent strive to repay their debts by their new year at

Hallowe'en time, and thus we might work to pay off our credit card balance in the fall, before the Yuletide gift-giving rush begins.

The following are some common magick customs and rites associated with the solar holidays.

Hallowe'en

Hallowe'en is celebrated between October 31 and November 2 by modern practitioners. It is also called Hallows, Hallowmas, All Hallow's Eve, or Hallowed Evening, shortened to Hallowe'en. It was and is celebrated in many locations, including western Britain, Ireland, the Isle of Man, Scotland, and Wales. In Irish Gaelic, it is known as *Samhain*, which means the end of summer. It is also called *La Samhne*, *Oidhche Shamhna*, and *Gam* (beginning of winter). Cornish people call it *Nos Galen Gwaf* or Allantide. The Scots call the holiday *Samhainn* or *Samhuinn*, while in Manx Gaelic it is *Hop-tu-Naa* or *Sauin*.

Hallowe'en night is considered to be New Year's Eve by many magickal people of Celtic descent. In the Cymraeg (Welsh) language, the holiday is called *Nos Calan Gaeaf*, the night before the new year. Celtic cultures marked it as the first day of the winter season and the darker half of the year.[43] In several locations, the festivities last for three days. Thus, it is one of the most important holidays for participants in British-based folkloric magico-religions.

For my ancestors, Hallowe'en marked the final day to harvest the crops. Late fall was a time to slaughter cattle, sheep, and pigs. Fall was also the time for hunting wild animals for their meat, hides, and furs. Rituals and workings accompanied these processes, including giving thanks to the animal's spirit. Since butchering is messy, bloody work, it's no wonder that we focus so much on death, spirits, and frightening stories around Hallowe'en time.

Other concerns included harvesting enough medicinal herbs, firewood or peat, and animal fodder to last throughout the winter season, when snowy and rainy weather made finding supplies difficult. People made a contest of foraging for nuts, apples, berries, and the last of the wild greens. Rites were performed while drying, pickling, salting, and preserving foods. Sea deities were offered ale in exchange for fish and seafood. Failure to prepare for the harsh winter season could mean starvation or hypothermia.

---

43. Ruth Edna Kelley, *The Book of Hallowe'en* (Whitefish, MT: Kessinger Publishing, 2008).

Another reason that Hallowe'en is spooky is because the day is considered to be outside of the calendar, a time when the boundaries between this material world and the unseen realms are able to be crossed. As this day is considered a liminal period, occurring not only between seasons but between the past year and the new year, the normal rules of linear time and space do not always apply. Spirits and fairies are believed to be able to move about freely. Hallowe'en night is the time to visit with departed loved ones, divine the future, appease the spirits of the land, and do rituals of protection against malevolent beings.

Hallowe'en is traditionally a fire festival, when bonfires are burned for ritual purposes.[44] Fire is used as a symbol of fertility and immortality, to scare away malevolent entities, and in some cases to light the way for friendly spirits. In the past, some farmers lit bonfires on hilltops to walk cattle around or between, to use smoke to protect them and prevent illnesses, and to sanctify the animals before slaughtering them for meat. In some locations, the hearth fires in each home were extinguished and rekindled from a village bonfire. This is a perfect time and place to ceremonially burn talismans and ritual objects that have lost their protective qualities with continued use.

Other smaller fires were and are ritually burned for Hallowe'en in Britain. A "need-fire" is supposed to be kindled with flint and steel or the friction of two sticks, then used for wishing upon. Participants must stay awake until the fire is reduced to ashes to gain their wish. Welsh folks participate in an augury rite of *coelcerth*, placing stones into the hearth fire for divination. If a stone is broken or cannot be found the next morning, it is an ill omen. Fiery torches or rushes are paraded through some towns. Turnips, rutabagas, or beets are hollowed out and filled with oil, or carved and placed over a candle, to create a light to scare off baneful specters or welcome ancestors to the home. These were called punkies, which sound very similar to a familiar orange gourd. When immigrants brought the punkie tradition to America, they soon found that pumpkins were much easier to carve into jack-o'-lanterns.

Bonfires naturally invite storytelling. A large variety of bogeys, or supernatural beings with baleful intent, haunt Hallowe'en folktales. The *Cailleach Bheur* is a fearsome crone goddess representing winter in Ireland, while the *Mallt y Nos* is the night hag of Wales. The Wild Hunt is said to be riding the skies, collecting

---

44. James Bonwick, *Irish Druids and Old Irish Religions* (New York: Hippocrene Books, 1986).

spirits to bring to the underworld. A ferocious pack of albino or coal-black hounds with glowing red eyes pursue the souls of the dead. The hunt is led by various dark figures, including *Gwyn ap Nudd*, the White Son of Nobody, who is the King of the Fairies; Arawn, the god of the underworld; Herne the Hunts-man, a horned figure who may be an incarnation of Cernunnos; the broom-riding hag, Mallty Nos; and in more Anglicized areas, the God Odin, Oðin, Wodin, or Wotan.

In several Brythonic cultures, death is personified as a specter or frightening entity. Our modern version of the Grim Reaper looks a great deal like the Welsh *yr Angau*, which is Cymraeg for "the death," and the Cornish Ankow, or L'Ankau, found in Brittany. This bony spirit, wearing all black and carrying an arrow, sickle, crossbow, or scythe, comes out on Hallowe'en night to strike down the living and haul them away in his rattletrap cart, drawn by a skinny white horse. In Wales, an enormous black female pig with a cropped tail chases pedestrians. She is called the Cutty Black Sow or *yr Hwch Ddu Gwta*. The monstrous Gray King, a "wild man" figure, dragged people away to the mountains. In varying locations, goblins, baleful spirits, and evil fairies could attack travelers. A jack-o'-lantern or will-o'-the-wisp lured unsuspecting people to their deaths in a swamp. The devil himself was said to be abroad, stalking graveyards and lurking at crossroads. Many place-names in the British Isles carry the moniker of the Christian entity associated with evil, such as "Devil's Bridge." The fairy mounds, or *sidhe*, are said to open on Samhain night, disgorging all manner of spirits. Numerous Hallowe'en rit-uals involve protecting oneself from these beings' wrath. Poetic charms are spo-ken to prevent being taken by malevolent entities. Turning clothing inside out is believed to protect a person from malicious fairies. Wearing charms, whistling, reciting prayers, carrying talismans, and crossing water can foil the spirits.

Dressing up in costume on Hallowe'en is a means of hiding from malign spirits or tricking the gods of death. It may also be related to hunting rituals. In past days, people wore animal skins and skulls, masks, antlers or horns, tails, and other animal costumes.[45] This helped to ensure a successful hunt as well as to identify with spirits of nature.

---

45. John Brand and Henry Ellis, *Observations on the Popular Antiquities of Great Britain* (Lon-don: H. G. Bohn, 1853).

Trick-or-treating may derive from the ancient Celtic practice of giving wayfarers a dinner to show them hospitality. It is considered good luck to feed the first person to cross your threshold on New Year's Day.[46] After the harvest was in, the fall hunt had been undertaken, and animals had been slaughtered for meat, people in unfortunate circumstances, or those seeking charity for others, would perform short dramas or songs, asking to be rewarded with food and money.[47] Another food-related ritual is feasting in honor of ancestor spirits. Fairies and unhappy ghosts are considered responsible for playing tricks, so they are offered food to placate them.

Since this is the final harvest, Hallowe'en is celebrated by plentiful feasting. Fruits, nuts, vegetables, grains, and plenty of meats are part of the feast. Toasts of beer, mead, and whiskey are offered. Lamb's wool, a drink made from roasted apples crushed into pulp and then added to milk or cream, ale or wine, and spices, is traditional in England and Cornwall. A wedding ring is hidden in the punch bowl, and the person who ladles it up will soon be married. Welsh folk eat *cawl*, a stew made of beef, pork, or mutton with vegetables, including carrots and rutabagas, and spiced cakes made with treacle or molasses. People in the West Country of England enjoy black sausages. Speckled bread filled with raisins, called *bairín-breac* in Ireland, *bara brith* in Wales, or barmbrack in both places, is enjoyed on Hallowe'en. In England, bread pudding with concealed trinkets is eaten as a symbol of prosperity and to tell fortunes. For example, a ring means marriage and a penny symbolizes wealth.

Apples, quite abundant during autumn, are considered the symbolic fruit of Avalon (Island of Apples), representing the fairy realm and the underworld. Cider vinegar is fermented from apples and used in cleansing rites. Bobbing, ducking, or "dooking" for apples are folkloric rituals that are called a trial, meaning a competition. These games also have divinatory significance. Apples are placed in water in a bucket or pot or hung on strings from the ceiling. Each player puts their hands behind their back and tries to capture the apples using just their teeth. One way of doing an augury is naming particular apples for various people and then attempting to catch the apple in their mouth. In Wales, *twcofala*, or bobbing for apples, has a special meaning—the young lady who retrieves the first apple

---

46. Kelley, *Book of Hallowe'en.*

47. Brand and Ellis, *Popular Antiquities of Great Britain.*

is most likely to be married in the coming year. Another custom is peeling the apple in a long, unbroken strand, tossing the peel over the left shoulder, and looking to see if a letter of the alphabet appears. The letter is believed to be the initial of a potential suitor.

While the jack-o'-lanterns are still lit and people are safely disguised in costume, it is the time to visit with ancestors, spirits, and energetic beings related to nature. Many Hallowe'en rites involve augury. This includes descrying or "kenning" using the flames of a bonfire or candle, gazing into a bowl of water or a dark mirror, and using natural objects such as stones or nuts for ritualized fortune-telling. Trees without leaves are more likely to show "tree writing" of Runes or Ogham at the end of October. People also seek to have visions and "dream walks" on Hallowe'en, in which they view future events.

The "dumb supper" is not only a prognostication rite, but also a way of communing with the departed. It involves preparing a meal in silence, setting a place at the table for an ancestor, and eating dinner without speaking. The table is to be set backward, with the forks on the right. The departed person's favorite foods are offered to honor them, and they are also given glasses of whiskey or mead. This can be equated with offerings left out of doors for the spirits of ancestors. Photos and beloved items formerly owned by deceased loved ones are placed on altars or in their preferred chair. When participating in a dumb supper myself, I've often heard my dear dad reminding me to put oil in the car, change the furnace filters, or clean out the screen in the water softener...sound advice indeed!

Another version of the dumb supper includes leaving empty plates to represent future marriage prospects. Young ladies then dream of the gentleman they are to encounter. Both ceremonies require all participants to prepare the food and eat silently. The custom was brought to Appalachia by Welsh and Scottish-Irish immigrants.

Folk magick traditionalists often hold a Hallowe'en vigil to honor the departed. Sometimes a gateway to the otherworld becomes visible in the evening mist, or as a shimmering in the air, like mirages seen above overheated asphalt roadways or lakes at sunset. One of our legends says that the goddess Rhiannon goes underground and causes winter, similar to the Greek myth of Persephone and Hades. On Hallowe'en night, Arawn, the god of death, is busy hunting or celebrating his honeymoon with Rhiannon; thus, he doesn't notice that spirits of the dead have escaped from the underworld. Another folktale says that graves, ancient tombs, and barrows open on Hallowe'en, allowing ghosts the freedom to wander.

Hallowe'en is especially good for interacting with spirits. Protection rites beforehand are an absolute must, and wearing an amulet for spiritual safety is advised. It has been discovered that a ritual circle sometimes impedes the free flow of energy and hinders access to the sacred space by the ancestors, who may be confused about being dead. Offerings of their favorite foods and beverages, items that connect the spirits to their former lives, and contagion magick items, like shoes or a hairbrush, are used to invoke loved ones who have passed on. Magick users may wish to enter a trance state to effectively communicate with spirits.

Once Hallowe'en is over, pumpkin or turnip jack-o'-lanterns are composted or smashed. They've served to protect our rituals from malicious spiritual beings and negative energies, and thus should be allowed to decompose.

The Winter Solstice

This day is also called the hibernal solstice and occurs around December 21. Some practitioners call this Midwinter's Day because Hallowe'en is considered the onset of winter. The winter solstice is the shortest day and longest night of the year. The sun appears lowest in the sky on this day. In parts of North America and Britain, daylight only lasts for about nine hours, and dusk can begin around four o'clock in the afternoon. For this reason, the winter solstice is strongly associated with the symbolic loss and return of the sun. This may account for merry Yuletide festivities, designed to bring hope at the darkest time of the year.

The Romans brought their feast of Saturnalia to Britain, observed on December 17, the Bacchanalia of December 19, and the celebration of Sol Invictus, the unconquered sun god, whose sacred day is December 25. Some of these festivals' customs were syncretized with British traditions. The Anglo-Saxons followed with their own Yuletide customs. Yule, also spelled Iul, Ylir, Jul, Jule, Juul, or Jól, may derive from the Anglo-Saxon word *yula*. The name Yule may have come from the old Welsh *heul*, which means sunlight, or the English word yew, as in the tree.[48]

---

48. Robert K. Barnhart, *The Barnhart Concise Dictionary of Etymology* (New York: HarperCollins, 1995).

In Wales, the winter solstice is called *Gwyl Canol Gaeof*, or *Alban Arthan*. It has been translated as "light of Arthur." Alban Arthan might also mean "point of roughness," perhaps describing the stormy winter weather. These terms may have come from Welsh poet Iolo Morganwg.[49] In Irish Gaelic, the winter solstice is called *Mean Geimhridh*. It is called *Montol* in Cornwall and *Mōdranicht* in Old English, meaning mother's night.

The Yuletide season can begin as early as Saint Nicholas Day on December 5 or 6 and last all the way until Candlemas in early February. Some practitioners celebrated from solstice day until New Year's Day on January 1. Christians celebrated Christmastide from December 25 to the Epiphany, or Three Kings Day, on January 6, also called Twelfth Night, the original "twelve days of Christmas." Plough Monday follows, the first Monday past Yuletide. These customs were syncretized with common magick traditions. Traditions attributed to various nations were brought by British immigrants to the US and other colonial locations.

Decorating with greenery at the winter solstice is a custom practiced by people of Celtic ancestry. Boughs of pine and fir trees, bay, laurel, holly, ivy, and mistletoe all remain green throughout the winter months, symbolizing life and the promise of spring. The branches are carried indoors to adorn mantles, doorways, and staircase bannisters. Mistletoe should be harvested with one swipe of a sickle-shaped bronze knife called a *boline*, as cutting mistletoe with iron destroys its magickal properties. Allowing mistletoe to touch the ground also ruins its powers, so it was caught in a white muslin sheet or the hem of Druids' robes, according to Roman writers.[50] Besides having curative features, mistletoe is said to prevent house fires. Standing beneath a sprig of mistletoe hung above a doorway means you're free to be kissed. Priests and ministers of Christian faiths preached against its use and forbade bringing mistletoe into a church.[51]

Prickly holly repels negative energies and burglars, but it should not be brought indoors before the winter solstice. The customary Yuletide colors of red and green imitate holly branches and berries, although winter colors also include gold, silver, black, white, gray, and ice blue. Wreaths are constructed from evergreen boughs and holly sprigs, ornamented with ribbons and pine cones, and used

---

49. J. Williams ab Ithel, ed., *The Barddas of Iolo Morganwg*, 2 vols. (Abergavenny, Wales: Welsh Manuscripts Society, 1862).

50. MacCulloch, *Religion of the Ancient Celts*.

51. Brand and Ellis, *Popular Antiquities of Great Britain*.

to decorate the front door, bringing protective energies to the home. Wreaths are a sign of welcome, and the endless circle represents the cycles of the seasons and of life. Greenery is a talisman for good luck, but it should be removed by either Twelfth Night or Candlemas. At that point, the plants' magickal capabilities have been used up. Decorative greenery should be composted or burned, as simply throwing it away is considered bad luck.

Fire rituals are an older winter solstice tradition in Britain as well.[52] The custom of lighting bonfires on hilltops around the winter solstice continued well into the twentieth century. Fires are lit to attract the sun god, enticing his return, as well as to light up the longest night. More recent ceremonies included setting fire to brush piles, old furniture, and wagon wheels. In some locations, tar barrels are ignited. This custom is also practiced on New Year's Day in Scotland.

The Yule log, also called a Yule clog or Yule block, was a tradition brought to Britain from the Scandinavian countries,[53] symbolizing luck, warmth, fertility, and the returning sun. Burning the Yule log ritually turns darkness into day on the longest night of the year. In Wales, the Yule Log is called *y blocyn Gwylian*. In some places in Ireland, the log is called the "Cailleach Block," referring to the crone goddess who represents death, winter, and darkness. The Yule log is customarily a sizeable piece of ash, yew, or birch wood—sometimes even a whole tree trunk—designed to last for twelve days and nights of continuous burning. It is considered bad luck to allow the fire to go out before the entire log is reduced to charcoal. The Yule log is believed to ward off chilblains and frostbite, protect a building from being struck by lightning, and prevent the home from catching fire for an entire year. A piece of charred Yule log is kept under the bed until next year, and a new log should be lit from the old one. If a neighboring house catches fire, remnants of Yule logs are thrown inside to placate the fire spirits. Lighting candles from a flaming Yule log should be done in silence. After the candles are lit, the family gathers to make wishes and sing carols. Candles are not snuffed out, but instead are allowed to burn all the way to the end. In the West Country of England, an "ashen faggot," or bundle of ashwood sticks, serves the same purpose as a Yule log. (The word "faggot" was not a pejorative back in the day; it simply meant an armload of branches.) The ashes of wood burned on Yule are said

---

52. Bonwick, *Irish Druids and Old Irish Religions*.

53. Brand and Ellis, *Popular Antiquities of Great Britain*.

to have healing properties and should be put into the garden to increase crop fertility. A more symbolic Yule log is a block of wood with holes drilled for candles and decorated with greenery, ribbons, and pine cones. Another, sweeter option is a cake frosted with chocolate in the shape of a log.

The winter solstice is the last feast day before the onset of freezing temperatures and snowy blasts, and thus it's the time to begin monitoring the food and supplies of heating fuel. January and February are sometimes called the "famine months." In the past, the slaughter of surplus farm animals continued, as well as hunting for wild animals. The Celtic sun god Lugh was asked to bless hunting arrows. Sacrifices were made in thanks to the gods, and birch twigs were used to sprinkle blood across the threshold of the home, called a "redding" or "reddening." This was believed to have ritual-cleansing qualities.

After the Roman incursions, bulls and horses were sacrificed for the holidays surrounding the solstice. The Saturnalia celebrated by Romans is the feast of the god Saturn. He is viewed as the source of gifts exchanged during his holiday.[54]

The custom of decorating a Yule tree comes from the Norse incursions.[55] It appears very similar to the raggy bushes or clootie trees found throughout Britain, although those are not holiday specific. Choosing to decorate with glass ornaments may have been inspired by the spherical glass balls used for divination, called glains, and home protection, called witch's balls. As with many other customs, the decorated tree was adopted by Christians. The Anglo-Saxons were responsible for many other English Yule traditions. The custom of eating a whole pig, or a boar's head with an apple in its mouth, came from the Saxons.[56]

Two characters in folklore represent the dark and light side of the winter solstice, the long night and the beginning of the lengthening days. Many common magick practitioners tell the tale of two deities or kings, representing summer and winter, who have a battle or play chess. The winner rules over the next half of the year. This is quite similar to Robert Graves's Oak King and Holly King folktale.[57] For Celtic-based folkloric Pagans, the two contestants are Owain and King Arthur, or the Celtic god Lugh fighting the monstrous Balor. The spring-

---

54. Brand and Ellis, *Popular Antiquities of Great Britain.*

55. Ibid.

56. Ibid.

57. Graves, *White Goddess.*

time robin is said to battle the wren, who represents winter. There are sometimes enactments of Sir Gawain versus the Green Knight, or Robin Hood versus a villain called Guy of Gisborne. All of these entities have the symbolism of an agricultural figure versus a figure of death, the waxing year opposing the waning year, or the darkness being displaced by sunlight.

Several of these stories which feature dark and light, or winter and summer, are expressed in the form of ritualized dramatizations or folkplays. These performances often include a procession from house to house, songs, dances, a type of street theater, and a reward or treat. Some modern mummers' plays have similar characters. Other folkplays included ritualized hunting dramas as well as a custom of walking or dancing with representational animal mascots though town. In Wales, a horse skull draped in ribbons and trinkets is called a Mari Lwyd, or gray mare. One hunt-related folk story, brought by Welsh immigrants to the US, involves the sacrifice of a man who shapeshifts into the form of a stag. The deer is hunted and killed during the hunger months of winter.

In Ireland, the Isle of Man, Wales, and parts of England, people engage in "Hunting the Wren" on December 26, which is the secular Boxing Day, or January 6, Twelfth Night. In past days, a real bird was killed, but more recently, a taxidermized or facsimile wren is hidden, then hunted. In Ireland, the hunt is called *Lá an Dreoilín*. When the wren is found, it is displayed on a pole or put into a wreath. Or, on the Isle of Man, the wren is placed in a small, triple-hoop structure decorated with greenery and ribbons. Lads called wren boys wear straw costumes and parade through town, dancing and begging for pennies, ostensibly to pay for the wren's funeral. The "Cutty Wren" song is sung by participants. Since "cutty" in a Northumberland dialect means old, worn out, and shabby, it may refer to the past year.[58] The wren symbolizes winter and is killed to bring about springtime.

Mummers' plays are presented during the Yuletide season in many British and Irish villages. These, sacred hunts, processions, and other winter solstice customs, including sword dances and singing carols, are believed to bring luck and prosperity in the coming year. Mummers and carolers are traditionally given bread and cheese, fruits, beverages, treats, and small change.

---

58. Brand and Ellis, *Popular Antiquities of Great Britain.*

Speaking of caroling, several older Yuletide songs are still around in the present day. Groups of singers and minstrels playing instruments go from house to house in the early morning and at dusk. The traditional Welsh carol "Deck the Halls" makes reference to decorating with greenery and burning the Yule log. The song was originally called *Nos Calan*, meaning new year or night of calends in the Cymraeg language, which tells us that the song may have first been sung at Hallowe'en.[59] Wassailing, or singing from house to house and enjoying an alcoholic drink, is performed throughout the Yuletide season. "The Holly and the Ivy," "The Twelve Days of Christmas," "Christmas Is Coming," "The Boar's Head," and several versions of these songs are historically older and/or of British origin, and they contain Pagan themes or elements.

There are many delicious foods and beverages associated exclusively with the winter solstice holiday besides the legendary boar's head. Rich desserts include figgy pudding that hides a sixpence or a plum pudding that contains objects used for divination. Gingerbread cookies were originally baked during the harvest holidays, but today they are a popular Yuletide treat. Cookies are shaped to represent human and animal figures as a talisman. Frummety is wheat boiled in milk with sugar and spices and can also contain talismanic or divinatory objects.

Alcohol is popular as well. Wassail is a drink made from hard apple cider, mulled wine, or brandy that is mixed with spices. It is sprinkled on apple trees to ensure their fertility and imbibed during holiday parties. Several wassail bowls dating from medieval times can be found in British and Welsh museums. The name may derive from the Anglo-Saxon *wæs heil* or *wæs hail*, a greeting that means "be well."[60] Lamb's wool is a similar beverage. Hot buttered rum, eggnog with rum, glog, brandy, ale, wine, and beer are also consumed.

Winter solstice presents were originally fruits, nuts, sweetmeats, handmade gifts such as knitted scarves, small coins, and the famous sugarplums. Oranges pierced by cloves, small toys, and chocolate coins were given as gifts. The presents were put into shoes or stockings hung by the fireplace or at the foot of the bed. This custom likely originated in Britain, moved to US with settlers, but then died

---

59. Jack Goldstein, *10 Amazing Christmas Carols*, vol. 2 (Bedfordshire, UK: Andrews UK, 2013).

60. *Merriam-Webster*, s.v. "wassail," accessed April 2, 2020, https://www.merriam-webster .com/dictionary/wassail.

out in many places in England.[61] In both locations, Christmas was celebrated by playing games such as blind man's bluff, puss in the corner, hide and seek, tag, and an early version of "truth or dare" which demanded forfeits of those who refused to answer. All of these activities can be incorporated into modern common magick practice as a way to connect us to our past, to raise energy, and to celebrate the season.

Imbolc

Imbolc is pronounced Ihm-bōllk, and means "in belly," referring either to the pregnancy of a mother goddess or to farm animals. It can also be translated as "in the bag." The holiday is also called *Eimelg*, also spelled *Oimelg* or *Oimelc*, which means ewe's milk in the Gaelic language, referring to the lactation of female sheep. In Cymraeg, the holiday is called *Calan Fair* or *Gŵyl Fair Canhwyllau*, but is not widely celebrated in Wales. This was one of the four sacred days that scholars believe were celebrated by the ancient Celts,[62] and it remains an important Irish holiday in the present. It commemorates the onset of springtime.

The Festival of Februata was commemorated by the Romans who occupied Britain, which included rites of purification.[63] Feasts were held where males did the cooking and women were served the meal, allowing them an afternoon of rest. Men were also responsible for the cleanup and doing the dishes afterward.

Imbolc is also called the festival of Brigid, or *Lá Fhéile Bríde* in Irish Gaelic, named for the goddess Brigid (also known as Brighid, Brigit, Bríg, or Bríd). Her name means "exalted." In Scottish Gaelic, the holiday is called *La Fheill Brighde*, and in Manx, *Laa'l Breeshey*. Brigid was one of the Tuatha Dé Danaan and was likely a triple goddess figure, with representations of springtime fertility and healing. She may be related to Brigantia or Brittania, from whom Britain gets its name.[64] Brigid is the goddess of early spring, the dawn, poetry, fire, metal crafting, dairying, brewing, and midwifery. A Christian legend says Brigid was the Virgin Mary's midwife. Brigid was later canonized by the Catholic Church and became the matron saint of Ireland.

---

61. Brand and Ellis, *Popular Antiquities of Great Britain*.

62. Ibid.

63. William Smith, ed., *Dictionary of Greek and Roman Biography and Mythology* (Boston: Little, Brown: 1867).

64. George, "Brigantia."

Brigid is also a goddess of fire, so candles, hearth fires, or bonfires can be ignited, which also represents the onset of spring and return of the sun. Blessings and purifications of the self, animals and pets, and homestead can take place. Many Catholics celebrate the holiday as Candlemas. Candles symbolize light in the darkness, as the days are becoming longer. The shrine to St. Brigid at Kildare in Ireland has an eternal flame. Old-line Pagans fire up torches, rushes, witch's candles (mullein spikes), or old brooms—in addition to or in replacement of candles—and walk around the outside of the house three times deosil. This ceremony protects and purifies the home. Common magick users sometimes light candles for ritual or leave a candle burning all night in anticipation of the lengthening days.

Imbolc is a day to honor women and to do magickal rites that are related to the hearth and home. In England, February 2 was observed as the Wives' Feast or Lady Day. The night before Imbolc, many Irish women prepare a "Bríd's bed" for "Bridey dolls" who represent the goddess or saint in her aspect as a mother and bringer of fertility. The effigies are constructed of straw from the last sheaf of grain harvested in the fall, then dressed in white lacey cloth. The dollies are taken to sacred wells to be anointed and blessed. As the Bridey dolls are placed into the bed, participants chant, "Bríd is come. She is welcome!" Similar customs take place on the Isle of Man and the Hebrides, where the beds are constructed of a basket, rushes on the floor, or hay from the barn. Sometimes a birch or whitethorn wand is placed in or near the bed, a symbol of the male principle. In the Western Islands of Britain, a sheaf of oats left from the harvest is used as the dolly. A club or wand is placed in the basket, symbolizing Brigid's magick wand, which she uses to command the crops to grow.[65] This might also symbolize the male principle, and the dolly and the club together form polarity magick for fertility. At night, ashes from the fireplace are raked smooth in hope of seeing the impression of Brigid's footprint, viewed as a good omen.

In Kerry, Ireland, a festival of the "Biddy," or Brigid, culminates in a house-to-house procession. Participants wear white robes and woven straw hats and carry a dolly called a *Brídeóg*. Like other folkplays, there is music, dancing and singing, and ritualized begging. In Killorglin, Ireland, this includes a parade of torches,

---

65. Brand and Ellis, *Popular Antiquities of Great Britain*.

along with the effigies. The Biddy figure in the procession ensures abundance, fecundity, and good luck for all who see her.

A symbol of Ireland, as well as the seasons, is a four-armed Brigid's cross made from rushes or basket withes, used as a talisman to bless and protect the home or barn. The equal-armed crosses are woven into a diamond shape in the middle and tied off with woolen yarn. They can represent the directions and be a talismanic symbol.

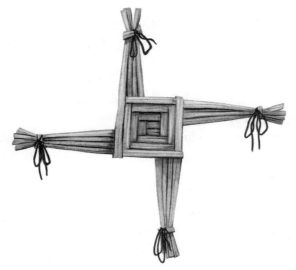

Figure 4: Brigid's cross

There are several other plant-based customs related to Imbolc. The national emblem of Scotland is a milk thistle. It is said that on Candlemas day, milk from the breasts of Brigid (or the Virgin Mary) fell onto the plant, leaving white spots. It is also called the blessed thistle or lady's thistle. The custom of dressing a straw man or straw bear and parading him through the town is part of the Imbolc holiday in Scotland, Ireland, and Northern England. The figures symbolize an agricultural entity. There is a straw bear festival held every year for tourists in Whittlesea in the east of England, taking place in mid-January. This tradition, called *skeckling*, is also practiced in Germanic countries. At Imbolc, any greenery leftover from the winter solstice should be removed from the home, as its protective qualities have expired after six weeks' time. Greenery is ritually burned or composted, not discarded in the trash.

Since Imbolc means "ewe's milk," the holiday coincides with the birth of lambs, which in past times was a crucial farming and herding event. Stored food may be running short or become rotten, so our forebearers sought any sign of fecundity and growth. All-night vigils were held as farmers and shepherds assisted the ewes with lambing. This symbolized new life after a long fallow period, as it had been three months since the final harvest. Rituals were performed to increase the fertility of the herds, such as adorning them with ribbons and blessing them or placing talismans in the sheepfold and barn. Other sheep-related rites include drinking ewe's milk and eating the last stored mutton or the first slaughtered lamb. Cottage cheese made from sheep milk is served for breakfast. Children craft images of sheep from yarn or use cotton balls glued to a sheet of paper.

On Imbolc, shepherds and farmers await the dawn in order to forecast the weather for the remainder of the quarter. Sunrise and bright skies on this day mean storms and snow until springtime. In England, a badger is the omen for weather, rather than the groundhog of the Americas. If the sun is shining and the badger sees his shadow, it means colder weather is likely ahead. In Scotland, snakes emerging from their holes are weather auguries. In the northern US, a bluebird appearing around Imbolc is a sign of forthcoming spring. A legend about the crone goddess, the Cailleach, says that if the sun is shining in early February, she can gather more firewood, and thus, a longer winter will ensue. On the Isle of Man, the Caillagh takes the form of a crow, gathering sticks in preparation for cold weather.

In past days in Ireland, Imbolc was the time to begin plowing the fields, while in Britain, this occurred on Plough Monday, the first Monday after Twelfth Night, or the Christian Epiphany on January 6. Plows are also used to cut turf for heating fuel. Plowing games and races are held, along with decorating plows with ribbons and trinkets. Rituals are performed in colder climates to "break the back of winter," including chopping wood, shoveling snow or manure, or anything that is strenuous exercise using upper-body strength. Modern practitioners engage in contests of physical fitness for the purpose of raising energy.

Imbolc foods include Irish stew, roast mutton, soda bread, and colcannon. Offerings are made to Brigid by setting a plate of food outdoors and pouring beer in libation. Pancakes or crepes were and are eaten in parts of England, Cornwall, and Brittany for the Imbolc holiday. Their round shapes represent the sun. The pancakes are supposed to be flipped over without breaking them, symbolizing good luck.

People also decorate holy wellsprings on Brigid's Day, including the fount at Kildare in Ireland, which is dedicated to St. Bridget. Other common magick activities related to veneration of Brigid include brewing and drinking beer, writing and reciting poems, reading folktales, making butter and cheese, and creating handicrafts, especially knitting or crocheting with woolen yarn.

Spring Equinox

Also called the vernal equinox, the first day of spring takes place around March 20. The equinoxes mark a time of equal daylight and darkness as well as the dates when the sun crosses the celestial equator. Earth's hemispheres are equally aligned with the sun, which rises due east and sets due west. The spring equinox begins when the sun enters the constellation of Aries. It is said that on the spring equinox, when the sun is directly overhead around noon, a person standing up cannot see their own shadow.

This holiday is called Oestara by some modern Pagans, also spelled Ostare, Oestar, and Eostare, possibly deriving from the Old English word *Eostre*.[66] The origin of the name is unclear. It may have came from a Teutonic springtime goddess, who was descended from an Indo-European goddess of the dawn.[67] Oestara or Eostre might originate from the Norse *aestur* which means to "grow warm."[68] The spring equinox is called *Alban Eilir*, or *Gwyl Canol Gwenwynol* in a Cymraeg dialect. Alban Eilir can be translated as "time of spring" or "light of earth," which may have been the invention of the Druid revivalist and Welsh nationalist Iolo Morganwg.[69] In Irish Gaelic, the spring equinox is called *Mean Earraigh*, although the day is not widely celebrated in Ireland.

The Romans used either March 1 or the spring equinox to mark the first day of the new year. The Romans celebrated their famed Rites of Spring around the

---

66. Barnhart, *Concise Dictionary of Etymology*.

67. Amanda Borschel-Dan, "The Pagan Goddess Behind the Holiday of 'Easter,'" *The Times of Israel*, April 5, 2015, https://www.timesofisrael.com/the-pagan-goddess-behind-the-holiday-of-easter/.

68. Jacob Grimm, *Teutonic Mythology*, trans. James Steven Stallybrass, 4 vols. (London: George Bell & Sons: 1882).

69. Williams ab Ithel, *Barddas of Iolo Morganwg*.

equinox time. Lady Day, celebrated by some Christians and traditional witches, takes place on March 25 and is considered a quarter-day in England and Scotland.

The Christian holy day of Easter is held on the Sunday following the first full moon following the spring equinox, which has distinct Pagan overtones. The name Oestara or Eostre is likely where the word Easter comes from.[70] After the rise of Christianity, the Venerable Bede wrote about "Eostur Monath" or "Eastre," which took place in April on the European continent.[71] It's notable that he used this name rather than calling it "paschal month" for Passover or the passion of Christ.

Oestara is an important holiday to common magick users who follow a Norse or Anglo-Saxon tradition. It is the beginning of the summer half of the year. Many British spring equinox and Easter traditions likely came from the Teutonic peoples, including the custom of coloring eggs.[72] Eggs symbolize fertility, new beginnings, good health, and the return of spring. On the farm, baby chicks and ducklings begin hatching from eggs around the equinox.

Eggs were and are dyed with madder, woad, beets, and any number of green plants. Eggs were also colored with red pigments to represent birth. In his *Observations on the Popular Antiquities of Great Britain*, John Brand cited a British amateur folklorist who witnessed the exchange of colored eggs for Easter in the mid-1700s. Participants wrote on the eggs with wax or tallow from candles so that the white eggshell showed through the dye.[73]

Hiding eggs and finding them relates to searching for bird's nests containing eggs because birds will not usually lay their eggs until the weather is warm enough for their survival. This information would be vital to an agrarian society, and would influence the planting of crops after all danger of frost had past. Hanging colored eggs from tree branches symbolizes fertility and protection of the home. It can also be a sympathetic magick rite to persuade wild birds and domestic fowl to begin laying eggs, thus bringing about good weather.

---

70. Borschel-Dan, "Pagan Goddess Behind 'Easter.'"

71. Faith Wallis, trans., *Bede: The Reckoning of Time* (Liverpool, UK: Liverpool University Press, 1999).

72. Grimm, *Teutonic Mythology*.

73. Brand and Ellis, *Popular Antiquities of Great Britain*.

Pace egging endures as a working-class tradition in rural England and Ireland. The name likely derived from "paschal."[74] Around Easter, eggers or eggmen go from house to house singing songs and begging for colored eggs or treats in exchange for a folkplay performance in which a knight character defeats an evil dragon. Eggers in Lancashire originally wore animal skins, linking the custom to hooded animal rites.[75] The term "egging him on" is about the bad puns and insults which eggmen yell at those who refuse to give them a treat.

Common magick users decorate their homes and businesses with flowering branches hung with colored eggs for the spring equinox. A thorough cleaning of the house must first ensue; both the mundane variety—washing fusty bedding, hanging clothes outdoors, airing out the home after a long winter shut inside—and ritualized cleansing, smudging, aspergating, and renewing protective talismans. Houses' walls and floors are washed with saltwater or water mixed with baking soda. According to my father-in-law, thatched roofs in Britain were repaired in early spring and homes were given a fresh coat of whitewash, along with cleansing ceremonies. Stables and barns were mucked out, and the manure was put onto fields and gardens as fertilizer. The homes and outbuildings could then be blessed for springtime.

Beating the bounds was practiced in parts of England, Cornwall, and Wales[76] and has continued or been revived there and in other locations. It is also called perambulation, commonriding, or ganging. Landowners walk the perimeter of their property, or church members walk around the edges of their parish, checking fences and boundary markers. This is an opportunity for instilling magickal wards, such as burying eggs to absorb negative energies, and performing ceremonies for protection. A bundle of sticks, willow withes, or a besom is used to "beat" or smack trees, bushes, cornerstones, and the ground to drive away baleful entities. In past days, a group of young boys were also brought along on the journey. The notion was that youngsters could remember the boundary markers into adulthood. Sometimes a boy was turned upside down at each corner and symbolically "switched" with the willow fronds, which resembles enduring an ordeal

---

74. "Pace Egg Play," *World Wide Words*, accessed April 2, 2020, http://www.worldwidewords.org/weirdwords/ww-pac1.htm.

75. Ellen Castelow, "Pace Egging," Historic UK, accessed April 2, 2020, https://www.historic-uk.com/CultureUK/Pace-Egging/.

76. Brand and Ellis, *Popular Antiquities of Great Britain*.

for a rite of passage. Walking the entire perimeter of a large estate or parish could take up to a week. Afterward, participants celebrated with ale and a feast. The custom was made obsolete by modern surveying, although New Hampshire and Vermont in the US still require walking the state boundaries every seven years.

Folklore relating to hares and rabbits may not be ancient, but it is older than the recent neo-Pagan movement. Stories linking rabbits to Oestara can be traced back to German writers, including Jacob Grimm of fairy tale fame.[77] However, rabbits and hares were prevalent in Celtic, Anglo-Saxon, and Germanic mythology. The moon in March is called the hare moon, and the saying "mad as a March hare" refers to the crazy behavior of mating bunnies. Witches were said to transform themselves into hares, which may be the remnant of a visionary ritual or belief in animal totems. Seeing a hare before sundown is believed to bring good luck, but after sunset it can be an ill omen. "Hare pie" was a favorite dish of the peasants and nobility alike. I speculate that the lore about hares or rabbits laying eggs could have come from farmers who noticed that the home of a lapwing, grouse, or snipe—all ground-nesting birds—resembled a hare's nest.

Traditional foods for the spring equinox, besides eggs and the ubiquitous Easter candy delivered by the rabbit, include fresh cheeses, puddings made of milk and bread, and root vegetables cooked in shepherd's pie or stew. In past days, food suffered from the lack of refrigeration, so pickled vegetables, sauerkraut, dried fruits, and sausages or dried, salted, and pickled meats were eaten for the spring equinox holiday. Corning beef, or preserving it with spices, was one way of keeping the meat from spoiling. Corned beef and cabbage is commonly enjoyed in the US for the equinox. People went out hunting for fresh edible greens, including wild garlic, garlic mustard, campion, sorrel, and dandelions. Hot cross buns may have been originally baked as a Pagan tradition before their use as an Easter treat.[78] The cross can represent the directions, the quarters of the moon, or a solar cross. In some locations the pastries were hidden away in the attic as talismans against fire. Hot cross buns are thought to never get moldy, and some folks believe they have curative properties.

77. Stephen Winick, "Ostara and the Hare: Not Ancient, but Not as Modern as Some Skeptics Think," *Folklife Today* (blog), Library of Congress, April 28, 2016, https://blogs.loc.gov/folklife/2016/04/ostara-and-the-hare/.

78. Brand and Ellis, *Popular Antiquities of Great Britain*.

Springtime was and is celebrated in Wales with sowing and planting activities, including plowman games. This is similar to the Roman Rites of Spring, which was also a time of feasting, sporting, and games. Farmers race their horses with plows attached or try to beat a time for completely plowing a field. Plows are decorated with ribbons, trinkets, and cloth flowers.

Beltane, or May Day

The merry first day of May was and is celebrated across the British and Irish Isles. Emigrants from these areas brought May Day traditions to the US.

Beltane, also spelled Bealtaine or Beltain, is pronounced Bell-tayn, Be-all-tay-in-eh, or Bell-tawn-yah. This holiday marks the beginning of summer for many Celtic-based folkloric Pagans and is the most important fertility holiday. The day is sometimes called Lady Day in English and was called Floralia by the Romans, whose springtime goddess Maia lent her name to the month. It is called *Nos Galan Mai* or *Calan Mai* in Cymraeg, meaning the calend of May. Irish people celebrate the holiday on May 6 or 7 and call it *Beltaine, Beltene, Beltine, Cetsamhain*, which means the beginning of summer, or *Sam*.

Bel is an older Irish and Welsh word for fire or brightness, as well as the name of a solar deity, while *tain* is a word for fire in Welsh, or raid in Irish. An Irish and Welsh sun god is called Bel or Beli. Beltane was one of four Celtic fire festivals.[79] In past days, Bel-fires were kindled on hilltops on the night before May Day and were often the focus of all-night festivities. Some of these fires burned for up to three days. In some localities, hearth fires were extinguished only to be rekindled by an ember from the community fire.[80] According to the Irish king and bishop called Cormac, cattle were driven between two fires on Beltane Eve to protect them from diseases.[81] Fires are kindled by friction, and revelers leap through the flames for good luck, health, and fertility.[82] May Eve is believed to be a time when "witches" are abroad, hence people hold all-night vigils around a bonfire. Divination and rites to honor spirits are performed at the fires, similar to Hallowe'en.

---

79. Bonwick, *Irish Druids and Old Irish Religions*.

80. Ibid.

81. *Encyclopaedia Britannica Online*, s.v. "Beltane," accessed April 2, 2020, https://www.britannica.com/topic/Beltane.

82. Bonwick, *Irish Druids and Old Irish Religions*.

The Beltane holiday is often celebrated with weddings, with couples jumping the fire together to ensure their fecundity.

The greening and blooming of the woodlands means that summer is on the way. Cutting greenery in the woods and decorating a home with boughs during the early morning of May Day is a generally older tradition, also practiced at Yuletide.[83] Numerous accounts exist, from the high Middle Ages up to the mid-1800s, of townsfolk going into the forest and gathering wildflowers, green branches, and flowering boughs.[84] These are paraded through town and used to adorn every doorway, mantle, porch. and shop counter. This rite is called "bringing in the May" or "garlanding." Young men sometimes take the opportunity to secretly decorate their beloved's home. The flowery branches and green leaves represent summer and fertility. Yellow flowers, such as primrose and cowslip, symbolize the sun. The woodland journey is accompanied by courtship rituals, from a secretive kiss to an engagement to "wearing the gown of green," or outdoor lovemaking. Churchmen were forbidden to participate.[85]

One British ceremony includes "bauming the thorn," adorning a hawthorn tree or bough with ribbons, flowers, and trinkets. This may have been an older custom which was Christianized,[86] as hawthorns are sacred in many old-line Pagan traditions, providing visionary capabilities, homes for fairies, and protection against baneful magick. In some locations, bauming the thorn takes place at Midsummer. Lore about the hawthorn tree includes the belief that bringing the flowers indoors on May Day is good luck, but prior to that date, the blooms are considered unlucky. Hawthorn flowers on a twig are worn as a corsage or in a hat for good fortune. Thorn tree branches are nailed to the door of the home or business for protection and to show esteem for the inhabitants. Similar folklore applies to rowan trees, said to be found at the center of fairy rings.

The May bush is a custom that looks similar to a decorated Christmas tree and the cloth-adorned clootie or raggy tree, used for healing rites. On May Day, a shrub or bush is cut down and placed outside the home. It is decorated with ribbons, streamers, bows, trinkets, and flowers. Some folkloric traditionalists create

---

83. Brand and Ellis, *Popular Antiquities of Great Britain*.
84. Ibid.
85. Ibid.
86. Ibid.

a Maypole, May gad, or May gam, which is a wand made from a green branch stripped of bark, painted or wrapped with ribbons or flowers, hung with trinkets or bells, and topped by a pinecone, acorn, or bundle of flowers. These wands are also used by a jester or fool, but their scepter is crowned by a baby doll's head or inflated pig bladder balloon. The May wand represents the male principle.

May branches decorated with streamers and flowers are a Welsh tradition. Dollies or poppets symbolizing life and death, or a May King and May Queen, are sometimes hung from the bough. Another custom involves adorning the May branch with hollow, colored eggs, which is also done at the modern celebration of Oestara and Easter. Three hoops crossed in a "flower of life" design can be decorated with foliage and blossoms, rather like the hoops used for hunting the wren during Yuletide. May hoops represent the female principle. The wands, branches, and hoops are used for sympathetic magick to bring about fertility and for contagion rites of protection, banishing winter, and welcoming spring.

Some Beltane traditions may have come from the Roman Floralia, or Flora's day, when revelers adorned their homes with flowers in honor of the spring goddess Flora.[87] The "Furry," "Faddy," or Flora's Dance of Helston, Cornwell, is listed on a Cornish tourism website as an older custom which may have an origin in Celtic festivals.[88] Participants garland buildings with greenery and flowers and dance in processions through the village, singing folk songs in a day-long celebration. This event may culminate in an evening at a pub or in the local manor house for a fancy-dress party. In some coastal locations, a wreath of flowers and leaves is created to decorate fishing boats or thrown into water to honor gods of the sea. Some of the materials used include hawthorn flowers, birch branches, apple blossoms, or greenery from the rowan tree.

Young men wearing elaborate leafy costumes called "Jack in the Green" (or Jack o' the Green) parade through the streets of England and Cornwall on May Day, accompanied by young ladies in milkmaids' attire and men dressed as chimney sweeps. The foliate figures resemble animated pine trees and can symbolize entities such as the Green Man or wild men like the Woodwose. These traditions are believed to honor various forest deities and fertility goddesses. While Jack in

---

87. Smith, *Greek and Roman Biography and Mythology*.

88. John Ravenscroft, "The Helston Furry Dance," *TimeTravel-Britain*, 2005, https://www
.timetravel-britain.com/articles/history/helston.shtml.

the Green can only be traced to the mid-1700s,[89] practiced by chimney sweeps in urban areas, the custom could have been brought to the cities by rural youths longing for greenery. Conversely, it might be an invented tradition. A similar ritual is enacted in several English locations, including the construction of a female foliage statue.[90] The young people also create garlands for sale. This custom died out around the two World Wars but was revived in the 1980s.

The tradition of the May basket is related to courtship. Decorated wicker baskets filled with flowers (or bouquets called poseys, nosegays, or a tussy-mussy) are hung from a door knob before knocking and running away. As well as a love interest, flowers are also given to mothers, teachers, and wives. May baskets or hoops of flowers are also placed at the top of some of the Maypoles. In the present day, folkloric magick users fashion a May flower from tissue paper and pipe cleaners, using the principle of sympathetic magick.

The modern Maypole decoration and dance is a syncretized tradition, with roots in Celtic, Roman, Norse, and Teutonic cultures. Some Maypoles are painted in spiral patterns, using gold and black, green and white, or red and white. This practice was mentioned by Shakespeare when the character Helena calls her rival "a painted Maypole" in *A Midsummer Night's Dream*.[91] The iconic ribbons probably were added after the Germanic incursions into Britain, merging with the tradition of tying cloth streamers to a May gam or wand, the May branch, and decorating a May bush. Originally the ribbons were red and white, which may symbolize either bandages and healing or a maiden's first menstruation. Later societies used various colors of ribbon.[92]

The Maypole represents the union of earth and sky, evoking the law of polarity. The long pole seated in the ground is believed to symbolize a sexual union between a solar deity or woodland god and an earth goddess. The clockwise perambulation, or the back-and-forth pattern interweaving the ribbons, is similar to several other British folk dances. It raises a great deal of energy and is said to be a ritual of springtime fecundity, growth, and regeneration.

89. Brand and Ellis, *Popular Antiquities of Great Britain*.

90. Ibid.

91. Shakespeare, *A Midsummer Night's Dream*, 3.2.305. References are to act, scene, and line.

92. Brand and Ellis, *Popular Antiquities of Great Britain*.

Young people are chosen to represent springtime, called the May King and May Queen. The royalty and their court lead May Day processions and initiate the Maypole dance. On the Isle of Man and Isle of Lewis, the court of the May King and May Queen stage a mock battle,[93] while in some locations, the factions are headed by a young Maid Marion versus the elder Malkin, which seems quite similar to folkplays about the Summer King versus the Winter King.

Mummers' plays, or folk dramas performed by street actors, and the popular English morris dance are current British May Day activities. The famous hobby horses (or 'Obby 'Oss) of Padstow and the 'Ooser of Dorset are favorite spectacles that can accompany mummers or dancers. Folklorist Ben Jones wrote about the similarities of the hobby horse traditions to other hooded animal dances or processions.[94] Robin Hood plays were and are also frequently performed.[95]

Of course, you can't have a dance without music. May Day was and is a celebration with travelling minstrels and stationary bands, playing harps, bagpipes, fiddles, tympani and other drums, bells, clarinets, flutes and fifes, brass instruments, and whistles made of hollowed sycamore twigs or tin whistles called tintarrems. British folk dances performed in a procession, circle, or square, such as the traditional morris dance, are often accompanied by an accordion or melodeon player. Some musicians begin parading through the streets at midnight, signaling the time to get up and gather flowering branches from the woods. Songs include "Hal-an-Tow" (Heel and Toe), "Summer Is a'Comin' In," and various hobby horse melodies, all of which can be heard online. Several of the songs have lyrics that are quite suggestive.

Popular Beltane foods include a "syllabub" made of milk, sweet cakes, and fruit wine; a "caudle" or stew served from a cauldron; and green salads containing sorrel, chives, dandelion greens, and other freshly picked woodland plants. Fresh meat, including veal, suckling pig, fish, and lamb, sustained the May Day revelers. After the feasting come contests and sports tournaments, including footraces, sack races, three-legged races, wrestling contests, and archery competitions related to the folkplays about Robin Hood.

---

93. Ibid.

94. Ben Jones, "Traditions Similar to Hoodening," Hoodening, last modified December 2019, http://hoodening.org.uk/hoodening-similar.html.

95. Brand and Ellis, *Popular Antiquities of Great Britain*.

Since 1988, the Beltane Fire Society has hosted a Beltane Fire Festival in Edinburgh, which has revived the May Eve bonfire tradition that petered out in the early twentieth century.[96] The festival also includes modern events and revelry, with both a magico-religious and secular approach.

Midsummer, or the Summer Solstice

This holiday falls between June 20 and 23, whenever the sun is at its zenith. As mentioned previously, the word "solstice" has the connotation of the sun standing still. Midsummer is the exact opposite on the solar calendar from the winter solstice; hence, it is the longest day and shortest night of the year. The earth's northern pole is tipped the farthest toward the sun, which makes it seem as if the sun is at its highest position of the year in the sky. This is also the day that the sun enters the constellation of Cancer. Midsummer, as the name implies, was the midpoint of summer to the Celtic nations, whose summer season began at Beltane. In modern times, the summer solstice is considered the first day of summer. In most places, the days are growing warmer and summer crops are beginning to ripen.

Modern Pagans call this holiday Leitha, Lietha, or Litha, which is a word for "mild" in an Old English dialect.[97] Bede called both June and July "Litha Monath."[98] *Alban Hefin* or *Alban Hefyn*, pronounced All-ban Hev-ihn, are Welsh names for the holiday, but these may be Iolo Morganwg's contribution.[99] In Cymraeg, the day is also called *Gŵyl Canol Haf* or *Alban Heurin*. *Golowan* or *Goluan* is the name for the holiday in Cornwall. Christians celebrate St. John's Day anywhere from June 23 to June 25. The Irish observed the solstice anywhere from June 21 to 24, calling it *Mean Samraidh*, which can be translated as "summertime." This is the agricultural midpoint between sowing seeds and harvesting the crop, thus called Midsummer. For Wiccans, it is a lesser sabbat, while many common magick users consider the solstice a major holiday.

Several stone age monuments, including the famous Stonehenge, and the ruins of tombs and other buildings have architectural features corresponding to the sol-

---

96. "About Beltane Fire Festival," *Beltane Fire Society*, accessed April 2, 2020, https://beltane.org/about/about-beltane/.

97. *Wiktionary: The Free Dictionary*, s.v. "Litha," accessed April 2, 2020, https://en.wiktionary.org/wiki/li%C3%Bea.

98. Wallis, *Bede*.

99. Williams ab Ithel, *Barddas of Iolo Morganwg*.

stice sunrise, sunset, or moonrise. The Scottish dolmens at Callanish on the Isle of Lewis feature summer solstice markers, and a legend says that "the shining one" visited this monument at Midsummer.[100] Modern Pagans flock to Stonehenge each year on the summer solstice, watching the sun rise over the dolmens and enjoying a festival.

Fire represents the zenith of the sun during the longest day. Some folkloric traditions related to flames are generally older,[101] and persevere today. Sacred fires are kindled on hilltops and kept burning from Midsummer's Eve until the following day. Fireworks can accompany the bonfires. In Ireland, parades of revelers carrying burning rushes go from town to town. In some cities in England, celebrants hold lanterns on poles. Others bear lit torches. In Scotland, people carry flaming barrels or buckets of lit tar. Shepherds use straw fires to prevent diseases in cattle and sheep, driving the herd animals through or around the flames. In Cornwall, cloth tarpaulins are soaked with tar and waved in a circular pattern. Wheels representing the sun are packed with straw, pine pitch, and other flammable materials, lit on fire, and rolled down a hill, symbolizing the sun descending to the earth. Christians attribute this rite to burning St. Catherine's torture device, yet it can also represent the sun or a solar deity.

Dancing clockwise around a fire is believed to bring good luck and wishes that come true. In Cornwall, folks join the "serpent dance" through the embers of a bonfire. Common magick users often hold an all-night vigil near a fire, then greet the dawn. Keeping watch beside a fire all night and awaiting the sunrise is called a wake. The ashes from the Midsummer night bonfire are believed to repel evil spirits and cause the soil to become healthier for gardening. The burning of a wicker man on summer solstice night was recorded both by Claudius Caesar and the Normans, and the custom survived until the mid-1880s, described by folklorists.[102] Straw effigies were set on fire as well. This ceremony is replicated in present times by stuffing a wicker basket with fruits, vegetables, and nuts and casting it into a bonfire to make an offering. Some practitioners write words of thanks or requests on slips of paper and tuck them into the basket. The popular "Burning Man" celebration is said have its basis in the wicker men of old.

---

100. Brand and Ellis, *Popular Antiquities of Great Britain.*

101. Bonwick, *Irish Druids and Old Irish Religions.*

102. Brand and Ellis, *Popular Antiquities of Great Britain.*

Divination is practiced at bonfires on Midsummer night. One type of augury rite uses a glass ornament or crystal called a glain or glane, a witch's ball, or Druid's glass. A glain is also called serpent glass, said to have been created by the saliva of a ball of snakes, but that is not true. The glass is also called dragon glass when found on sandy beaches. These glains are formed by lightning hitting the sand, forming blobs of molten silica that hardened into glass. Finding these glass objects on Midsummer's Day is considered very lucky. The objects might simply be hollow glass floats for fishing nets. A glain is held up to a fire and used like a crystal ball, with images projected into the glass by the flickering flames and dancing smoke.

Plants are used on the summer solstice to determine whether or not a romantic partner is monogamous. Flowers of the orpine plant are assigned the names of the lovers in question and then hung in the bedchamber. If the flowers turn toward one another as they dry, all is right in the relationship. If one turns away, it means that partner is having an affair. Young ladies also gaze into wells, pools, or still bodies of water on Midsummer in order to view an image of their future husband.

Common magick practitioners travel to the woodlands on the summer solstice to cut sprigs of oak, ash, and thorn leaves, immortalized in Rudyard Kipling's "Tree Song."[103] Oak represents strength, abundance, and the male principle; hawthorn is a protection against harmful magick, fairies, and the more mundane thieves; and ash was commonly used for arrow shafts. Ash is also used as a talisman against fire because in a forest fire, ash wood often does not burn. The three twigs are tied together with red ribbon and used as a charm to protect the home, barn, or workplace. Garlands containing leafy birch branches, fennel, white lilies and roses, motherwort, vervain, and violets are created as well. Gathering fern seed is a common Midsummer custom. Powder ground from the seeds is believed to have all kinds of healing properties. Fern leaves and seeds symbolize the male principle, said to have regenerative qualities. Saint John's wort is tacked above doorways to discourage harmful entities from entering a building.

Many Midsummer customs involve fairies and other nature spirits, either the desire to commune with them or to seek protection against their pranks. Elves

---

103. Rudyard Kipling, "A Tree Song," in *Puck of Pook's Hill* (originally published 1906; Project Gutenberg, 2010), http://www.gutenberg.org/files/557/557-h/557-h.htm.

are believed to tangle "elf locks" in the manes of horses or the hair of lovers caught sleeping outdoors. Sleeping beneath an elderberry bush on Midsummer night will likely result in a visit with the Fae, but the seeker is advised to wear their clothing turned inside out and to carry a twig of rue or a rowan cross bound with red thread to avoid being "pixie-led" or bewitched. Milk, bread, and strawberries are left outdoors to appease the fairies, as well as beds of rose petals and moss for them to sleep in. On Midsummer, there is supposedly a truce between humans and the Fae; they will grant wishes, heal people and animals, or impart wisdom in return for a coin. Of course, Shakespeare's *A Midsummer Night's Dream* chronicled the exploits of the king and queen of the fairies, as well as the playful Puck.

Midsummer is a favorite time for pilgrimages to sacred wellsprings in order to decorate them with flowers, green branches, straw effigies, and trinkets. These holy founts, often dedicated to goddesses, fairies, water nymphs, or (in later times) folk saints, are believed to have purifying or healing properties. (A "folk saint" is one who is uncanonized, or unrecognized, by the Catholic church. An example is the Cornish Modron or Madron, who is considered to be the matron of various sacred wells.) Seekers approach the wellspring before dawn, circumnavigate the water three times, leave an offering of silver, wash in the spring for healing or purification, and pray to the spirit of the well. Maidens bathe their faces in the wells, or with morning dew, to improve their complexions. Some do this at Beltane as well.

Another popular tradition is "dressing the well," which occurs in the Peak district of England in small villages each summer. Well dressing involves pressing flowers, leaves, and other natural materials into a clay-lined frame to create a design or picture. The image is paraded through town and displayed at the site of a sacred well (or lacking that, the public water pipe or horse trough). Well dressing is an older Celtic custom.[104] The first modern reference to dressing the well is from Tissington in Derbyshire, documented in 1349.[105] The practice has since become Christianized with Biblical pictures and blessings by local ministers, yet it is still a common magick ritual as well.

Gathering the first fruits and vegetables is part of many summer solstice celebrations. This day is considered the onset of the harvest season. In the past, huge

---

104. David Ross, "Well Dressing in Derbyshire," *Britain Express*, accessed April 2, 2020, https://www.britainexpress.com/counties/derbyshire/Well-Dressing.htm.

105. Ibid.

agricultural feasts, carnivals, and fairs, where livestock and farm wares were sold, took place throughout all of Europe. In Britain, fairs at Covington, Banbury Cross, and Scarborough, remembered in folktales and song, still take place each summer. All kinds of seasonal foods are enjoyed, as well as breads, dairy products including butter and cheese, and alcoholic beverages. This was also an opportunity for neighbors and family members to visit. Games such as horse races, teams of oxen pulling increasing weights, and contests of skill are held. Some of these customs have been duplicated at modern Renaissance fairs and county fairs.

In past days, as now, lovers chose June as the optimal time for weddings. The weather is warm, the land is green, and flowers are abundant. Lovers' bowers are constructed of birch or willow wicker and decorated with blossoms, cloth birds, and bells. Like at Beltane, making love outdoors on Midsummer is believed to increase the fertility of crops, animals, and human couples. Jumping over a bonfire together is said to promote fecundity.

Marriages, anniversaries, and Midsummer agricultural celebrations include folk music, juggling, tumbling and acrobatics, boat rides, and outdoor games and sports. Individual and group dances are performed in town squares and parks, as well as around bonfires. One dance includes joining hands as a formation in the shape of an X and skipping sunwise in a circle. Another is the popular "spiral dance." Folkplays are enjoyed as well. A ritualized battle between a Summer King and Winter King takes place again at the summer solstice, this time with the summertime entity winning the fight. This can be incorporated into games, such as tug-of-war or arm wrestling, at modern folkloric gatherings. In modern times, neo-Pagans may attend one of the many outdoor festivals in celebration of nature spirituality.

Harvesttide, Lughnassadh, or Lammas

The name *Lughnassadh* is Irish Gaelic, pronounced Loo-nah-sah. In modern times, it is spelled Lúnasa. The word has to do with the feast of the god Lugh, whom some view as a solar deity. The name *Lunassa*, or *Luanistyn*, was used on the Isle of Man until recent times. In Scotland, it was called *Lùnastal*. The celebration is called *Guldize* in Cornwall, but the harvest rites can also be held later in the autumn. It was and is only a minor observation in Wales, where it is called *Calan Awst, Nos Gŵyl Awst, Gwi Awst,* or *Ffaile Llew*. Modern Pagans may call the holiday Lammas, which derives from the Old English *hlaef masse*, meaning "loaf mass" or "bread ritual," celebrated by the early English church.[106] While Lughnassadh has a Celtic origin, Lammas derived from Old English. Many English speakers simply call this holiday celebration Harvesttide.

While August 1 is the midpoint between the summer solstice and the autumnal equinox, Brythonic folkloric magico-religions do not necessarily observe their harvest holiday on any one consistent calendar day. It usually takes place whenever the gleaning is underway or finished. The Harvesttide festival could last anywhere from one day to two weeks to a month.

Harvesttide is the first "corn" gathering, which meant any grain, including barley, wheat, rye, or oats. It was and is a time of thanksgiving. In the past, stores of flour and beer would be running low, so farmers were likely pleased to refill their granaries. This was also a season for cutting hay and other fodder plants. Harvest celebrations mark a brief respite between the long process of chopping down the crop with a scythe, stacking it in sheaves, threshing it to separate the grain from the chaff, and making it into useful products. It is also time to do preservation magick.

Farmers play several games while reaping, including a race to see who can bring in their crops the fastest. The final sheaf standing is called the gullet, the neck, or the knack. Effigies are made from the last sheaf harvested to represent the personification of the grain, which is called a corn maiden, corn king, corn dolly, corn mother, John Barleycorn, the harvest dame or harvest queen, or the corn or cern baby, sometimes spelled kern. The heads of the corn and the straw are fashioned into a human shape and dressed in the clothes usually associated with females. These effigies are sometimes used in a dance, hung up in a barn for good luck, or kept over the winter so they could be used for other holiday ceremonies. The figures represent the spirit of the grain or an agricultural deity.

The custom of baking trinkets into a loaf of bread, or "Lammas Loaf," was documented in the Middle Ages.[107] Each item represents a prediction, such as a coin for wealth, a small clay pig to represent luck, or a ring symbolizing marriage. In Scotland, the loaves are called *lunastain*. Some loaves are shaped like a sun; some are made to represent an animal. Some are glazed with honey and sugar,

---

106. *Merriam-Webster*, s.v. "Lammas," accessed April 2, 2020, https://www.merriam-webster .com/dictionary/Lammas.

107. George C. Homans, *English Villagers of the Thirteenth Century* (Cambridge, MA: Harvard University Press, 2014).

eaten in gratitude for the earth's bounty. In England, bits of a Lammas loaf are broken off and placed in the corners of buildings to ward away harmful entities.

Throughout Europe, August is the time to begin brewing beers and ales from grain and hops. Barley for beer and rye for whiskey are abundant. This is a way to preserve extra crops, and also to put something aside for later celebrations. Mead and wine are also fermented around Harvesttide. A folksong dating back to the 1600s, "John Barleycorn Must Die," commemorates the practice of planting, harvesting, threshing, and brewing, told from the hapless grain entity's point of view.[108]

Several small towns in England, Scotland, and Cornwall still hold harvest ceremonies in early August. Harvest feasts are held to celebrate abundance and featured a whole pig, a side of beef, or a sheep or lamb. Garden vegetables are also consumed, as well as fruits baked into tarts, pies, and other rich desserts. In several locations, a whole lamb or entire side of mutton is roasted over an enormous fire on the closing day of the Lammas festival. In Ireland, an entire bull is sometimes cooked and eaten at a Lughnassadh feast. Picking bilberries is a traditional pastime, documented in the theatrical production *Dancing at Lughnasa*. Raspberries and blackberries take their place in other locations.

In older times in Ireland, the entire month of August was traditionally the season for trade, convening court, making contracts, matchmaking, and settling debt.[109] Lammas in England and Scotland is a quarter-day, originally used for paying rents and making donations to the church.[110] Christian ministers took the opportunity to bless the harvest and to collect the tithings. Modern common magick practitioners can use the occasion to look over contracts, such as rental agreements, and do workings to ensure that they're getting the best deal.

Harvesttide was and is celebrated with fairs, open markets, dances, rituals of thankfulness, kissing games, and other fun activities. Games of capture the flag pit various factions against one another. The Irish Tailteann Games were reconstructed in 1924 as athletic contests and feats of skill (hurling, weight throwing, and archery competitions) and agricultural games (horse races, sheep-shearing contests, and greased pig chases). This event is mentioned in the legend about Cucullain wooing his wife, Emer, a manuscript that dates back to the eighth century. The name Tail-

---

108. Ralph Vaughan Williams and Albert Lancaster Lloyd, eds., *The Penguin Book of English Folk Songs* (New York: Penguin Books, 1990).

109. Bonwick, *Irish Druids and Old Irish Religions*.

110. Brand and Ellis, *Popular Antiquities of Great Britain*.

teann might have come from Tailltiu, who was Lugh's mother, and the games might have originally been celebrated on the occasion of her funeral.[111]

Other rites in commemoration of Lugh included throwing a rock with a sling, which is in imitation of the god's battle with the giant or monster called Balor. A folkplay involves Lugh harvesting grain as a gift for humankind, or seizing it from a dark entity called Crom Dubh, and overcoming the enemies of blight, rodents, and insects, which could destroy the harvest. These symbolic contests between Lugh and Balor, Lugh and Crom Dubh, or the opponents of the harvest are similar to the other representational contests between summer and winter. Poetry, song, and storytelling were also done in honor of Lugh.

Climbing hills or small mountains on Lughnassadh is a generally older Irish custom that has persisted into the current day.[112] Seekers enjoy watching the sunrise (or sunset) from the top of a hill. A carved stone head was sometimes placed at the mountain top to symbolize Balor or Crom Dubh, then knocked down by an actor who represented Lugh.[113] People carried flowers up the hillside, burying them to signify the demise of summertime. Sometimes the last sheaf of grain that was harvested was taken to the hilltop and ritually buried as an offering to ensure fertility.[114] Christians have borrowed this practice, turning the hill climb into a pilgrimage.

In modern times, Lughnassadh celebrations are still held across Ireland, while other customs have been revived. The annual Puck Fair in Killorglin, County Kerry, Ireland, has been around since the mid-seventeenth century and features a goat who is crowned as a king, a farmer's market, folk music and dances, and historical reenactments. Common magick users can celebrate the Harvesttide holiday by attending local agricultural fairs, playing outdoor games, holding picnics, and enjoying the fruits of the harvest.

---

111. "Teltown; the Táilteann Games," Discover Boyne Valley, accessed April 2, 2020, http://www.discoverboynevalley.ie/boyne-valley-drive/heritage-sites/teltown-t%C3%A1ilteann-games.

112. *New World Encyclopedia*, s.v. "Lughnasadh," accessed April 2, 2020, https://www.newworldencyclopedia.org/entry/Lughnasadh.

113. Brand and Ellis, *Popular Antiquities of Great Britain*.

114. Ibid.

Autumnal Equinox

The final solar holiday falls between September 20 and 23 and is a day of equal darkness and light. It is also when the sun enters the constellation of Libra. In the Cymraeg language, the autumnal equinox is called *Gŵyl Canol Hydref* or *Alban Elfed*, possibly an invention of Iolo Morganwg.[115] Merry Night is celebrated whenever the harvest is finished. In Irish Gaelic, the equinox is called *Mean Foghamar*, but it is not widely celebrated. In England, this holiday is sometimes called Harvest Home or the Ingathering, which are Christian commemorations of the harvest season. These holidays took place anywhere from the end of August to mid-September as a time to express gratitude for a bountiful year. Christians observe St. Michael's Day or Michaelmas on September 29, which has become syncretized with harvest traditions. Modern Pagans call the holiday Mabon, a name which came from author Aidan Kelly in honor of the Celtic legend about Culhwch seeking a lost prince called Mabon.[116]

The autumnal equinox is considered the second grain harvest. One older custom was throwing a sickle at the last standing barley or wheat so that the spirit of the corn would not blame any particular individual for its death. Gleaners would chant, "Well-cut, well-bound, well-shocked, saved from the ground," as they were reaping, binding, and stacking the sheaves.[117] As mentioned in the entry on Lammas, farmers used straw from the final sheaf of grain to create various ornaments, including woven wheat/straw figures. The sheaf was often adorned with white clothing and ribbons in honor of the deity or spirit of the corn. This object takes on a talismanic quality. Sometimes the straws were saved to make Brigid's crosses or Bridey dolls in the early spring. In some traditions, the corn dolly is burned at the end of the year.

Another autumnal equinox personification of the grain is creating a "bickle," "bikko," or straw dog and jestingly award it to the farmer who was the last to gather his harvest. Threshers would playfully spank the slowest farmer with a sheaf of his own grain. Other traditions included building a huge pile of straw on the back of a wagon and then parading it through the village, singing songs

---

115. Williams ab Ithel, *Barddas of Iolo Morganwg*.

116. Aidan A. Kelly, *Crafting the Art of Magic, Book I: A History of Modern Witchcraft, 1939–1964* (St. Paul, MN: Llewellyn Publications, 1991).

117. Brand and Ellis, *Popular Antiquities of Great Britain*.

with both celebratory and funereal themes. This procession was accompanied by a bagpiper, fiddlers, harpers, tin whistlers, drummers, and a host of cavorting farmers. They usually marched to a neighboring barn for a harvest festival.

Other farming customs are observed as well. Herding communities hold a party for washing and sheering sheep, a filthy job that involves reluctant animals. Hence, there is much good-humored jesting, as herdsmen ended up as dirty and wet as their sheep. The animals are ritually cleansed and blessed at the same time. Fishermen honor their boats and the seas. Apples are abundant at this time of year, and thus feature prominently in harvest rites. Pressing cider, making applesauce in large cauldrons, and drying apples all had their own attendant magickal workings. Threshing the grain was a time for farmers to gather and have fun, which often culminated in a barn dance. In the US, corn husking parties were held, and those who found a red ear of corn could claim a kiss from their sweetheart.

Of course, after all this harvesting comes the feasting. This is called a ploughman's dinner or a mel supper, which probably was a shortened version of "meal." Celebratory dinners include meats, fowls such as a capon, or a whole roast goose, due to the belief that someone who ate goose on St. Michael's Day would never starve. Honey, butter, garden vegetables, fruits, nuts, cheese, cream, and buttermilk accompany each meal, as well as multiple breads and pastries. Bannocks are cooked—without the use of any iron implements—as gifts for the Fae. Grain is soaked and boiled in milk for dessert, along with plum pudding, cheesecakes, and fruit pies. Alcohol flows like a river, so drinking games are a common pastime. Prayers and rituals are done to ensure that the food stays preserved in order to ensure plentitude throughout the long months of cold. And people eat until they groan, giving thanks for the bounty of the land.

This plentitude is usually shared with deities who represent the harvest. Offerings are given to the Celtic agricultural god Amaethon (sometimes a folk deity called Grain or Bran), the Roman goddess Ceres, the Norse god Freyr, or the local version of the grain goddess or harvest god, often at small roadside shrines. Some of these locations later became dedicated to Catholic saints. This tradition of sharing abundance includes offerings left outside for the fairies. In many places, any fruit, grain, or vegetables left in the fields or gardens after a certain date becomes the property of the spirits or the puka, which may be a euphemism for allowing the impoverished to collect the last of the produce. One legend says that any blackberries left outside after Michaelmas belong to the devil.

Filling a cornucopia, or horn of plenty, was a custom that came from the Romans. Various goddesses are portrayed holding these woven wicker baskets overflowing with fruit, including Ceres, Hecate, Diana, and the three Matronae or matrons, statues of whom have been discovered in Britain. This might be a parallel custom to the Celtic wicker effigies that contain fruits, vegetables, berries, and nuts, which are ceremonially burned. The cornucopia is a surviving tradition, most often seen during the American Thanksgiving.

Autumn is also a time for hunting and sacred rituals dedicated to the hunt. Costumed rites including folk dances and folkplays are performed before going hunting. The famous Abbots Bromley Horn Dance, a folk custom at least 800 years old, occurs each year on Wakes Monday in early September.[118] Dancers called deermen carry wooden stags' heads fitted with real antlers, perhaps to commemorate the deer-rutting season or in memory of a hunting ritual. The horns have been dated to be around 900 to 1,200 years old and come from a species of reindeer now extinct in Britain … or perhaps the antlers were imported from Scandinavia.[119] The dance, which has been performed continually with the exception of the Reformation and during the two World Wars, is quite similar to the morris and to some of the costumed hunting rituals. A young lad with a bow and arrow (representing Robin Hood), a man dressed as a woman called Maid Marian, a hobby horse, a fool, and a melodeon player accompany the deermen's procession and dance. This ceremony used to be enacted during Yuletide but has since moved to its current time. Deermen visiting a home or business are said to bring good luck. The Horn Dance can be seen every year in Staffordshire, or in videos online.

Throughout the world, many modern Pagans host Pagan Pride Day celebrations in late August, September, and early October. This gives magick users an opportunity to educate non-Pagans about our customs, to interact with our fellow celebrants, to learn new magickal techniques, and to gather food to share with the less fortunate. Locations of nearby Pagan Pride Day gatherings can be found online.

For most of these traditional solar holiday activities, the point is to raise energy for immediate use or to refill a magickal pool. It helps that many other people are

---

118. "About the Horn Dance," *Abbots Bromley Horn Dance*, accessed April 2, 2020, https://www.abbotsbromley.com/horn_dance.

119. "The Abbots Bromley Horn Dance," *Revels*, accessed April 2, 2020, https://www.revels.org/experience-revels/cultural-traditions/abbots-bromley-horn-dance/.

participating in the rites. Common magick users can also connect with the rhythms of the seasons and of nature. Deities and other entities can be honored, along with interacting with a traditional folkloric culture. Plus, celebrating the holidays is a whole lot of fun.

nine
MAGICK AND NATURE

Common magick is intimately allied with natural forces. In the past, most folkloric practitioners lived close to nature. They worked on farms, in mineral mines, and near woodlands. Homemakers grew and gathered herbs for remedies and food. Even city dwellers kept vegetable gardens. Working with nature requires intuition, as magick users need to make good choices when interacting with beneficial animals and plants. It was also essential to develop magickal coping strategies for things like the weather and health. In current times, an association with nature is still vitally important. People crave contact with the natural world. Interacting with spiritual entities who are connected to our environment is mutually beneficial.

Natural items can contain their own intrinsic, organic power. The four-leaf clover that signifies luck is well-known, but there are many more natural objects that have a talismanic or divinatory quality. Animals can be omens of good fortune, and plants have symbolic meaning. For example, catching a falling leaf means a wish will be granted, acorns represent prosperity, finding hay or cut grass on a path predicts wealth, and birds' nests mean home and family.

As mentioned in the sections about ethics and magickal beings, working with nature has some boundaries. The spirits of places and elemental forces may require communication, a mutually satisfactory agreement, and some type of payment or reward, including offerings or a show of appreciation. Rituals can be enacted for blessing and thanking natural powers.

This chapter is dedicated to the magick of animals, water, stones, trees, and plants. It includes the symbolic meaning of natural objects, as well as auguries related to nature. There are also some nature spirituality ceremonies for working with natural energies.

Figure 5: Celtic boar totem with knotwork designs

Animals in Magick

Animals have special meanings as omens, symbolizing a particular state of being or a future event. Their products can be used as protective talismans or as ingredients in spells and workings. Animals can serve as familiars, guides, or magickal helpers. They can also have a totemic purpose. Folktales are full of magickal animals, such as the white stag who appears as a prophetic messenger from the otherworld in Celtic legends.

All animals are represented in common magick beliefs, not just the furry or cute ones. They can include insects, reptiles, and amphibians. Fungus and bacteria, which were called "ill humors" by early healers, nonetheless have a role to play in nature. Smaller animals count as well; many people are proud of their eagle totem, but according to a British Isles folktale, the wren bested the eagle to become King of the Birds.

The following are some of the animals associated with common magick.

Horses

Horses, associated with heroes and gods, are integral to many folk stories of the British Isles. The horse represents work, nobility, placidity, wildness, virility, bravery, strength, wealth, and plentitude. A class of esoteric horseshoers, horsemen, or "horse whisperers" were said to have powers over equines and were adept at healing livestock who'd fallen ill or injured. This led to a magickal guild centered around the horse.

Horses can be ornamented for safety and protection by using paint, brass talismans, bells, and ribbons in their manes and tails. The sweat from a horse can motivate a lazy person. The "old gray mare" symbolizes death and rebirth, while a foal born with a white spot on its forehead is a sure sign that all is well. A baby passed beneath the belly of a horse will thrive. Witches supposedly transformed people into horses by using a special bridle, "hag-riding" them until exhaustion. If you encounter a white horse, quietly make a wish. Horsehair charms are used for binding and protection, while a single hair from a strong horse's tail is used for a pendulum in divination.

Much of the lore and folk magick associated with horses can be transferred to our modern vehicles and homes. Symbols of horseshoes and the rune Ehwaz, representing a horse, are painted on or placed inside a vehicle to prevent accidents and breakdowns. A sigil of a horse is painted on a home to ward away evil. Horseshoes nailed above the door ensure good fortune; hang them like a U to contain the luck.

Rabbits

Stories about rabbits and hares are prolific throughout the British Isles. Witches were said to transform into hares, dancing and cavorting at night. British folktales describe a hunter who shoots a rabbit, but it remains alive and flees, limping. The hunter tracks the animal to the home of the village witch, who has been shot and is injured in the same place on her body as the rabbit was shot. British emigrants took this story to Appalachia, where it was told to the folklore collectors of the 1930s.

Other stories tell of rabbits and their penchant for speed, cleverness, and avoidance of danger. The Mad March Hare is actually doing a mating dance; observing it grants fertility. Saying "rabbit rabbit" on the first day of the month will bring good luck, while stating "I hate rabbits" at a campfire will prevent smoke from getting in your eyes. There is an image of a leaping hare on the moon, and a constellation called Lepus is the image of a hare, complete with long ears. The Teutonic tribes who came to Britain used hares and rabbits to represent fertility and the springtime goddess Oestara.[120] White hares are viewed as messengers from the underworld, like the rabbit character Lewis Carroll wrote about, who introduced Alice to Wonderland.

Cats

A black cat is considered fortunate when on a ship, and if a black kitty comes toward you on your path, they bring luck. However, if they cross your path or run away from you, they take your luck away with them.

Pure black cats, Siamese kitties, and gray, brown, and black tabbies seem to be the best familiars, although don't discount the fluffy calico, who may surprise people with her magickal adeptness. The notion of cats as witches' familiars has been around for a long time; the word *grimalkin* in Middle English means both a cat and an ill-tempered old woman, and in Shakespeare's *Macbeth*, one of the three witches calls her cat Graymalkin.[121; 122]

Animal shelter workers tell me that black cats and dogs are the last to be adopted because of superstitions about bad luck, but pet parents report that black animals make excellent companions. Hallowe'en folklore about black cats has little to do with misfortune: The black cat sitting next to someone foretells good luck, and if the cat jumps on a person's lap, it means excellent luck. A yawning black cat means an opportunity is coming your way.

---

120. Katie Edwards, "The Very Strange History of the Easter Bunny," *The Conversation*, March 24, 2016, http://theconversation.com/the-very-strange-history-of-the-easter-bunny-56690.

121. *Dictionary.com*, s.v. "grimalkin," accessed April 5, 2020, https://www.dictionary.com/browse/grimalkin.

122. Amanda Mabillard, *Macbeth* Glossary, *Shakespeare Online*, August 20, 2009, http://www.shakespeare-online.com/plays/macbeth/macbethglossary/macbeth1_1/macbethglos_graymalkin.html.

Dogs

Britain has numerous black dog folktales, including Grim, who guards church-yards; the *Cwn Annwn* who accompanied Arawn, the Welsh god of death; the *Cu Sidhe*, fairy dogs; the black Shuck; dandy dogs; ratchet hounds; Gabriel hounds; the Garm; Barget; Herla's hounds; and ol' Padfoot. To see them was an omen of death, as the hounds of the otherworld came on Hallowe'en night (or during Yuletide) with their master to gather souls. The dogs accompanying the Wild Hunt could be black, or they could be crop-eared white hounds with red eyes.

Pigs

The pig, sow, or boar was considered by the Celts to be good luck and a sym-bol of strength, fertility, and wisdom, but it could also symbolize misfortune. A boar with a magickal comb in its bristles was hunted by King Arthur and his knights on a quest; after finding him, the boar gave directions to find the lost prince Mabon. Isolde predicted the death of her lover, Tristan, during a dream about a boar. The goddess Cerridwen was associated with a white pig and, in some versions of her myth, transformed into a sow. Warriors wore the symbol of a boar on their helmets or shields, and the Romano-British sometimes deco-rated their helms with boar bristles. The Welsh *hwchddugwta*, or black sow with a cropped or cut tail, is a type of spectral pig that is said to chase after humans on *Nos Calan Gaeaf*, or Hallowe'en. The Norse deities Frey and Freyja, both symbol-izing virility, sometimes rode in a chariot drawn by a pig. In folktales, the swine-herd is often really a prince.

Pigs are associated with grain, fertility, and plentitude. This could be why toy money banks are often formed in the shape of a pig. A pig token on a charm bracelet means luck and abundance.

Insects

Decomposers such as beetles, carrion worms, and insect larvae have a role in physi-cal and magickal transformation. Bugs can represent change; for example, consider an insect that evolves from egg to larvae, chrysalis, adult form, gravid, old age, and finally death.

Insects including crickets, dragonflies, butterflies, ladybugs, bees, beetles, and others are symbolic of luck and power and are sometimes considered messengers of the gods. A bumblebee in the house means a welcome visitor will arrive soon.

Spiders

Spiders are viewed as weavers of the sacred web. They represent storytelling and bending or shaping types of magick. They are symbols of industry and earnings. If a spider descends on a thread in front of you, it means you will receive a message.

Bats

Bats are a conveyance for air spirits and a guide from the underworld. A single bat flying in circles is a beneficent omen. Bats can also represent nighttime, darkness, and the unseen.

Toads

Toads have long been associated with witchcraft as a familiar spirit and as a type of charm. A living creature was sometimes used by a "toadman," or healer, to draw negative conditions or sickness away from a person and into the animal by employing contagion magick.

A dried, mummified toad or a toad skeleton were used in magickal rites, sometimes ground into a powder and put into a healing ointment or potion; sometimes pierced with pins to repel harmful energy. Toad skeletons were also used in talismanic magick or in a ritual where they're thrown into running water.

Toads are also beneficial helpers in the garden, viewed as the "fairy steed" or conveyance for the wee folk. A toad house constructed of a flower pot on its side can shelter a little friend.

Snakes

Snakes symbolize healing powers in many cultures. Think of the caduceus, or the staff entwined by a snake that represents medicine and first responders. A snake is the guardian of the Norse Midgard, or material realm. A snake also symbolizes wisdom.

Underwater Critters

Sea creatures are magickally important as well. Welsh mythology tells of the salmon of wisdom and the dolphins who rescued sailors, and Irish legends recall the seal who transformed into a female fairy or *selchie*. All of these animals are found in the coastal waters of the US, while salmon also dwell in the Great Lakes. Trout, bass, haddock, cod, and the panfish living in American lakes and rivers represent abundance. So do the herrings or kippers of the sea. Eating sea creatures may transmit their qualities to humans.

Fantasy Creatures

When we think of animal symbols, let's not forget the creatures of fantasy, including unicorns, gryphons, water monsters, and the firedrake. They might be considered spirit beings. For example, dragons sometimes represent the energies of fire and are said to live inside volcanoes, but they are also associated with other elements. The red dragon, *Y Ddraig Goch*, depicted on the Welsh flag, was said to fight against a white dragon representing England. The red dragon was defeated and disappeared underground, but will reemerge to fight another day.

The Scots use the symbol of the elusive unicorn as a magickal figure. Scotland is also the home of the watery, mythological Loch Ness Monster called Nessie. There are water beasts to be found in the US, including a similar creature in Lake Champlain named Champ. The Welsh have the Afanc, which resembles a giant beaver, comparable to a watery creature that is rumored to live in Lake Michigan.

Some magickal animals are combinations of species. For example, the gryphon has the qualities of a lion, serpent, and eagle. These capabilities have mystic significance; the lion's strength, the wiliness of a serpent, and the eagle's power are all wrapped up in one creature. Combined, these characteristics signify a much stronger being.

Spirit and Familiar Animals

Spirit Animals

A spirit animal is usually defined as a physical being or spiritual entity that represents a person, family, clan, profession, or other group of people. Many cultures employ a similar concept, including British society. For example, the practice of heraldry often uses animals to signify a family or royal house. Spirit animals can help us as we perform rites, serve as a guide, or be a messenger from a deity.

Birds, fish, insects, amphibians, reptiles, and mammals can be spirit animals in British folkloric magick. Some folktales or fables assign a trait to an animal, such as a clever fox or trickster snake, and use those qualities as a teaching tool about nature, certain events, and consequences. The animal spirit can symbolize natural characteristics, such as the strength of a horse, the motherly instincts of a wildcat, or the prickly, protective capability of a porcupine. The animal can represent a valuable human quality, like the wisdom of the Celtic salmon, the cleverness of a raven, or the sexual prowess of a stag.

Some spirit animals embody all the characteristics of a certain animal and every member of its species. For example, the Great Bear might represent all bears and the virtues of all bears: strength, loyalty, and protectiveness. By calling upon or invoking the spirit of the Great Bear, the magick user takes on those particular aspects and summons the desired qualities of the animal. For a magickal connection to the animal, physical representations of an animal can be used, such as fur, claws, or bones, as well as representational art or symbols.

Animals in folklore may help a hero achieve his goals, perform the role of a trickster, or simply represent a person as their symbol. They can serve as a guide or as a messenger from the spirit realm. They can serve as a foil or opponent to the hero as well.

Familiar Animals

In my tradition, a familiar can be a living animal that works with a person, offering emotional and magickal support. They might be a pet, a farm animal, or a wild animal in nature that lives near human dwellings. A pet cat can yowl in the presence of disquieting energies, and a horse may sense when we are feeling vulnerable and nuzzle us. A squirrel in the yard offers energy for a magickal working by running up and down a tree trunk, chattering along with the spell. Patting a dog soothes people when they are upset, which could be the reasoning behind emotional support animals. Living familiars can also lend us their energy during difficult times.

In other common magick traditions, a familiar is a spirit that takes on an animal form to serve as a magickal helper. In folkloric magico-religions with a Norse background, the *fylgja* is a spirit animal that connects a person to their fate, or *wyrd*. Meeting a particular animal might auger, or foretell, certain conditions; for example, seeing the *fylgja*, or spirit, of Brock the Badger can mean that a person is loyal, stodgy, digs in to solve problems, and has some fierce qualities. Disembodied animal familiars can intercede with the spirit realm, serve as a watcher or ward during rituals, prevent psychic attack, act as a guide, and have other powers beyond a living animal's capacities, such as human intelligence.

Deified Animals

Often, a deity or other entity may embody the spirit of an animal or manifest the characteristics of an animal. There are dozens of deities in British pantheons who have animal symbols, traits, characteristics, and associations. Some have animal helpers, such as the hunting hounds of the Celtic lord of death and the Anglo-Saxon master of the Wild Hunt. Celtic deities transformed into horses, eagles, owls, rabbits, deer, fish, and other creatures. As the British and Irish are seafaring people, there were also mermaids, mermen, and people who could change into seals.

Many worldwide cultures revere some form of wild forest or hunting deity that symbolizes both fertility and death. This deity is usually male and typically has horns or antlers. Several of them are found in the British Isles, descended from the folkloric traditions of Celtic and Roman civilizations. This includes Cernunnos (also known as Kernunos, Cerunincos, Ciarán, Karnayna, Carenus, Cern, and Herne), Atho (also known as Addo Dhu), Faunus (also known as Pan, Sylvanus, and the satryr), the Buca (also known as Puck, Pook, and Damh), Frey, Robin Goodfellow, the roebuck, and Ol' Crockern. All of these woodland deities appear as an antlered huntsman and forest god in folklore. The Horned Lord of Wicca or British traditional witchcraft is a similar construct. Images of a horned or antlered man were stamped on British coins that date back to 60 to 30 BCE, believed to be Cernunnos … or perhaps his representative priest.[123] The Anglo-Saxons brought the woodwose to Britain as a type of mascot—the Wild Man of the Woods that is part beast.

Animal Omens

Some creatures symbolize good or ill fortune. Seeing a robin redbreast, catbird, or mockingbird means good luck, while a sparrow in the house is bad luck. Butterflies and hummingbirds signify good fortune, as does a house wren, an albatross, twin calves, or goat kids. A catbird singing after dark is good luck, and means you'll soon be "sitting in the catbird seat." Bulls, pigs, deer, horses, and cattle represent prosperity, especially to the Celts. Honeybees mean plentitude. Believe it or not, roaches symbolize bounty, as they are attracted to a plentiful food source.

---

123. Chris Rudd, "Horned God or Druid Priest?," *Celtic Coins*, December 2014, https://celticcoins.com/wp-content/uploads/2014/12/Horned-god.pdf.

Swallows nesting nearby have a positive connotation and are favorable to a voyage. Wild turkeys mean abundance. Geese represent the harvest, prosperity, and protectiveness.

Some animals presage mortality. Pigeons flocking around a house, seeing a single magpie, and dogs howling outside can foretell a human death. A whippoor-will that only cries three times foretells a death. A bird tapping on the window is bad luck. Killing a swan is the very worst of bad luck. And a hoot owl speaking like a human means that person is not long for this world.

Wild animals are frequent prognosticators of weather and the seasons. House mice coming indoors in September means winter is soon to follow. During autumn, expect frost soon after snakes and amphibians disappear. Blackbirds flying south before Labor Day predict an early winter. Fat mammals with thick fur in autumn predict a cold winter. Woolly bear caterpillars with russet at both ends and black in the middle represent the winter season; more black means longer snows. Busy squirrels mean a hard winter. Yowling cats foretell a heat wave. Cowering dogs predict a thunderstorm. Mosquitoes bite more before a rain, while crabby bees mean a storm. Birds hush before strong winds. Redwing blackbirds singing on a cloudy day portend luck for fishing.

According to *The Old Farmer's Almanac*, crickets' chirping can predict the warmth of the air. Faster chirps mean a higher temperature. Count the number of chirps in fourteen seconds, add forty, and that number is the air temperature in Fahrenheit.[124] Often, esoteric symbolism has a solid basis in the material world. House crickets are also considered good luck.

One of the oldest forms of divination involves using the scapula, or shoulder blade, of an animal that was hunted or slaughtered for food, usually a deer, pig, or sheep. The scapula is heated in a fire, and the cracks that form on the bone's surface are read and interpreted. This was called scapulimancy by the Romans and *slinneanchach* in Irish Gaelic.

Travelling up a hill and meeting an animal is an omen. Burrowing animals symbolize stability, grounding, and well-being, while a deer means either fleeing a harmful situation or gaining prosperity. An opossum might mean someone is trying to pull off a sneaky trick. Raccoons symbolize cleverness. Red birds, such

---

124. Catherine Boeckmann, "Predict the Temperature with Cricket Chirps," *The Old Farmer's Almanac*, June 24, 2019, https://www.almanac.com/content/predict-temperature-cricket -chirps.

as cardinals and tanagers, are an omen of good luck. A flock of crows or jaybirds signify a bountiful harvest.

Some animal signs might not mean what we think. For example, a dead fish at the edge of the water may seem like a bad omen, but it is also a sign of plentitude and rebirth. The corpse is teeming with new life, including insect larvae and bacteria.

Some cultures see various birds as good or bad luck, including crows and vultures, who are viewed as either messengers of the gods or an augury of death because they enjoy eating roadkill. Biologists who study animals have realized that crows can be as smart as a seven-year-old human child.[125] These birds can solve problems and use tools. In British folklore, crows were often considered good fortune and represented prosperity.

Animals in Rites

Animal products can be used as talismans and for spells and workings under the principle of sympathetic magick. Anything containing a part of an animal can represent the traits of that critter, including snakeskins, teeth, hides, hooves, rooster spurs, owl pellets, shells, bones, and any other discarded products. Items that come from animals can symbolize generalized intangible qualities, like cats' claw sheaths for protection or antlers for fertility.

Fish scales are cast on a board or cloth for divination. The tail of a horse can be used as a ceremonial fly whisk or scourge. Bird feathers symbolize communication and wisdom; they can also alert us to messages from the gods. Entrails are used for divination. Bear or wolf claws can symbolize protection. And the famous rabbit skin of the folk poem is used as baby bunting.

Old-timey meat markets kept the back left foot attached to a rabbit carcass to ensure that an unscrupulous butcher was not serving his customers a small dog or a cat instead of rabbit meat. Their feet were later sold for magickal implements. The Celts believed that hares are good luck.[126] Rabbits' or hares' feet are carried as lucky talismans in the British Isles. In Britain, stroking a sick person's face with

---

125. "Crows' Reasoning Ability Rivals That of Seven-Year-Old Humans," Press Association, *The Guardian*, March 26, 2014, https://www.theguardian.com/science/2014/mar/26/crows-reasoning-ability-seven-year-old-humans.

126. Charles Panati, *Panati's Extraordinary Origins of Everyday Things* (New York: William Morrow, 1989).

a rabbit's foot is said to facilitate healing, and if the foot is hung near a cradle, the baby will stay healthy. Carrying the rabbit's foot is believed to prevent rheumatoid arthritis.

Now we must come to the difficult topic of animal sacrifice. This subject makes many magick users feel uncomfortable, but if you've ever eaten a hamburger, gone hunting or fishing, or even slapped a mosquito, you have been a participant in a sacrifice. Common magick users recognize that in order to make an omelet, we must break an egg. Animals killed for food must be thanked and comforted, and we must try to end their lives with little pain or suffering. All parts of the animal should be used, and we must understand their meaning and purpose in order to honor their gifts. Welsh herders have a saying: "Use every part of the sheep except the baa." My ancestors had proscriptions against killing baby animals, instead allowing them to grow and reproduce. When we go hunting or slaughter an animal for food, we wash our hands before and after, thank the animal's spirit, perform a ceremony to release it to be reborn, and give an offering of a coin, song, trinket, or beverage to the deities of the wilderness.

Some animal-based rites have been falsified, especially those described during the witch trials. For example, a rite called the *Taghairm* in Scotland is used for divination. A type of shamanic practice, this includes sitting in a cave or the space behind a waterfall and covering oneself from head to toe with the freshly slaughtered, skinned hide of a bull or stag. "Taghairm" means spirit calling, and thus the magick user speaks to the ancestors. The wind in the cave or the rushing sound of the water becomes the voices of the dead. The darkness of the animal-skin covering facilitates astral travel. However, during the times of persecution, this rite was bastardized; it was said that witches practiced the Taghairm while hurting and killing black cats in order to speak to the devil.[127] Supposedly, dozens of cats would appear during the rite, stalking and yowling. While the Taghairm did in fact use the product of an animal—the hide of a bull—the other story is untrue.

Water in Magick

Water has always had magickal connotations in the British Isles, as there is so very much of it. Salt water is considered purifying and cleansing. Still bodies of

---

127. M. Martin, *A Description of the Western Islands of Scotland* (originally published 1703; Internet Archive, 2009), https://archive.org/details/descriptionofwes00mart/page/n4.

water, like ponds and small lakes, are filled with calmness or stability, while flowing water, especially from a southbound stream, implies movement, change, and transformation. Many older spells advise drawing water from a swiftly running, southbound river and using it for changing a situation, like washing the floors of a workspace to promote industrious behavior. It can also be used for healing. The water of a wellspring is great for health, clairvoyance, and communication with water spirits. Bottled water works nearly as well.

Morning dew gathered at Beltane or Midsummer is used to bathe the face and improve the complexion. Laying a cotton sheet, towel, or cloth in a meadow and wringing out the dew water provides enough to be used in spell workings all year. Rainwater, pond or river water, or well water is gathered to use for washing and healing. A crystal can be placed in water and set beneath the full moon to cleanse its energies. A stone that has been well rinsed, placed in a glass of rainwater or well water, and left outside under the new moon will imbue the water with the crystal's quality when used as a beverage or wash.

Gazing into water is used for divination, particularly water in a *tarn*, or a still, dark pond with decayed plant matter creating *marl*, or rich organic mud, at the bottom. Water scrying can also be done at an old-fashioned yard well or cistern, a calm lake, or a bowl of water. The vessel should be lit by a candle over one's left shoulder. Other diviners use a mirror to gaze into, with the body of water or the well behind them. However, if the image is disturbed by a jumping fish or a thrown pebble, the envisioned sequence of events will likely be disrupted in consensus reality.

One divination ritual from the north of England uses south-running river water. The water is put into a glass or ceramic bowl. The user will also need a ring or coin suspended by a horsehair, which serves as a pendulum. After asking a question, the user will watch the pendulum for movement. The ring hitting the side of the glass once means a "yes" answer, not touching the side means "no," and multiple clinks of the coin or ring against the side means that more information is forthcoming.

Certain wellsprings are considered sacred to a water nixie, spirit, or goddess. Many of these holy wells survive in the British Isles, including a few in downtown London. Some of the wells were and are used continually. The spirit of a sacred wellspring can be asked a question, with a coin or crystal offered in return for a vision. Water from these sacred wells was and is used for bathing and drinking, for the reasons of purification and healing. Any water taken from holy wells should be boiled to ensure it's safe to drink. This may reduce its magickal properties, but it also kills bacteria and protozoans that are harmful to humans.

There is documentation from the Medieval period onward of sacred wells being visited by seekers, and while some Reformation-era ministers chided their congregations for using them, it does not seem to have slowed anyone down.[128] Healing rites at St. Madron's Well (also known as Maddern, Matron, Motran, or Modron; possibly a folk saint, possibly a name of a Celtic goddess) in Cornwall were recorded around 1777, long after some scholars assumed these Pagan ceremonies had died out.[129] Seekers partake of the waters, then make equal-armed crosses of straw that are sealed in the middle with a bent pin. These are used as an offering in exchange for health. Bubbles rising from the well are counted by young ladies, corresponding to the year of their marriage or the first letter of their future husband's name. Brigit's Well of Kildare in Ireland is now associated with the saint, but it was originally sacred to the goddess Bríd and is still considered a holy well with mystic properties. The fount, situated in a grotto, has offerings of Catholic prayer cards, Brigid's crosses, ribbons, jewelry, and votive images lining the walls.

Seekers leave votive items in trees nearby the sacred wells—or in the wells themselves—including trinkets, coins, crystals, bent pins, buttons, photographs, drawings, ribbons, and bits of cloth tied to the tree branches. A person in need of healing will wash their afflicted body part with a piece of fabric dipped into the well water, say prayers or words of power, then hang the cloth on a nearby tree limb.

In folklore, whitecaps near a shoreline or riverfront were said to be the "white horses" ridden by water spirits. A river running backward foretold a life-changing event. Items found along the edge of water, such as driftwood or hagstones, contain the properties of earth, sea, and sky and can be used in magickal workings. Any offerings in return must be biodegradable.

---

128. Robert Charles Hope, *The Legendary Lore of the Holy Wells of England: Including Rivers, Lakes, Fountains, and Springs* (London: Elliot Stock, 1893).

129. Robert Hunt, ed., "Maddern or Madron Well," in *Popular Romances of the West of England: The Drolls, Traditions, and Superstitions of Old Cornwall* (London: Chatto and Windus, 1908), https://www.sacred-texts.com/neu/eng/prwe/prwe148.htm.

The Magick of Stones, Crystals, and Minerals

Stones, crystals, and minerals have become a media trope. In television and movies, witches are often seen using crystal balls for divination, and healers use colorful stones for magick. These portrayals are common because we really do these things, and they work.

Certain stones are said to possess something resembling intelligence, such as the quartz crystals used in radios, watches, and computers. Some magick users believe that crystals have an energetic vibration. These stones are thought to contain powers such as amplifying memory, healing, or enhancing other abilities. They can be a source of, or a container for, magickal energy.

People have been using rocks for magick for centuries. An inscribed pendant that was 11,000 years old and made of shale (and may have belonged to a shaman) was found at the Star Carr site in Yorkshire.[130] Agates can be found on beaches throughout Britain and America; also known as chalcedony, they were used by Neolithic peoples as jewelry.[131] These stones are thought to provide strength and gentle healing. The crown jewels of the British royal family have many uses besides being pretty; they convey authority and have healing properties. Most common people did not own rubies and sapphires, of course, but amethyst, tourmaline, beryl, jet, amber, topaz, clear quartz, pearls, and cairngorm are native to the British Isles. These gemstones were and are sometimes owned by the middle classes, tradespeople, and merchants, including cunning men and women and other traditional healers. Cairngorm is a type of smoky quartz from Scotland's northern mountains. It is the Scottish national stone and can be used for grounding, stabilizing, and preventing nightmares. Many Wiccan high priestesses wear amber and jet; these gems have also been used for invoking and banishing, respectively, since ancient times. Neither of them are actually stones, but instead organic mineralites: amber is petrified resin from an extinct species

130. Abigail Beall, "'Magic' Mesolithic Pendant is Oldest Art Ever Found in Britain: 11,000-Year-Old Jewellery May Have Been Worn by Shaman to Ward Off Evil Spirits," *Daily Mail*, February 25, 2016, https://www.dailymail.co.uk/sciencetech /article-3464192/Magic-Mesolithic-pendant-oldest-art-Britain-11-000-year-old -jewellery-worn-shaman-ward-evil-spirits.html.

131. "Fossil Agate Meaning and Properties," Fire Mountain Gems and Beads, accessed April 5, 2020, https://www.firemountaingems.com/resources/encyclobeadia/gem -notes/gmstnprprtsfssl1.

of pine tree, while jet comes from compressed, decaying wood. Both carry a slight negative electrical charge, and both are believed to have curative abilities.[132]

One natural item that can be found on most rocky beaches is a hagstone or holey stone, also called a fairy stone, peep stone, eye of God, or seer's stone, meaning a pebble or rock with a hole worn all the way through it by natural means like water or compression. In Britain, these rocks were sometimes called adder stones, believed to relieve snakebite. Pliny the Elder wrote that the stones were formed by a grouping of snakes casting slime, although this isn't true.[133] More likely, that type of "stone" was actually a piece of amber, and while it has healing properties, antivenom isn't one of them. Neither amber nor hagstones are the product of snakes. Anyway, holey stones are used for clairvoyance, viewing fairies and other beings, seeking truth and clarity, helping to heal ailments of the eyes, and to represent the female principle. They can be hung in the window by using a bit of leather, string, or yarn in order to repel negative energies. A hagstone suspended above the bed prevents nightmares. Holey stones should not be painted, as it can reduce their power.

Another common rock found in Britain and the US is limestone, often containing fossils. These are used to represent permanence and stability, and they carry the properties of life and death as well as water and earth. Fossils are good for polarity, but if you find yourself becoming stodgy, they might not be the best choice. Petoskey stones and limestones containing seashells, ferns, and even small prehistoric animals can be found in rock shops and nature centers, as well as in the wild.

The sacred, white, powdery limestone rock of the chalk cliffs of Britain is good for drawing magickal sigils and figures onto hard surfaces. One art form was cutting turf away from a hillside to reveal the white chalk beneath it. There are more than twenty figures of men, horses, and other animals in England, some of which are up to 3,000 years old.[134] These include the Long Man of Wilmington, the Uffington White Horse, and the Cern Abbas Giant. Couples who wish

---

132. Scott Cunningham, *Cunningham's Encyclopedia of Crystal, Gem & Metal Magic* (St. Paul, MN: Llewellyn Publications, 1988).

133. Pliny the Elder, *The Natural History* (London: Taylor and Francis, 1855).

134. Ellen Castelow, "Chalk Hill Figures," Historic UK, accessed April 5, 2020, https://www .historic-uk.com/CultureUK/Chalk-Hill-Figures/.

to become pregnant lie down inside this figure's huge erection. A hill figure can be replicated elsewhere by outlining an image with white stones.

Of course, stone circles had and have great significance in the British Isles. Each year at the summer solstice, modern Pagans meet to celebrate at Stonehenge and other places that are surrounded by a ring of gigantic hewn rocks, which are considered sacred spaces. Psychics state they can perceive a high energy within these stone circles. Tall stones are called dolmens, god-stones, a god stane, and standing stones, while the monuments themselves are called megaliths. Some standing stones had or have capstones across their tops, while others form tables, arches, and possibly altars. Stone cairns, or piles of rocks, and tombs made of stones are also considered to be megaliths, many of them containing magickal energies. Some are believed to be home to the fairies, gnomes, or spirits. The passage tomb in Newgrange, Ireland, has a feature where the sun shines through one end on the winter solstice, while Stonehenge and other megaliths have a portion that lines up with the sun on the summer solstice.

Many of the megaliths were and are used by common magick practitioners for worship rites and magickal rituals. For instance, ladies crawl through or beneath large stones with a hole or monuments with an arch or capstone in the hopes of becoming pregnant. This rite uses the female principle as well as a type of contagion magick. Babies are passed through the opening to ensure their health. One large perforated stone, called the Mên-an-Tol, located in Cornwall near Penzance, is still in use. Circumnavigating a dolmen three times going deosil creates positive energies and well-being. Rubbing or touching the stones brings health. Funeral rites were conducted at the monuments, some of which contain buried grave goods. Burials of dignitaries took place at several megaliths. At some of the cairns, it is customary to add a rock, both to honor the dead and for good fortune.

The paths between stone circles and other megaliths are also considered to have magickal significance. These paths are called *Heilige Leinen* in German, meaning holy lines, and fairy paths by the Welsh and Irish. They were also called green roads. In 1921, amateur archeologist Alfred Watkins wrote a book called *The Old Straight Track* about the lines between the monuments, which he found to be geometrically important. Watkins called these paths ley lines, and theorized that they may have been arranged deliberately, may align with magnetic fields, and were possibly used as roads.[135] Some people believe that building anything other than a monolith, graveyard, or place of worship on a ley line is unlucky, and that the fairies may destroy the structure or otherwise cause havoc. Ghost roads are similar lines, but are mainly used by spirits walking toward the underworld. Churches, cemeteries, tombs, and barrows can be built along ghost roads. Some common folk believe that standing on a force line could access "dragon power" or "serpent breath," and they may use a glain or serpent stone to do so.

A common magick rite to check for the presence of negative energies uses three small plain gray pebbles found at the edge of a lake or stream. Seekers place the rocks in a bonfire or hearth fire and look at them after the fire has burned away to ash. If one stone is cracked, a person is causing trouble. Magick users carry the one cracked stone with the two unbroken ones to confront the suspected troublemaker; they will inadvertently reveal themselves and their motives. If two or three are broken, the culprit is a spirit being. If none are broken, there is no problem.

A lucky rock or a penny made from copper brings good fortune. People can pick up a stone, carry it through a dangerous location for protection, and drop the stone as soon as they leave. Some British villages had their own sacred stone, blessed by a saint or magicked by a "cunning man," used for healing, divination, and to remove negative energies. Some of these rocks were even rented out for use by other practitioners. Common backyard stones include granite (representing strength), pigmented sandstone (used for drawing sigils), volcanic rocks (embodying fire), and sparkly multifaceted quartz, which can augment power.

Plants and Trees in Magick

Trees have considerable significance in British folk magick. Various trees are associated with the moons and seasons, such as oak for June and holly for December. Each tree is said to have different magickal properties. Plants are used as food and clothing, employed as curatives, used for augury, and burned for cleansing rites and heat. Plants and trees of Britain can be substituted by others found in the Americas as long as the practitioner is aware of their qualities. For example, while there are few larch trees growing in the American northeast, Douglas fir can be used instead for talismanic purposes and Yuletide decorations.

---

135. Alfred Watkins, *The Old Straight Track* (New York: Ballantine, 1973).

There is considerable folklore related to trees, from the spirits who dwell within the forests to the uses and meanings of various species of tree. For instance, oak, ash, and thorn are three magickal trees written about by Rudyard Kipling in his "Tree Song." [136] The following are some of the trees and plants used for common magick.

Ash

Ash trees symbolize community. Ash is said to represent the male principle. Ashwood bows are highly prized, as the wood is supple—bending, but not breaking. If there is a forest fire, ash trees usually do not completely burn, and thus they are said to bring about safety from house fires. Ash sap is believed to have curative powers, although it tastes really bad, in my humble opinion. Burning ash wood at Midsummer and inhaling the smoke brings about prophetic dreams. Ash wood is used to create stangs or staves, especially those with three prongs or branches at the top. An ash wand can ward off negative energies. The World Tree of the Norse people, Yggdrasil, was an ash tree.

Oak

Oak trees symbolize strength and the male principle. They also represent plenitude because of their abundant acorns, which are food for many wild creatures. A necklace of acorns is used to evoke wealth, while acorns in a bowl on an altar brings prosperity. The Welsh words *duir, dewr,* or *drui* and the Irish Gaelic *dar,* referring to wrens and oak trees, could be the origin of the word Druid. Pliny the Elder wrote of Druids gathering mistletoe from oak branches and meeting together in a *drunemeton,* or oak forest grove. [137] Touching an oak tree on Midsummer can bring about health all year long, and an oak leaf poultice is said to heal sores. Acidic oak leaves are also used for tanning leather. The Oak King, written about by author Robert Graves as the ruler of summer and the opponent of the Holly King, may have come from folktales about two deities or heroes fighting for sovereignty and the right to control the seasons. [138] Legends of Llew say that the god turned into an eagle and perched in an oak tree. Sap flowing

---

136. Kipling, *Puck of Pook's Hill.*

137. Pliny the Elder, *Natural History.*

138. Graves, *White Goddess.*

from an oak branch in the fireplace presages a war. An oaken wand topped with a pinecone, called a priapic wand after the Roman fertility deity Priapus, is used for summoning fecundity and plentitude. Many of the Green Man foliate figures have oak leaves as hair.

Thorn and Rowan Trees

Folklore about lightning cautions, "Beware of an oak, it draws the stroke; avoid an ash, it courts the flash; creep under the thorn, it can save you from harm." [139] Thorn trees feature prominently in British folktales, including whitethorns, blackthorns, and hawthorn trees. Whitethorns, hawthorns, blackthorns, and rowans are considered sacred, the province of wizards, and homes to the wee folk. They are believed to have magickal properties.

Thorn trees represent the female principle and fertility. These trees will often flower before they produce leaves. "Bauming the thorn" means decorating a living tree with ribbons and trinkets. Sharp thorns and the wood of thorn trees are said to repel malicious spirits and baneful energies, as are rowan branches. Wands made from these woods are used to direct power and to make wishes.

Two rowan twigs, when bound with red thread in the shape of an equal-armed cross, prevent malicious workings and repel harmful entities. Rowan's white blossoms symbolize purity, although their flowers or branches should not be brought indoors between Harvesttide and Beltane for concerns about bad luck and disturbing the fairies. Nail a whitethorn or rowan branch that is flowering but is without leaves above the main doorway of a home on Beltane to bring about goodwill and blessings all year long. Rowans are also called mountain ash. Their wood should not be cut by metal. Red rowan berries have a pentagram shape. These are used to make sloe, as in sloe gin.

The blackthorn was used by Cornish pellars as a "blasting rod," a wand to zap negative energies and even cast curses (not recommended). The saying is "whitethorn to bless, blackthorn to blast." Blackthorn was also used to craft a *shillelagh*, a cane or weapon.

If one takes a branch from any one of these trees for magickal use, a gift of a coin, trinket, or beverage must be left in its place.

---

139. John Simpson and Jennifer Speake, eds., *The Oxford Dictionary of Proverbs*, 5th ed. (Oxford: Oxford University Press, 2008).

Fruit Trees

Fruit trees are blessed, or "sained," during a rite around New Year's Day, called "wassailing the trees." They are watered with apple cider and given toast to eat, and songs are sung for them. The Apple Tree Man is the elderly spirit of the oldest tree in the orchard, according to British folklore. He is wise and is offered reverence while saining or wassailing the trees.

Apples are considered food of the gods; cutting the fruit across the middle—between the stem and the bottom—reveals a pentagram within the seed cavity. Apple blossoms symbolize springtime, happiness, beginnings, and several of the states in the US.

Birch and Willow Trees

Birch is considered to have female energies. Folk in the British Isles often use birch for broom handles, with twigs of the broom plant for bristles, wrapped by a willow withe.

Willow, which bends easily when fresh, is used to create baskets. It represents the female principle, water, and the power to bend and change reality. Anything made of wicker, such as furniture, the walls of homes, and baskets, was likely constructed of willow bent around the framework of a stronger wood. The Old English word *wican* could have been derived from the same root word.[140] Willow withes used in holiday rites are called wickens.

Evergreens

Since holly and mistletoe are considered sacred trees within my heritage, they're being listed here. Most people are familiar with the symbolism of evergreens at Yuletide. Not only were pine, fir, holly, and mistletoe used for winter solstice festivities, but species of ivy and bay and laurel leaves are also part of the Yuletide rites.

Holly symbolizes the return of spring after winter as well as everlasting life, since the leaves stay green all year. Prickly holly can repel intruders and prevent theft. Sometimes it was considered bad luck to bring holly into another person's home, yet talismans are made from holly for good fortune. People may wish to

---

140. *Online Etymology Dictionary*, s.v. "wicker," accessed April 5, 2020, https://www.etymonline
.com/word/wicker.

wait to decorate with holly until the actual day of the winter solstice, as doing so beforehand can mean bad luck. Decorated evergreen wreaths on the door help to welcome visitors and prevent malevolent beings from entering all year long.

The popular mistletoe, often associated with the Druids, is a parasitic plant that grows on many different trees, including apple and oak trees. Because it has no roots, mistletoe is said to subsist on air, and thus is considered magickal. The plant inadvertently killed the god Baldur in Norse mythology, when an arrow of mistletoe struck him in his unprotected foot. For that reason, mistletoe was condemned to never touch the earth while alive. Mistletoe is believed to be good luck if it grows on ash or hazel trees. Bronze knives should be used to harvest this plant so that its magickal properties are not disturbed by iron. Mistletoe is considered to have healing properties, although the berries are toxic. Making an eye wash of mistletoe in an infusion of water can bring visions. At Yuletide, the legend about kissing under the mistletoe to seal a relationship was long held in the British Isles, and the plant brought indoors can also prevent house fires. Its evergreen leaves and white berries promise springtime. The clusters of three leaves symbolized the trisula/triquetra, or holy trinity.

Mistletoe and other evergreen boughs should be removed from the home by Twelfth Night or Imbolc, as the plants' talismanic properties will have worn out by then.

Other Tree Magick

+ Several ancient yews are still growing in churchyards in the UK, with dire prophecies if they are ever cut down.

+ Juniper trees should not be cut, lest ill luck follow.

+ Juniper berries are used to flavor gin.

+ Quaking aspens are said to be homes for air spirits.

+ Those suffering from epilepsy, palsy, or other diseases that cause nerve tremors can tie a lock of hair to a quaking aspen for the purposes of sympathetic repulsion magick, in the hope of removing the ailment.

+ Green broom twigs should not be brought indoors before Beltane.

+ Dowsing rods in the US are usually constructed from a forked hickory limb; they are sometimes dogwood or peach or applewood.

+ Maples represent food and survival, as do apple trees.

+ Witch hazel wands are used for healing, while a tisane of witch hazel is good for curing skin conditions and piles (hemorrhoids). Hazels can also be used for purifying sacred ground, said to be "enhazeled."

+ Elder trees are homes of fairies and elves, so no furniture should be made from elder wood. However, the withes can be braided or knotted while still on the tree to prevent arthritis. This is a type of sympathetic magick, as the supple elder branch represents ease of movement.

+ Fairies can sometimes be spotted beneath elderberry bushes at midnight on Midsummer.

+ Whistles were constructed from hollow sycamore twigs at Beltane, used to make a ruckus and drive away evil.

Clootie Trees

Clootie trees are often found near sacred wells, said to be the home for nature spirits who aid in healing and who grant wishes. They are usually gnarled old hawthorns, although other deciduous trees or even pines could serve as clootie trees, covered with decorations all year long. They can also be called cloutie trees, fairy trees, raggy bushes, or wishing trees. People bathe themselves in the water of the nearby holy well with a piece of fabric, then tie the material to a tree branch. This not only serves as a votive offering, it is also an example of contagion magick. As the cloth decays, the illness dissipates.

People also leave offerings of trinkets, coins, stones, images, and strips of cloth in or near clootie trees in exchange for the spirit granting a wish. Other wishing trees have coins stuck beneath their bark or nailed to them, some of the coins dating back to the Roman era. Other trees have images cut from tin attached to them. People also hang a dead person's chair in a tree to remove negative energies after a death.

Clootie trees, raggy bushes, and wishing trees can be seen in photos online, or when visiting rural locations in Britain and Ireland. A biodegradable fabric should be used to enact the healing or wishing rite. Some of the clootie trees are dying under the weight of hundreds of strips of polyester and nylon, which is sure to displease the spirit associated with the tree and the wellspring.

The Magick of Plants, Foliage, and Flowers

There is considerable folklore related to the esoteric properties and magickal use of plants. Allies are plants that are helpful to humans. While some plants are viewed as symbols or augurs for divination, others are used physically for healing purposes. Some plants are used for their intrinsic magickal properties but are not consumed. They can be mixed into a potion, used for sympathetic magick, and then discarded. For ritualistic purposes, plants gathered during the waning moon are for banishing; plants gathered during the waxing moon are for invoking. Plants can be considered hot or cold and dry or wet, according to their qualities. For instance, mint, ginger, and black peppers are adjudged as hot and dry, while jewel weed and cattails are considered cold and wet.

Plant Symbolism

Hazelnuts represent Cernunnos and other forest deities, as well as male fertility. Leeks, the symbol of Wales, and garlic represent strength, victory, and repel negative energies. Leeks growing on the roof of a thatched cottage are good luck; people with rooftop gardens can plant leeks in early spring, then harvest them near Hallowe'en for the purpose of drawing good fortune. Garlic has intrinsic healing properties. Garlic and roses grow well together, complimenting one another as a type of polarity—stinky and sweet. Thistles represent Scotland, and thistles have protective powers.

Hay and straw scattered on a path means good luck, but hay, chaff, or straw scattered on the doorstep means an adulterer or wife beater is living in that building. He draws the wrath of the agricultural gods.

Wearing a "green gown" or "rolling in the hay" are euphemisms for making love outdoors, which might be why green wedding dresses are considered favorable to maidens in folkloric tradition. "Green Gowns" are also a type of nature spirit.

Plants for Spells

Any of the symbolic plants listed previously can be used for sympathetic magick. In addition, vervain leaves can be worn to attract the opposite sex. The fairies were said to ride brooms of ragwort, so hanging that herb outside can attract them. Carrying a pinch of dried thistle leaves can help a runner to never tire. The withes of hazel or willow, dried-out blackberry brambles, heather stalks, and herbs such as mint, rue, and tansy are all used for smoke cleansing or smudging.

Thistles, briars, and the thorns from a rosebush or thorn tree are traditionally used to repel negative energies, beings, and feelings, and for protection of a location such as a home, barn, or workplace.

The leaves, root, and fruit of a mandagore, wood byrony, or mandrake plant (or its American equivalent, the mayapple) is sometimes called a hand of glory. This replaces the illegal use of an actual dead person's hand. A mayapple can be harvested while it has fruit. It can be pulled up from the roots. Then the leaves are wrapped around the flower and apple and tied off with the stem and root. It is burned ceremonially, said to add a boost to any other magickal rite.

Plants for Divination

Hazelnuts are used for divination, painted and cast like stones or bones, or put into a fire to see which way they move when heated. Thick corn husks can foretell a hard winter. Seeds of fern or bracken gathered at Midsummer and tied in a white handkerchief give the "second sight."

Flowers

Flowers were and are used to convey emotion, such as sympathy at funerals or admiration for a love interest. Different colors of flowers represent various emotions; red roses are for love, white for purity, yellow for a message, and pink for friendship. Planting or giving flowers on Mother's Day not only symbolizes love for Mom, but also brings good luck and harmonious feelings to the home.

Flowers are used to garland or decorate horses, wells, doorways, a woman's hat or circlet, and ritual items such as a May branch for the solar holidays. Men usually wear ivy or green branches, but there are no gender limitations. Altars are dressed with flowers during spring, summer, and fall. Blossoms are carried by brides and scattered before a married couple to represent fertility. As with any other plant, the flower should be thanked for allowing its use in ritual.

Peonies are associated with the moon because once their flowers open, they never close, not even at night. Peonies growing near the home offer good luck and protection. A charm called an *alraun*, carved from a peony root in the shape of a baby, is used to protect children.

Where I live in southwestern Michigan, if lilacs bloom on Beltane, the weather and planting season is on point. Lilacs flowering any earlier means that garden plants may be killed by a late spring frost, so transplanting should be delayed. Any lilac blossoms occurring later means that harvest season might be late.

Witches' Herbs

Some plants are associated with the practice of traditional witchcraft, which means they might have "darker" qualities. This can include affecting a person's physical, mental, and emotional state. Some witches' herbs are soporific, while others are toxic, even poisonous. Wiccan author Gerald Gardner used the term *dwale*, an older Welsh word for "poison," to mean a soporific plant, one used in anesthesia or a sleeping potion. In his "Ardanes," Gardner wrote, "Be sure, if steadfast you go to the pyre, Dwale will reach you," which meant that if a witch was going to be executed by burning, someone would give them an herb to reduce the pain of immolation.[141]

Entheogens

These are plants that can bring about a change in consciousness, but they can also be harmful when ingested. One of the more benign entheogens is good ol' hemp leaves and seed heads, currently becoming legal in many locations. Hemp can either cause a calm, relaxing high or paranoia and disorientation. Its admirers believe it can cure many ailments, from chronic pain to eating disorders.

Nervines

These are plants which are said to help with "nervous conditions," such as stress, anxiety, or depression. These are also called adaptogens or sedatives. Catnip, linden leaves, valerian, damiana, and lemon balm are all herbs that are brewed into teas that can help calm the nerves. Mrs. Rabbit gave her wayward children some soothing chamomile tea before bedtime in Beatrix Potter's tales about Peter Rabbit.[142] St. John's wort can be used as a mood enhancer, as can wood betony. Mistletoe was said to calm the nerves and prevent "fits."

People are cautioned to read up on any possible side effects of these herbs, but many of them are sold over-the-counter at commercial stores. Of course, if one suffers from clinical depression or anxiety, it is best to consult a medical professional.

---

141. Gerald Gardner, *The Gardnerian Book of Shadows* (1961), https://www.sacred-texts.com/pag/gbos/gbos38.htm.

142. Beatrix Potter, *The Tale of Peter Rabbit* (London: Frederick Warne, 1902).

Hallucinogens

These are more risky entheogens that can bring about visions. Artemisia or wormwood leaves are used to make absinthe, a tincture in acidic white wine. One small tea strainer full of leaves, left soaking in the white wine and put in a warm place, can infuse the wine with oils from the herb. All of the plant material must be strained out, as ingesting wormwood leaves can cause serious nausea and vomiting, to the point of dehydration. If one glass of wine makes someone tipsy, then half of a glass of absinthe will bring visions. A wormwood tisane will also get rid of intestinal parasites.

Skullcap can cause hallucinations, as can mescaline, salvia, ergot fungus, and moonflower and morning glory seeds. The latter two contain arsenic and should be used with great caution, scraping the outer coating of the seed away before ingesting. The psilocybin fungus, or "magic mushroom," and the amanita muscaria, or fly agaric mushroom, are powerful hallucinogens, used by shamanic practitioners of Europe.

It is suggested that practitioners use a good plant field guide that contains pictures (or look at images online) before gathering any wild herbs or fungi. All of these substances can be dangerous under the wrong conditions, so it is wise to consult an herbalist.

Atropines

These are plants that can cause a hallucinogenic or soporific effect. Their use is very risky. Atropines include henbane, aconite, black hellebore, both black and red nightshade (American bittersweet), belladonna (European nightshade), *Datura* (thornapple, loco weed, jimpson weed), and mandrake (Mediterranean mandragore, rather than English byrony, *Bryonia alba*). Several of these plants have pentagram-shaped flowers, while aconite is called monk's hood, as it resembles a cowl.

Atropines should never be ingested. They can be made into an unguent using melted fat, also known as the famed witches' "flying ointment" or "lifting balm," which can be applied topically. While it may bring visions, it can be dangerous. Extreme prudence should be used if trying any of these herbs.

Poisons

Several atropines come under the heading of poisonous, as they can be deadly. Poisonous substances were sometimes used for destroying vermin. Hemlock (the plant, not the tree) should just be left alone, as it's very dangerous. It looks somewhat like wild parsley or Queen Anne's lace, so caution is advised. Oleander leaves and twigs are poisonous as well.

Practitioners who harvest plants that are toxic or poisonous may wish to wear gloves to prevent their alkaloid-laden sap from touching the skin. Hellebore can actually cause chemical burns. Ingesting these plants can make a person violently nauseous, have convulsions, or even cause death…a nasty, painful, twitching, vomiting, bleeding death. I am not exaggerating; I once saw a goat that ate thornapple die of poisoning. It was awful. Most atropines are best used as potions, not for human consumption in any manner.

Psychedelic herbs should only be taken under ceremonial conditions, as using them for recreational purposes wastes their energies. They may have an effect for anywhere from an hour or two to all night. The shadow self or unpleasant realities might be confronted while working with them. There might be aftereffects like psychological disruptions and difficulty assimilating back into consensus reality. Practitioners may want to have a "watcher" or helper when indulging. Driving a vehicle, minding children, or operating machinery is out of the question while using any visionary herbs. It's wise to undertake some journeying or astral travel without use of entheogens before experimenting with these plants. If someone has a medical condition like high blood pressure or a nerve disorder, entheogens are not for them. For others, a fermented beverage like wine or beer can be enough. And if anyone has a propensity toward addictive behaviors, it might be best to just leave these substances alone.

Emmenagogues

Also called women's herbs or ladies' friends, these are plants used to bring about menstruation. This can be dangerous, so caution is advised. Timing is everything; if administered over a month after a missed period, emmenagogues can cause terrible cramping and even severe bleeding. No more than one teaspoonful per one hundred pounds of body weight should be taken. Some emmenagogues include pennyroyal, rue, tansy, and black cohosh. The seeds of Queen Anne's lace can be used as a prophylaxis (birth control) or as a morning-after contraceptive.

As with any item taken from nature, practitioners should leave an offering at a place where they've harvested a plant or a portion of a tree such as a twig or fruit.

Folk magick traditionalists thank the spirit of the plant for its contribution to our magickal practice. Watering and fertilizing plants and trees is also appreciated.

Other Natural Objects

Some other natural objects used for common magick include mud or clay, sand, and graveyard dirt; tree bark, seeds, leaves, nuts, fruits, and fibers; insect galls, cocoons, and shed exoskeletons; hollowed-out bird eggs; and dried fungus. Fox-fire, a glowing fungus, is highly prized by magick users but lasts for only one or two nights. It can be used for protection, divination, and clarity of thought. The sawdust from a woodpecker hole in a tree summons blessings to the home. Graveyard dirt can be used for necromancy or banishing curses, but it also has the property of being a rich fertilizer. Natural clay used to create ritual vessels has the special ability of containment and connection to the land. Milkweed fluff (minus the seed) is employed for pillow stuffing and absorbing menstrual blood. Afterward, it is buried in the garden to bring about crop fertility. Milkweed, like dandelion seeds, could also be blown in the air to make a wish. Cockleburs, or burdock seeds, symbolize "stick-to-it" persistence.

Common Magick Nature Rituals

Natural magick can be the wildest, most unpredictable type of working. The spirits of nature have traits and capabilities that exist separately of human control. Some may be personified in poetry, lore, and stories; think of a tranquil lake, a mighty oak, a frightsome swamp, or a mystic mountain. Nature spirits can be beneficial, such as those of animal or plant allies, which enjoy the company of humans and other entities. Others can be baneful. Rudyard Kipling's "Tree Song" tells of a tree that enjoys dropping branches on people.[143] A spirit animal may cooperate, but it may also run away or bite.

Many natural beings do not have the intention of helping or harming humans, they just "are." A nature spirit might have a consciousness, yet not be sentient; for example, lightening may not realize that it is electric, wild, and capable of doing harm. It simply exists. Some entities can operate on a different timetable than humans—for instance, the spirits of rock formations may "think" very slowly and

---

143. Kipling, *Puck of Pook's Hill*.

not notice the passage of eons. Rivers are ever-changing. Grass may consider life in terms of a season.

Working with nature requires patience. A magick user will need to ground, center, and anchor themselves to consensus reality. A change in consciousness or perception may be required. Expectations must be left behind, as the spirits can open us to new possibilities.

When an animal appears as an omen, it is up to the practitioner to interpret its meaning. For example, an augury of a hawk might mean someone is being preyed upon, or it could signify that they are gaining personal strength, keen vision, and mental clarity. An animal can symbolize more than one aspect of its personality—deer are fleet and strong, but they are also timid and don't make the best decisions when caught in a car's headlights.

Folk traditionalists might call upon a spirit to find out information about the animal they represent or to manifest one of their traits. For instance, I might talk to the spirit of Cat to find out why my pet is ailing or summon the spirit of Mouse to politely request they not tear up important documents while dwelling in my cellar. If someone feels lonesome, they might interact with the spirit of an animal that lives in a colony, like barn swallows, or a herd, like bison.

When taking on an animal's or plant's traits, a practitioner should be careful to respect all aspects of their nature. Sometimes, people who call upon the very popular spirits of Raven, Wolf, Hawk, Bear, or Cat to manifest a certain desirable quality forget that there are beta wolves as well as alphas, or that bears spend half their lives asleep. Magick users can retain the desirable aspects, then politely thank the spirit as they would an energetic being with a human appearance. The person working with animal totems or spirits must also take care to not lose their human consciousness.

Things that are found during outdoor walks might have a special meaning in nature spirituality and can be useful in sympathetic magick. For example, paper wasp nests can designate an annoyance, danger, or protection. This depends on one's perception, other items combined with the nest, and the words of power used in a working. (Caution is advised to ensure that the nest does not contain eggs, larvae, or—worse—live insects!)

A folk magick user may want to preserve found objects and store them in an altar, cupboard, or another safe place in order to use the objects in later rituals and workings. Damp items should dry thoroughly before storage to prevent them from rotting. Other ideas include immersing things in salt, which has a drying effect, but this might overpower any intrinsic magickal capabilities. Hanging to dry works well for plants. If natural items are not handled by another human, they are unlikely to need cleansing, although they may require words of power to imbue them with a specific meaning and purpose.

Natural magick does not end in wintertime. Melted snow can be a fantastic cleansing agent, while ice can symbolically freeze an undesirable condition. Winter birds and animals are survivors, while those who hibernate represent the sleeping earth, contemplation, and the body at rest. New snow symbolizes purity, icicles can be used as wands, and objects can be buried in the snow for a ceremonial banishing. In locations where winter means rain, the liquids can be gathered for use in ritual. Winter months are used for introspection and repairing things, and this is a good time to sit indoors by a fire or lit candle, reading folktales and drinking a nice hot cuppa herbal tea.

Many animals can live inside a city, even turtles and deer, but the most common are birds, squirrels, rabbits or hares, raccoons (in the US), and hedgehogs (in the UK). The ubiquitous house sparrows, house finches, pigeons, and starlings are all residents of Britain. A bird feeder can provide hours of delight. Offerings of corn and peanuts can be given to the squirrels, crows, and jays. The summer hummingbirds, who represent happiness and acquisition, enjoy undyed sugar water. Walks in the forest or on trails in a park bring feelings of peace or, conversely, excitement when a chipmunk or woodpecker is spotted. Witches sometimes sit up all night, observing the local wildlife and discovering what the animals presage. Meditations can be undertaken outdoors, allowing us to soak up the energy of the surrounding environment. We also might just enjoy sitting and absorbing the beauty of nature and all of her phases and beings.

ten
COMMON MAGICK
SPELLS AND WORKINGS

Over time, folkloric magick users have discovered or invented certain ritualized actions in order to attract good experiences and avoid harmful situations. These procedures are commonly called spells or workings. Spell work is a type of active magick, or thaumaturgy, meaning that the practitioner is acting upon their environment for the purpose of creating external change. Many spells use the law of sympathetic magick: either like attracts like, or like repels like. A symbol represents a condition and is used to bring that desired circumstance into manifestation.

Many rites, workings, and spells have come down to us as the witchcraft we know today. These praxes really were common; everyone in the British Isles was at least aware of them. Common magick truly was *everywhere*.

For example, in 2016, a British historical society asked the public to help them find "witches' marks," or apotropaic symbols used to ward off negative energy from a building.[144] These are also called hex foils or protection signs. Previously, sigils and designs like this had been found in places ranging from Shakespeare's birthplace to the Tower of London. As of this writing, hundreds of protective symbols have since been reported in homes, barns, public buildings, workplaces, and in caves and outdoor locations. They were carved into wood,

---

144. Nicholas Molyneux, "Discovering Witches' Marks," Historic England, accessed April 5, 2020, https://historicengland.org.uk/whats-new/features/discovering-witches-marks/.

etched into stone, or inscribed with paint or charcoal. The witches' marks took the shape of daisy wheels or "the flower of life," a series of interlocking circles in the shape of blossom petals; equal-armed crosses; intertwining Vs, chevrons, Ms and Ws, which may have represented the letters for Virgin Mary; runes, concentric circles, and spirals; mazes and mazy crosses; Celtic knotwork; symbols of the stang or two- or three-pronged staff; representational drawings such as spectacles or axes; and yes, the pentagram associated with modern Wicca. People have also discovered concealed clothing and witch's bottles within their homes. Until 1967, no academic had made record of these apotropaic designs and items.[145]

The purpose of witches' marks or hidden objects is to deflect harmful energy from a building, act as a decoy, or entrap a malevolent being. Witches' marks were usually created by the common people, and as such, the media and scholars took no notice. Until recently, that is.

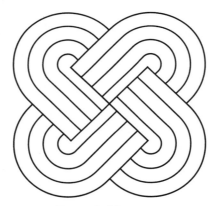

Figure 6: Mazy cross

Not only were protective symbols discovered in private spaces, a survey was done of the "medieval graffiti" found in British churches. The marks were scratched on walls, carved into wood, hidden in the rafters, and in one location, even placed on a baptismal fount. These marks included things like people's initials and doodles, just like modern graffiti, but they also contained numerous Pagan symbols, including pentagrams, a tree surrounded by two snakes, a hood-

---

145. Sally Coulthard, "6 Things You Need to Know About Witch Markings, According to an Ancient Graffiti Expert," *CountryLiving*, February 25, 2019, https://www.countryliving .com/uk/wildlife/countryside/a2021/witch-markings/.

ener's horse, sun wheels, a possible goddess figure with a pentagram and a stag, and what is believed to be an emblem of the Corn King (a representation of a sacrificial god honored by farmers). There were several designs of ships, which may have been used to ensure a safe voyage, and windmills, which could signify plentitude.[146] Researchers learned that widespread Paganism amongst the common people existed much longer than they'd originally considered, and that common magick was much more prevalent than they'd thought. The people's magick never really went away.

Spells and workings can go beyond making a mark within a building for protection. A spell is often done with ingredients combined together to create something—such as a potion or talisman—for representational or symbolic purposes. Ritualized actions help gather power from a source. The energy is then used to magickally "charge" the talismanic object, or to cause a transformation.

Words of power can be spoken to voice intent for a spell. Some people do not use ingredients at all, but instead go directly to using words and/or actions to channel power from its origin to its intended target. Chants, rhymes, and songs can help with performing a rite or spell. Besides voicing intent, the breath and will are harnessed to support the endeavor. It may get attention from energetic beings. Verbal spells and rhymes can trigger the subconscious, or the spirit, and help to focus on the objective. Many people chanting or singing in unison helps concentration and causes them to work in tandem to change their consciousness and direct power. Words that have been used repeatedly over time have built up energy, according to the principle of priordination. However, a spell need not be verbalized; it can be written, illustrated, or performed silently.

Many of the spells in this chapter can be done during the course of a liminal period, such as a holiday observance or astronomical occasion like a full moon. Some of these workings are actually part of a ceremony. For instance, corn dollies can be made to commemorate Harvesttide and can also be imbued with protective magick. These talismanic effigies are "charged" as participants play outdoor games, using the energy raised by an enthusiastic footrace. Magick users direct the power into the corn dollies. The talismans can then be used to attract plentitude.

---

146. Matthew Champion, *Medieval Graffiti: The Lost Voices of England's Churches* (London: Ebury Press, 2015).

An example of another common magick spell is performing an action to defend my barn against fire. On Midsummer, I gather herbs, crystals, and other items that have a protective quality, such as mistletoe, ash wood, a jasper stone, and an iron horseshoe nail. I put these ingredients into a wooden box inscribed with magickal sigils for protection. While chanting, "My animals and property are safe through any destiny," I use a forked stang to gather energy from the sun at its yearly zenith and channel it down the shaft, through my hand, and into my power objects. I then place the box on the wooden beam above the fire extinguisher in my barn.

Some of the information presented here may conflict with viewpoints found in other sources. Common magick developed over time; it developed within families or groups of peers who might have mutually decided that a certain symbol represented a specific condition, and that might be different from what was decided by people in the next village over. For example, some might think a seagull is favorable luck, an omen of fair seas and good weather. Others might see the seagull eating a dead fish and view her as an augury of death. Some believed seagulls contained the souls of people who were lost at sea. They were also viewed as messengers of the gods. Because of disparities like these, some of the symbols and workings in this book might be dissimilar to those found in other books or websites. Common magick is, by its nature, eclectic. That means it may have borrowed a bit of information from various sources, including Celtic, Roman, Anglo-Saxon, Christian, and indigenous populations of the US or Australia … often within the same ritual.

Crafting a spell is like experimental baking. There is a formula or recipe involved, but much of it requires one's own experience and intuition. I will list some of the ingredients and methods that people used in the past, but it is up to readers to experiment.

Spells

Spells are also called charms, rhymes, workings, onlays, conjurations, or incantations. Most people know dozens of common magick spells, but they've become so ingrained in our culture as superstitions, folks don't always recognize a spell for what it is. Break a dried chicken breastbone or "wishbone," and the person who gets the larger piece can request a boon. Keep your wish silent. Bless someone after they sneeze. Children sing "Rain, rain, go away, come again some other day," a popular weather charm. When salt is spilled, a pinch should be thrown over the left shoulder to avert bad luck. "Wash on Monday, churn on Tuesday" was advice based on planetary correspondences to days of the week. Water and the moon have a correlation because of the tides, so washing clothes was believed to be more effective on Monday, while the agitation of churning butter can be associated with Mars and the physical activity of "stirring things up."

Our predecessors were primarily concerned with health, wealth, and love. Many of our common magick spells fall under these categories. They can be modified for present-day use.

Spells for Health

In the days before antibiotics and surgeries, magick was used to help people stay healthy. While many of these spells employ the principle of sympathetic magick, they had no connection to a state of fitness. For example, wearing a blue cord, thread, or ribbon around the neck is believed to repel sickness. Putting an empty bottle on a ledge inside a chimney is thought to prevent illness from entering the home. Pouring a baby's bathwater onto a green bush helps both the plant and the child to thrive. A bellows placed on a chair is believed to prevent rheumatism (arthritis), while tying three or five knots in a living elder tree withe could remove the pain. Warts are supposedly cured with the brackish water from a hollow tree stump. Wearing a necklace of garlic is believed to banish illness. Walking deosil three times around a person wishes them well.

Some curative methods use sympathetic magick for repulsion. Black salt, which is ordinary table salt mixed with ashes or the burnt scrapings of an iron frying pan, is used in foods to prevent negative energies that caused illnesses. Burning certain herbs was considered to reduce the amount of "ill humors" (bacteria) in the air, and wholistic healers claim that burning sage (salvia) can improve air quality.[147] Some of these sympathetic magick practices can help, especially if belief is strong, but people are still urged to pursue conventional medicine as well.

Potions can be used during a rite for sympathetic magick; for example, a mixture of saltpeter (potassium nitrate), brimstone (sulfur), black salt, and molasses. These substances are combined in a cauldron, stirring clockwise to bring about

---

147. Arlin Cuncic, "The Benefits of Burning Sage," *Verywell Mind*, last modified March 18, 2020, https://www.verywellmind.com/the-benefits-of-burning-sage-4685244.

health or counterclockwise to banish a harmful condition or illness. Words of power are used to invoke healing and repel negativity. However, this potion should then be poured on the ground—*not* ingested—because the ingredients can be toxic. Saltpeter is used in the garden for removing stumps and killing weeds, and it is an ingredient in gunpowder. Sulfur can be applied to the skin in tiny quantities, like when killing acne bacteria, but eating a boiled egg is a better form of putting sulfur into the body. Neither saltpeter nor brimstone should be used near an open flame, as they are combustible.

Several crystals are traditionally used for healing rites. Bloodstones are believed to purify the blood and cure ailments affecting the kidneys and liver, imbuing a person with vitality. Amethyst is said to prevent drunkenness. Hematite is viewed as positively affecting the blood. Amber is used to heal problems with the eyes, to heal sprains, and for strength. Alabaster was said to prevent rabies. Green stones like chrysoprase, citrine, and malachite are said to have healing properties. Black stones or minerals, including jet, onyx, obsidian, and tourmaline, are used for grounding and banishing negative energies. Garnets and carnelians can improve sexuality. Clear quartz is used to augment the memory and to increase the power of other crystals. While some of these gemstones are native to Britain, others were imported by traders and used in healing rites.

Other workings are done according to the principles of contagion magick. Driving a pin into a wart and then casting it into a well is believed to draw it away, as is rubbing the wart with a piece of raw meat and then burying the meat. Cutting off half of a wart and then discarding or burning it is accompanied with the words, "By the powers of night and day, half draws half elsewhere away." The familiar saying "Hair of the dog that bit you," refers to taking a drink of alcohol to prevent a hangover. In medieval Britain, a dog bite was actually treated with the hair of the offending beast, for the reason of preventing hydrophobia (rabies).[148] In present times, people still need to take the series of rabies shots to ensure safety. Wearing a flannel scarf is thought to cure a sore throat. Water drawn from a holy spring at midnight on Midsummer is believed to have healing properties. Bathing in it is said to cure skin conditions. Washing one's face in the morning dew at Beltane is good for the complexion. Anointing a weapon is believed to

---

148. Gary Martin, "The Hair of the Dog," Phrasefinder, accessed April 5, 2020, https://www .phrases.org.uk/meanings/hair-of-the-dog.html.

heal its wound, so a knife that had sliced open a person's finger is smeared with ointment. The same medicine is used for dressing the cut. If a child has a sty in their eye, it is stroked with a gold wedding ring to remove it.

Fingernails and hair should not be cut on a Friday, lest health be cut away with the excess part of the body. Dispose of fingernail and toenail clippings by burning or burying them so "witches" cannot bespell you by using your nails for contagion magick. Hair should not be burned lest your home catch fire, but instead should be buried in the garden to drive away pests or left in a bush or tree for birds to make a nest, symbolizing fertility. People of some cultures did not cut their hair, believing it to contain a person's strength. This is described in the biblical story of King Sampson and in Welsh tales about the fairies, who refused to shave or cut their hair. Some common magick users from the British Isles believe hair should be cut only when a family member dies, as a sign of mourning. Cutting the hair at other times can bring about a death.

Many of the old-fashioned common magick spells for healing can be augmented by words of power, stating intent for the desired condition. When someone sneezes, they are blessed, as it was thought that their heart stopped. The German phrase *gesundheit* means "good health," but sneezers are also blessed in the name of a deity or told, "May the sun guard you." The blessing is also intended to prevent ill luck. Sneezing three times meant possible bad luck. Sneezing any number of times other than three was an augury of fortune.

Simple rites, like blessing a sneeze, do not require an extended ritual, but more complex potions and implements can benefit from calling magickal helpers, chanting, and enacting a ceremony to raise and direct power. Items used for healing can be charged with energy. For example, before wearing the blue string, bathing in a bottle of spring water, or eating an apple for health, a magick worker can bless the object in the name of a deity, hold it in one hand while walking three times deosil around a ritual space, fill the object with the power of the sun, verbally infuse it with healing qualities, and thank its spirit for assistance.

Of course, serious medical conditions will require the attention of a professional.

Spells for Love and Sex

These spells might attract a love interest, increase sexual pleasure, help in the conception of a child, or secure a marriage. When performing a love rite, the magick user should state intent and list qualities they want in a partner. Things such as gender, appearance, interests, and moral character should be considered. Or the practitioner can say, "Please bring the perfect love interest for me," and leave it open to the universal powers. Deities who represent love include the Welsh goddesses Rhiannon and Branwen, the Irish goddesses Brigid and Aine and the god Aengus, the Roman Cupid and Venus, the Norse gods Frey and Freyja, or heroes such as Culhwch and Olwen. Talismanic objects include rose quartz crystals, a rope tied into a lover's knot, silver pins to pierce the heart, and flowers like roses, violets, meadowsweet, and honeysuckle. Blossoms gifted to a love interest show a desire for chastity (white), fond emotions (pink), or sex (red). Lemons should be avoided while courting, as they can sour a relationship. Friday, being Freyja's day, is the optimal time for love magick.

Historically, before clocks and watches became inexpensive and common, people burned "hour candles," which had markings to indicate the passing of time. To evoke love, two pins were pushed into the candle at the final hour mark, the pins crossing one another through the wick. As the candle was burned, love would seek the magick user or client. A pink candle attracts love.

Two poppets bound together with red thread—one dolly containing the magick user's hair, fingernails, and blood, the other left blank—work to invite love. Both poppets should be filled with milkweed fluff for stuffing, lovage, rosemary, heart's ease, and bleeding heart flowers.

Placing two hazelnuts on the hearth near a fire can predict the longevity of a relationship, depending on whether the nuts move together, jump apart, or stay stationary in the heat. Nuts that catch fire (no pun intended) are said to be consumed by passion. Expressing a wish for a relationship at a need-fire can bring a lover.

For young ladies, sewing a handbag or knitting and chanting, "Witches and stiches, make me a missus!" is bound to attract a husband. Women curtsey to the new moon in March, asking to envision their potential beau. Young men sleep with a bay leaf beneath their pillow to dream of their future wife. Young ladies sow hemp seed in their dooryard or garden, saying, "Hempseed I sow, hempseed I grow, and then my husband will come to mow." This means that a courtship and marriage would take place by harvesttime; others believe this will cause the girl to dream of her beloved.

Maidens of the British Isles enact a "dumb supper" to envision the shade, or spirit image, of their potential swain. Like the quiet dinner performed on Hallowe'en to visit with ghosts, three young women prepare a meal and eat in silence. The spirit of their future husbands can join them then, or they can appear at night while the women dream.

Although this next rite is performed on the feast date of a Catholic saint, November 25 or Saint Catherine's day, it is *so* obviously a spell: Three to nine young ladies wear myrtle (periwinkle, vinca) in their bosoms all day. Myrtle is sacred to Aphrodite, Venus, Rhiannon, and Freyja. At eleven o'clock in the evening, the young ladies must light a brazier of charcoal and sprinkle frankincense and myrrh onto the embers. The myrtle is smudged in the ensuing smoke. It is then placed beneath their pillows to bring dreams of their future husbands.

Young gentlemen of Wales create elaborate "love spoons" to present to their intended. These are made of sycamore, linden, poplar, or another soft wood and carved during a long sea voyage or during the winter months. The tradition dates back to at least the 1660s and is possibly older.[149] Designs on the love spoons include spirals, Celtic knotwork, hearts, birds, flowers, wheels, wedding bells, and a lock and key for protection and a representation of the "key to my heart." The spoons originally expressed a desire to feed and care for a wife. The carving is so intricate that the spoons are mostly displayed on the wall as ornaments and house blessing objects.

In past days, young ladies of the British Isles and Americans of British descent would make a box supper for charitable events, which were then auctioned off to the highest bidder. Men who were interested in a certain lady would purchase her lunch in order to show his intentions, raise money for a cause, and to find out if the lady was a good cook. The food contained wishes and desires. Ladies also knitted garments for their fiancé, with prayers and wishes spoken with every stitch.

Here is a spell to help boost a current partnership. The magick user should let their loved one know that this is a symbolic rite to solidify feelings for one another. Three objects are gathered that represent love—the number three signifying both partners and the relationship itself. They must be things that cannot be spoiled by getting wet, such as jewelry, a crystal, a button, or a similar object. These are placed in the bottom of a mug. The couple pours their morning coffee

---

149. John Davies, Nigel Jenkins, Menna Baines, and Peredur I. Lynch, *The Welsh Academy Encyclopaedia of Wales* (Cardiff, UK: University of Wales Press, 2008).

or tea into the mug, over the objects, letting it sit for a minute. Then the liquid is evenly disbursed between the couple's favorite cups, leaving the objects behind in the mug. The couple then drinks their coffee or tea together.

Several magickal items and actions represent sexuality including stirring a cauldron or grinding herbs in a mortar with a pestle. Wearing lavender, vervain, and rose scents can attract a lover. The sigil of a heart could have originally been used to represent sexuality, as it resembles the female buttocks and genital region. A necklace of acorns enhances fertility. So does a priapic wand of oak topped with a pinecone or acorn. Kisses should not be wiped off until nightfall if you want a relationship to become sexual.

A "greenwood marriage" actually means having sexual relations in the woods on Beltane, while "wearing a green gown" means a roll in the hay. The lover's bower is an arch made of wicker with flowers and greenery woven into it, which is then placed in a shady spot with plenty of grass below. Wind chimes and tiny bells add to the ambiance. These are used not only for fertility of the couple and to enhance the relationship, but to help fertilize the surrounding farmlands.

Eating shellfish—particularly oysters—and red meat is believed to increase sexual stamina. Hazelnuts, apples, and red wine can enhance the sex drive. Placing lovage or vervain in the garters is said to attract members of the opposite sex. A garnet necklace emphasizes sexuality for ladies, while carnelians and antler or horn charms increase male vitality.

Wheat heads, spring flowers, and long, curling wood shavings placed in a wreath over the bed makes sexytime more pleasurable. Ladies who wish to get pregnant should unbraid their hair, open the cupboard doors, eat rhubarb pie, place their shoes facing forward and backward under the bed, and wear a circlet of braided wheat heads and warm-colored flowers, all before consummation. Wearing a red ribbon can enhance fertility, as can putting hair from a hairbrush into a tree for the birds to make nests. Cats with kittens, salmon, and baby animals such as lambs, calves, and shoats (piglets) represent fertility.

Spells for Home and Happiness

These workings are intended to bring about contentment within the home, ensure a blessed relationship, and bring about happiness for loved ones.

Once married, the gold or silver wedding rings represent continuity. Diamonds symbolize permanence, but so do other gemstones, including pearls, opals, amethyst, morganite, lapis, and emerald. Losing, breaking, or cutting the wedding ring can lead to marital discord, even divorce.

Hanging up the besom that a couple has used for "jumping the broom," decorated with cloth flowers, seeds, nuts, and ribbons, ensures a happy home. Eating bread and salt together and drinking from the same cup guarantees a lasting relationship. The husband carries the wife over the threshold to commemorate separating their new life from the old, but first, the front stoop is washed and sprinkled with sand or salt. The house is whitewashed with lime so that the married couple can start fresh. The couple should eat their first meal in their new home facing one another, with representations of earth, sea, and sky (such as vegetables or potatoes, fish or shellfish, and wine or a home brew). Dessert should be sugary and decadent to ensure a rich life together.

Anniversaries are celebrated by tying ribbons for each year of your partnership onto a load-bearing wooden house beam or a wreath. The customary anniversary gifts for each year came from Emily Post in the 1920s, but this is actually a much older common magick tradition.[150] Rather than gifts of paper or silver tea sets, the couple was given practical items to set up a household. Newlyweds often spent the first few years living with relatives as they were given work tools, furniture, livestock, and ritual household tools such as a besom and cauldron.

Milk, cream, honey, and raspberries or strawberries sweeten a marriage. Planting a pine tree outside the front door adds to marital happiness and good luck. For long-term relationships, remember that "Kissin' tires out, but cookin' don't."

A double-yolk egg indicates a pregnancy. Once babies came along, they must be sained, baptized, or blessed to prevent them from being stolen by the Fae. The birth cord (umbilicus) was preserved in salt to ensure the infant's health. New babies are blessed with gifts of bread and salt, which are kept for the child or offered to strangers. These gifts represent earth and are designed to keep babies on this earth and in this world. Sigils are embroidered on diapers and garments for protection. Children wear bracelets and necklaces as amulets to keep them safe. A baby's hair is not cut for its first year of life, and fingernails are not to be cut with metal scissors or clippers.

---

150. Emily Post, *Etiquette in Society, in Business, in Politics, and at Home* (New York: Funk & Wagnalls, 1922).

Apotropaic sigils, including a pentacle, heart, triquetra, or daisy wheel, are inscribed on the footboard of a cradle. Rocking a "toom," or empty cradle, is bad luck. Children's cast-off "milk teeth" are kept until their adolescence, when they are buried at a crossroads to help them separate from family, and in the interest that they become wise and beautiful.

At holidays, special breads are served with ceramic or metal talismanic objects baked into them. These could foretell a youngster's future life events. A coin signifies wealth, a thimble means establishing a household (or spinsterhood), a button means fame and new clothes (or bachelorhood), a small toy horse represents travel, a baby means childbirth, a small emblem of a pig garners abundance, a key means a new home or a journey, while a ring foretells a wedding for the recipient. This is not only divination of the future, but a working to ensure a particular outcome.

Spells for Luck and Wishes

Dozens of common magick rites have to do with luck and wishes. Many of our modern customs about making wishes are actually quite old. Wishes were made on falling stars, then as now. People wish on the first star they see at night, on the first sight of the full moon, and when they toss a coin into a well. Knocking wood brings good luck—and averts bad luck, as it awakens the dryad or spirit who lives within the tree. This is especially true if someone says something they don't mean; knocking wood can prevent speaking ill luck into being.

Wishing on birthday candles is a current custom. So as not to offend the fire spirit, candles can be snuffed out between finger and thumb, or with a candle snuffer, rather than blown out with the breath. When a fire is kindled with two sticks, a wish can come true. A flame that remains burning is a good sign, and wishes are made for the coming year.

On New Year's Day, people eat frumenty, or wheat boiled in milk, for good luck and abundance. The custom of the "first foot," or the first person to enter the house on New Year's Day, determines luck for the rest of the year. Encountering a chimney sweep is lucky, which might be why some folk dancers in the UK blacken their faces and hands with soot, wear top hats, carry brooms, and mimic that profession. Tokens representing wishes for prosperity, health, and love were cut from a sheet of tin and hung in trees. In more recent times, desires written on paper are put in trees or cracks in stiles (stone walls).

If a person can count an entire flock of sparrows before they fly away, good luck will be theirs. The numbers three, five, and seven are considered lucky. Picking up a penny that is faceup brings about fortune. In some British and Irish villages in the eighteenth and nineteenth centuries, lucky pennies were used for everything from healing to purifying water to bringing wealth. Sometimes the next town over wanted to borrow the penny for rites, so they'd have to pay a hefty sum of cash as a deposit.

Seafaring people have many magickal rites for luck. A "nautical star" symbol on dockside homes or inland taverns brings fortune. Tie a knot-cross shape using a single rope for luck onboard a ship. Bowing to the full moon brought good luck to a voyage. Eyes painted on a ship's prow prevent it from running into rocks. Sailing vessels should not embark on a Friday or on Candlemas, as these days are unlucky for sailors. Certain words spoken aloud on board are said to be bad luck, but tugging the collar of your shirt will avert harm. Cats, especially black or polydactyl kitties, are especially lucky aboard a ship. Keeping a penny onboard ship ensures a safe voyage.

Other spells are for averting bad luck. Drawing the ace of spades in a card deck is unlucky. Mine workers should not whistle underground, and sailors should not whistle aboard a ship. People should not look at the new moon through a window or at the full moon through tree branches, both of which are considered ill luck. Sweeping dirt out the front door causes luck to be swept out of the home. Instead, dirt should be swept into a dustpan and thrown away. Drawing a lynchpin (a cotter pin, used for keeping cart wheels attached to the axel) on a vehicle's hubcaps protects it from accidents. People should not loan a knife, but instead should put it on the table and say, "Here 'tis," to prevent bad luck and a rift in a friendship. If one inadvertently curses an acquaintance by wishing them ill, one must turn around three times and walk backward out the nearest door, then come back in again and apologize. Opening an umbrella indoors symbolizes stormy weather and ill luck. The umbrella superstition likely began as practical advice; the old-fashioned "brolly" or "bumperchute" was made with sharp metal spines, so opening it indoors could knock things over or poke people.

The number thirteen was considered bad luck. This may be because the thirteenth apostle was Judas. The thirteenth god in Asgard was Loki. It may have to do with the legend about the Knights Templar being betrayed (or arrested, or executed) on Friday the thirteenth. However, there are thirteen lucky full moons during most years.

Bad luck is said to come in threes. After one doleful event, magickal rites are performed so that the other two unlucky things will be minor irritations, like spilled milk, rather than disasters.

Spells for Money and Prosperity

These type of workings are an extension of the luck and wishes category of spells. Negative energies and conditions should first be banished before casting a spell to bring about newfound prosperity.

Keeping silver coins on the altar or mantle brings increase, although some witches suggest not putting money in a sacred space because coins carry the energies of so many people. Due to sympathetic magick, a found penny could attract more of the same. Burying a penny at the crossroads can make money symbolically grow; for example, in your investments. At the New Year, keep money in your pockets or purse for plentitude all year long. Likewise, cash in your pockets during the new moon means wealth. Keeping a sixpence or quarter in the right shoe when crossing a bridge will ensure happiness and wealth. Finding a coin in Hallowe'en bread, Yule pudding, or a Lammas loaf brings prosperity. Money washed in rainwater can't be stolen.

Mondays are lucky for starting a new venture, as is beginning a project on the new moon. One should enter a business with their right foot forward to ensure a mutually gainful encounter. The ace of diamonds in a card deck is lucky, and it was sometimes put in a pocket with money for increase. Tying nine knots in a green cord that is thirteen inches long summons wealth. Wrapping a buckeye in an old, wrinkled dollar brings wealth. So does keeping the buckeye in your pocket or a pouch.

Some spells improve material things, which brings about more wealth. If milk is poured on the ground on Brigid's Day and porridge is thrown into the sea, there will be plentiful fish for the remainder of the year. Putting mistletoe above cattle stalls causes an increase in milk. Cutting the first sheaf of grain means plenty to eat all year. Shooting a gun across a cornfield brings prosperity (not recommended in modern times, unless it's certain where the slug will land). Menstrual blood put in the garden causes plant growth, and thus an increase of wealth.

A lodestone, or magnet, will point a person toward money. The words, "Enough and plenty, come unto me, oh come," are believed to bring plentitude, meeting all of a person's needs without excess. To gain ideas about how to make money, a magick user must find an old, wrinkled, faded dollar bill (or a very old coin) and sleep with it beneath their pillow to dream up new methods to earn prosperity.

Much of prosperity magick has to do with good behavior and gratitude. Folktales and lore tell us that found money should not be questioned, and thanks should be shown by returning favors and offering gifts. For example, those who found fairy money and gave it back, or those who did a service for the wee folk, were often richly rewarded. A man who rescued a fairy maiden was given a walking stick that caused his sheep to have twin lambs every time they gave birth.[151] A woman who kept a basin of water near the hearth for the pixies to drink was given a sixpence, but after she bragged about it, she received no more money.[152] If anyone questioned the fairies' generosity or got greedy and demanded more, the gifts would cease, and occasionally the accumulated money or items would vanish.

Weather Spells

Weather was a big deal to common folk who relied on sailing, fishing, herding, and farming. The clangor of bells is believed to disburse thunder and lightning. Standing under a tall tree during a storm, especially an oak or ash tree, is dangerous because it attracts lightning. A lodestone can draw lightning. Old-fashioned lightning rods were said to protect a home from house fires, but actually, the lightning is drawn to the metal pole and the electric charge travels down a ground wire and is harmlessly earthed. Objects attached to the lightning rod can be magickally charged.

To calm a storm, an adept magick user would wade out into the thick of the wind, driving rain, and flashes of lightning, holding their arms high over their heads with their palms up. This is fairly dangerous, so it's best to calm the storm from within a building by whirling counterclockwise while holding a baling hook.

---

151. William Jenkyn Thomas, "Fairy Walking Stick," in *The Welsh Fairy Book*. New York: F. A. Stokes, 1908, https://www.sacred-texts.com/neu/celt/wfb/wfb26.htm.

152. Thomas Keightley, *The Fairy Mythology: Illustrative of the Romance and Superstition of Various Countries*, accessed August 14, 2020, https://www.gutenberg.org/files/41006/41006-h/41006-h.htm.

Chanting "Spirit of the ____ (west, south, etc.) wind, let there be peace between you and me," for each wind direction, or simply "Spirit of the sky, let there be peace," is said to quiet the winds.

However, the winds are also needed for work, such as turning a windmill or for sailing. To raise a wind, the sound of the breeze must be imitated through sympathetic magick, accomplished with whistles or a "bull roarer," which is a flat stone or piece of wood tied to a stick and then whirled around the head in a clockwise direction. Tying three knots in a piece of rope and then untying them one at a time can raise a calm wind, a faster wind, and a gale. Waving a feather fan, blowing a bellows, or whirling clockwise in place while holding a baling hook can cause a wind to rise. A small whirlwind is an air spirit at play; it can be asked to invite its larger brothers and sisters to fill the sails or turn the windmill.

Certain drum patterns can make it rain, particularly those with a seven- or nine-count beat. Stirring saltwater clockwise with a wooden spoon brings rain. During a drought, a person can dip a leaf of maize (corn) or a stalk of barleycorn into spring water and dash the droplets into the air. Shooting arrows into the air can make it rain, as can throwing a handful of saltpeter toward the clouds. A sieve taken outdoors, dipped in well water, and shaken onto the ground can bring rain. Sympathetic magick is used as the water drips out of the sieve. The three-pronged pellar staff, called a *gwelan* or stang, can be used to draw rain clouds and promote summer showers. So can a pitchfork. Rainwater is collected and used in rites of cleansing and purification, as is the first snowfall … or just clean, fresh snow. Most people have heard "Rain, rain, go away," which sometimes actually works, but there's also this saying: "If the cat washes over the ear, soon the day is fine and clear." This was not just a homily for divination, but a chant for fair weather.

Several actions were said to make spring and the sun return after wintertime, including burning a bonfire, burning a wagon wheel with flammable materials and rolling it down a hill, and dancing around a Maypole. A mullein spike or flowerhead, also called a witch's candle, can be used to invoke sunshine. It is soaked in lamp oil and set on fire (carefully). Brewing a potion of "hot" spices, such as ginger, cinnamon, nutmeg, and cloves, is said to halt snowfall.

Everyday Spells

These are the homey, domestic spells performed by the common folk for daily occurrences. These brief but potent workings really do enhance one's life.

Words of power can be spoken while cooking so that everyone who eats a meal attains good health and prosperity. Carving sigils into a bar of soap can bring about spiritual cleansing along with physical cleanliness, banish negative forces, and invoke beneficial energy every time you take a shower. A spell can be done every morning, such as raising one's hands to the sky, turning around three times deosil, and saying, "This is going to be a fabulous day!"

Common magick users often pray before we eat, remembering to thank the spirits of the plants and animals who gave up their lives for human sustenance. The people who cook, serve the meal, and clean up afterward should also be honored. Deities and other entities are appreciated for their contributions.

Before falling asleep, it is a good idea to set wards and draw a sphere of light around the bed, asking for protection, peace, and restful sleep. This is a nice rite to do with young children. They can also thank the deities or ancestors for all the blessings of the day. Mugwort beneath the pillow brings prophetic dreams. Drawing a daisy wheel under the mattress keeps negative entities from hiding beneath the bed. This sigil is a series of interlocking circles, said to confuse evil spirits or the devil. Malevolent entities can also become trapped in the never-ending infinity loop of the symbol. A daisy wheel can also attract benevolent entities.

Spells can be conjured while brushing a person's hair, especially for health and protection. The soothing feel of the brush on the scalp, the repetitive movement, and words of power aid in the working. My husband has very long hair, so each morning before he drove off to work, I'd comb and braid it while asking our deities and ancestors to keep him safe on the job. The magick was braided into my husband's hair, and a hair tie of green, brown, or dark blue sealed the protection rite. Mothers have told me they do the same thing for children going off to school.

Several different rituals are enacted to seal a deal. Men proclaim oaths of fealty on a set of antlers, called "swearing by the horns." Ladies link their little fingers of their right hands to "pinky swear." Oaths are made by earth, sea, and sky and sworn on the Bible or on the grave of a loved one. Some holy stones are used for making agreements. Wedding rings symbolize the vows a couple makes to one another. In olden times, Scotsmen swore upon their dirk, or ritual knife. Two people making a handshake agreement would spit into their palms before clasping hands. Pricking the finger with a brooch, thorn, awl, or burin and mixing the blood created "blood brothers," and drops of blood were placed on a contract. Neither spitting nor using blood is recommended these days because of the spread of diseases through body fluids. However, a lock of hair can be retained to ensure that a contract is honored. Breaking bread together and sprinkling each slice with salt is still used to represent peace.

Travelers can perform a spell before embarking on a long journey, or even before driving to work. Images of horses and related items such as carriages, emblems called "horse brass," the rune Ehwaz, or a lynchpin can be drawn onto a vehicle with essential oils or paint to help protect the car from accidents or breakdowns. "Protect this truck from all of man, all of nature, and all of their creation" prevents collisions. Carrying a lucky penny in the car keeps it safe. Words of power, "There and back again," help create the conditions for a safe trip. Practitioners make the sign of the horns, forefinger and pinky extended, and walk around the car clockwise before embarking. Knocking on the interior car roof three times if the light turns yellow can help to get through an intersection safely. If someone collides with a deer, they should try to gather some of its hair, which will prevent further car/deer accidents. Deer whistles attached to a car are said to help chase them away. When driving under a railroad bridge, my family moos like a cow; it works—no train has fallen on us yet!

Doing housework is a perfect time to do magick too. Washing, sweeping, and vacuuming can all present opportunities for home cleansing. Working around a room widdershins casts out dirt and negative energies. Adding a pinch of salt to wash water aids in esoteric cleaning. Anything with lemons in it, including cleaners and furniture polish, can banish harmful energies. Folk traditionalists avoid killing any spiders because they represent good luck, although their webs can trap baleful forces as well as bugs, so they should be swept down. Tossing out clutter and recycling can remove discomfort and feelings of chaos. Carrying incense or burning sage clockwise through each room, starting on the bottom floor and working one's way upward, can bless the home.

Scattering rock salt or sea salt on floors, thresholds, and windowsills prevents harmful entities from coming inside. Bells on doors serve the same purpose. Putting an egg in each corner of a room can absorb disquieting energies, but the eggs must be discarded or composted, not eaten. If the house has a spooky basement, scattering lavender on the floor during a waning moon, waiting three days, then sweeping it up and discarding it casts out baleful energy. Suncatchers in the windows bring light to the house. Hanging herbs to dry on south-facing walls brings harmony. The old-fashioned embroidered sampler with "home sweet home" stitched onto it can really work.

In the past, there was a whole class of witches who advertised that they could find lost items.[153] Methods include tossing a similar object over the left shoulder and then walking in the direction it lands, seeking an image of the lost item's location in a bowl of water, and whirling in a circle with the arm and pointer finger extended, only stopping when the witch became too dizzy to stand. The finger then pointed in the direction of the missing object, or pointed toward something that symbolized the place it could be found. Dowsing or divining can also be used to find something that was lost.

A witch's ladder is a string or cord that has a number of knots tied in it, corresponding to a number used in a poem or spell. The repetitive motion of tying the knots or touching the cord helps to fuel the working. It is also used as a binding to connect a spell to the string and to bind the intent to the outcome. There may be other items tied to the cord including feathers, stones, or beads. Nine knots tied with nine intentions voiced can help bring the will into manifestation.

Banishment and Protection Magick

The "evil eye" is believed to occur when a person looks at another malevolently, causing illness and bad luck.[154] To avert the evil eye, common magick practitioners make a ritual gesture with their dominant hand: the thumb in the palm, the two middle fingers folded over the thumb, and the pointer finger and pinky forming horns. This gesture represents the horned forest god or the lucky bull. There are several ways to break a spell caused by the evil eye: point the forefinger with a cocked thumb (think of a finger gun); put the thumb between the pointer and middle fingers; cross your fingers; or spit between the forefinger and middle finger. Backhanding the evil eye's malevolent energy can also break its power. The evil eye was also called blinking someone, overlooking, eye biting, or the stink eye. An owl blink is a euphemism for a curse.

---

153. Brand and Ellis, *Popular Antiquities of Great Britain*.

154. Becka Roolf, "Healing Objects in Welsh Folk Medicine," *Proceedings of the Harvard Celtic Colloquium* 16/17 (1996/1997): 106–15, https://www.jstor.org/stable/20557317.

To banish the evil eye, people can carry a hawthorn cross wrapped with red thread, amber beads, or water from a holy well in a small bottle. Ground ivy was worn by milkmaids to avert the evil eye.[155] Making a bull's eye drawing and wearing it inside one's hat, facing rearward, can prevent someone from casting hexes behind one's back. Paintings of eyes on the prow of a ship, an eye drawn on the palm of a hand, or a pair of circles with a connecting arch (like old-fashioned spectacles) inscribed on a lintel post can prevent the evil eye from working within a vessel or building. The *Carmina Gadelica* has several poems designed to avert the evil eye, one stating, "I will subdue the eye, / I will suppress the eye, / and I will banish the eye."[156]

Apotropaic items are intended to repel bad luck or evil creatures. These include hexfoils or witches' marks. Sharp objects, such as knives and sickles, are placed blade-side up to repel harmful fairies and other troublesome entities. Sometimes they are placed on shelves inside the chimney. Scissors left open on the windowsill or under the doormat have the same effect. Hanging a piece of flint over a child's bed prevents supernatural attack, as does a hagstone.

Red thread wound around the tines of a three-pronged stang made of ash or rowan wood creates a spirit trap, ensnaring malicious beings. Sprinkling salt across the doorway, sticking bent pins into window frames, and hanging bells on doors and animal collars keeps bad luck and dangerous energies away. Laying a broom across the door, or placing it bristles up, keeps evil spirits (or the devil) out of a building. Magickal tools such as a bellows, feather fan, or besom can also accomplish this purpose by blowing or sweeping away the malign force.

Some actions and behaviors are said to repel harmful energies. Walking three times deosil around the home while carrying a burning torch or "witch's candle" prevents malign entities from harming children and stealing things. Although accidentally breaking a mirror is considered unlucky, inscribing sigils around the edge of a round mirror and deliberately shattering the glass releases harmful forces into another realm. Christian folks use Bible verses and cross themselves to avert bad luck and banish malevolent entities. Harmful beings are said to be unable to cross water, so leaping a stream or crossing a bridge can thwart bogeys following you home. Walking widdershins, or counterclockwise, around a

---

155. Ibid.

156. Alexander Carmichael, *Carmina Gadelica* (Edinburgh: T. and A. Constable, 1900).

space three times can undo negative spells, as can magickally cutting them with a black-handled knife.

A box lined with mirrors can permanently bind a negative situation; place a symbol of the baneful condition into the box, then bury it or throw it into a deep body of water. A chalice can also be used to trap harmful energies. The vessel is filled with water as the magick user speaks intent. After a period of time, the water is discarded outdoors. The chalice is then rinsed three times in pure water, vinegar, or white wine and refilled.

Amulets, Charms, and Talismans

Talismans and amulets are physical objects used to contain magickal power. They are believed to repel harmful or baneful situations. They are also used to attract good luck and beneficial conditions, such as wealth or love, or to manifest certain qualities, such as strength. A horseshoe nailed above the door, a Bridget's cross, a sprig of rowan flowers, or a small pouch filled with crystals and herbs can all be considered talismans. Amulets are usually magick items that are worn as jewelry. Some common magick practitioners use the words "talisman" and "amulet" interchangeably or switch the definitions. Some say that either a talisman or amulet has short-term or long-lasting effects. Others believe an amulet has intrinsic powers while a talisman must be activated with an action such as a prayer, rubbing or kissing the object, or using ritualized movements. Some folk traditionalists use the word "charm" for a physical object that contains energy, as in carrying a rabbit's foot as a lucky charm, but this term can also mean the spoken words used to activate the object.

Amulets and talismans are believed to retain magickal power, releasing increments of energy over a period of time. They can last for a long time or a short while. For example, a pentacle necklace or St. Christopher's medal can keep the wearer safe for years. An oak, ash, and thorn talisman crafted at Midsummer can protect a car until the following season.

Items that represent a circumstance, such as coins, a pine cone, seashells, or a ribbon, can be used as a talisman for sympathetic magick. These objects are often put into a pouch or other container. Usually, this type of item must be bespelled, or charged with magickal energy. Words of power are spoken and rites are enacted in order to state intent, summon energy, and load the talisman or amulet with force. Objects that have intrinsic properties, such as iron nails to avert evil or a buckeye to summon good luck, can be used for their innate, natural powers. Something that has gained power over time, like an athlete's lucky socks, can also be considered a talisman.

An apotropaic talisman or amulet is used to repel negative energies or malicious beings. These can also be called a periapt. Talismans and amulets used to attract luck are sometimes called charms, lures, charismata, lucky pieces, or fetishes. Folklore is teeming with talismans, including magick rings, four-leaf clovers, lucky stones, magick beans, special shoes, lucky coins, religious symbols, mistletoe, and so on. A wedding ring is a talisman. So is the cross used to repel a vampire, or the wolfsbane herb used to scare off werewolves in folktales.

Types of Talismans

Elf Bolts

One fairly well-known power object of Scottish folklore is the elf bolt, also called an elf shot, elf dart, elf arrow, or a fairy arrow. These are flint arrowheads created by prehistoric artisans. To be shot by one was said to cause certain death. Farm animals who were taken with distemper were said to be shot by an elf bolt. Conversely, finding an arrowhead is considered very lucky. Elf bolts are worn or carried as talismans against the evil eye, as protection from illness, and as a shield against violence. They can be hung in a stable or kennel to protect animals.

Poppets

A poppet is a talismanic object that stands in for, or represents, a person or living being who is not present. A poppet is also called a poppi, pippi, dolly, voodoo doll, mommet, moppet, effigy, dagides, dossil, or fetish. An effigy can be constructed of wax, cloth, wood, leather, or clay. A carved root of a plant fashioned in the shape of a human or animal, called an alraun, is a type of poppet. The dolly can be designed to look as much like the living being as possible, using colored yarn to represent hair, adding beads for eyes, dressing it in clothing discarded by the person, and so forth. It can also be named for the person or animal.

Contagion magick is used to connect the poppet to the individual by putting personal items into it such as the individual's hair, sweat, or fingernails, or an animal's fur, cast-off claws, or a drop of blood. Sympathetic magick is used to cause the desired condition through the use of symbols such as crystals, herbs, sigils, or representational images. The poppet is ritually "brought to life" by the magick user breathing into it, using an incantation or song, and/or enacting a rite to raise energy.

Although the media has portrayed a poppet as being used for evil, such as sticking pins into a voodoo doll to cause pain or burning an effigy to represent a politician being deposed, usually a dolly is created for the purposes of healing and protection and to bring about love, prosperity, and well-being. Poppets might be used as a "fetish" item to contain a fetch, an individual spirit or a detached segment of an individual's consciousness.

Concealed Objects

Some apotropaic items are hidden from view inside a home or workspace. These objects are usually concealed within a wall, under a floor, in a ceiling, buried beneath the threshold or hearth, hidden in the chimney or a stone wall outdoors, or an outbuilding's rafters. Concealed items include clothing, written inscriptions, animal skeletons or skulls, and witch's bottles. When older homes in the British Isles were remodeled, dozens of shoes were found inside walls and beneath hearthstones or thresholds.[157] Concealed objects bring about health and well-being through the absence of curses that cause illness and bad luck.

Concealed objects are not only used to repel negative forces and entities, they also serve as a type of decoy. Harmful energies are attracted to the material item instead of to the individual that the object represents. For example, underwear can be worn for a few days to soak it in sweat and menstrual blood, then hidden inside a wall of the house. Because the object contains the "essence" of a person, a baneful entity will attack the underwear rather than the individual. It might seem gross to our modern sensibilities, but it works.

A witch's bottle is made of glass or ceramic. It contains items to connect it to a person through contagion magick, such as urine, blood, fingernails, and hair. The witch's bottle may also include objects for repulsion magick such as wine, vinegar, nails, needles, bent pins, fishhooks, broken glass or crockery, metal shavings, herbs, and written inscriptions. The cork, bottle top, lid, or cover is affixed to the bottle with wax, which can be inscribed with sigils. The container is bespelled and then concealed within a home or nearby outside. Buried and concealed

---

157. Katy Prickett, "The Shoes Hidden in Homes to Ward Off Evil," *BBC News*, December 10, 2017, https://www.bbc.com/news/uk-england-northamptonshire-41507752.

witch's bottles have been found throughout Britain and in places where emigrants moved, and there is even a survey to find more.[158] Some containers were jokingly called "Bellarmines" after a Christian official whose face was supposedly sculpted on the ceramic jar.[159]

Baneful entities, sometimes called witches or evil spirits, would be fooled into thinking the witch's bottle was actually a person, and they would attack it rather than the individual. A witch's bottle could also trap harmful entities or energies or repel them. Other witch's bottles were cast into a fire or boiled in a cauldron, where the heat made them explode. (This is not recommended due to biohazards and flying glass.) The practice was believed to end "bewitchment" or negative magick, and sometimes it revealed the person who caused harm to another. These objects often still function after hundreds of years. In the present day, a witch's bottle can be made from a fruit canning jar, sealed with a metal lid, and buried nearby the home.

Sigils

A sigil is an esoteric symbol that is inscribed, painted, written, embroidered, or carved onto an object. Sigils represent a specific condition through sympathetic magick, and thus have talismanic qualities. Sigils can be letters of a magickal alphabet, such as runic or ogham, but plain roman letters used in the English language work just fine. The *Coelbren y Beirdd* is a Welsh alphabet that may be authentic or the invention of Druid revivalist Iolo Morganwg.[160; 161] Regardless, this alphabet can be used for sigils. Religious emblems like the Christian cross, pentagram, Thor's hammer, or the Celtic triquetra/triskula are all sigils. So are representational drawings used for a magickal or religious purpose like an eye, a pair of crossed keys, a bird, or a windmill, and the symbols used for brands on horses and cattle.

---

158. Evan Nicole Brown, "Yes, It's a Witch Bottle Hunt," *Atlas Obscura*, April 23, 2019, https://www.atlasobscura.com/articles/witch-bottles-project-in-britain.

159. Ralph Merrifield, "The Use of Bellarmines as Witch-Bottles," *Guildhall Miscellany*, no. 3 (February 1954).

160. John Michael Greer, *The Coelbren Alphabet: The Forgotten Oracle of the Welsh Bards* (Woodbury, MN: Llewellyn Publications, 2017).

161. Williams ab Ithel, *Barddas of Iolo Morganwg*.

The pentagram, also called a pentangle, pentacle, witch's foot, goose-foot cross, or goblin's cross, is actually a very old sigil. There are apotropaic marks in British homes, businesses, and even churches that are shaped like pentacles and pentagrams, used to repel negative energies.[162; 163] The sigil of four Fs put together in an equal-armed cross or snowflake pattern represented a Saxon blessing for prosperity, "Fodder, Flax, Fire, and Frigga" (or Freyja, or Food, or Flags, as in flagstones).[164] These four things represented the human need to sustain life. The symbol could also be read as FFFF, sometimes used by traditional witches to identify one another.

A glyph, which means a series of lines that connect letters of the alphabet in a pattern, is a very potent sigil. To create a glyph, write the alphabet in a pattern, then connect the letters with lines to form a word or a magickal name. The line alone is then used as a sigil.

Sigils can be used on or in talismans or be inscribed on surfaces of a building, drawn or painted on a vehicle, or tattooed onto the skin. While some sigils have been used for so long that they have taken on intrinsic magickal energy, others need a statement of intent to imbue them with a specific meaning. Some sigils work as a demon trap or hexfoil. Daisy wheels, spirals, mazy crosses, or Celtic knotwork are used in common magick to capture negative entities, which bounce around and around inside the symbol, unable to escape.

Talismans cannot prevent all bad things from happening, but they can help to safeguard people and animals, places like homes and offices, and things like vehicles and work tools. I have personally seen an oak, ash, and thorn charm that was used to protect a car that got into a wreck. Although there was damage to the vehicle, everyone inside was unhurt. The talisman's leaves looked as though they had been burnt. Any talismanic object that survives a car accident, prolonged illness, or fire should be discarded immediately, with a new protection item replacing it as quickly as possible. A talisman that is "done for" will feel lifeless and worn out.

Used-up talismans can be composted, put into the trash, or burned in a bonfire. This should be done during the waning moon phase, the dark of the moon, Samhain, Hallowe'en, or Yuletide.

---

162. Molyneux, "Discovering Witches' Marks."

163. Champion, *Medieval Graffiti*.

164. The Llewellyn Encyclopedia, s.v. "Term: Flags, Flax, Fodder and Frig," accessed April 5, 2020, https://www.llewellyn.com/encyclopedia/term/flags,+flax,+fodder+and+frig.

Spells can help to increase the probability that beneficial, positive events will occur, and they can help prevent harmful circumstances. Performing a ritualized magickal working can attract favorable attention from energetic beings. The actions, verbalizations, and symbolism of objects, especially when put together during a spell, can combine to link will and intent to a desirable outcome.

eleven
DIVINATION, ATTUNEMENT, AND TRANCE WORK

Magickal rites and workings such as divination, participating in a mystical journey, and performing rituals of attunement are all examples of the type of magick called theurgy. As mentioned before, the word *theurgy* means a "divine working." It is a passive type of magick, which means the practitioner is seeking hidden knowledge rather than creating change in the material world. This type of magick is more intuitive and receptive than thaumaturgy, or active magick. Attunement simply means gaining an understanding of energetic beings or forces and becoming aligned with them.

Divination

Divination is discovering information about future events through magickal means. It can also involve gaining insight about the past or current situations by use of supernatural methods. Divination is also called prophecy, intuition, forecasting, prognostication, sortilege, fortune-telling, augury, presaging, second sight, foretelling, *kenning* in colloquial Irish, *frith* in Scots Gaelic, and soothsaying.

Some magick users believe they receive messages from the gods or the universe, perhaps channeling an entity that whispers secrets. Other practitioners think that a wrinkle in the space-time continuum occurs, allowing people to catch glimpses of the future, the past, and other dimensions. Some people believe it may be the human subconscious sending images. Some of us think that divination is like watching a program that is broadcast from the otherworld. In the past, old-line Pagans mostly looked for signs about the weather, or predictions to aid in farming and other work, while young ladies tried to determine their future spouse…in other words, love, money, and health.

There are dozens of British folktales about divination with animal omens, portents in the stars, and images seen in magick mirrors, water, or crystal balls. There are also dire predictions of doom by oracles, elders, bad fairies, and evil witches, although these are quite uncommon in reality. The most auspicious times for ceremonies of foretelling are Hallowe'en, May Eve, Midsummer's Eve, and during Yuletide. Divination is also most easily performed during the dark of the moon and the moon's waning phase.

Augury rituals can be enacted as any other rite (outlined in chapter 6), with preparation of oneself and a sacred space, shielding, grounding and centering, calling upon helpers if needed, raising energy if desired, and thanking and dismissing powers who lent aid. Analysis can be done during the rite or afterward and can involve looking up correspondences. Divination can be followed by spells and workings to create changes, based on the information that was gained.

Methods of Divination

Although tarot and astrology certainly were and are used in the British Isles, I'm going to stick with techniques that were employed by old-line working-class people, using everyday household implements or the tools of their profession. Of course, folks also "saw" mystic visions, had prophetic dreams, or used their intuition, all of which require no ritual tools at all. The following are some of the more common methods of divination.

Scrying

Scrying is short for descrying, which means looking at or into an object to see predictive visions. Wiccan author Doreen Valiente wrote about how scrying was used in Wicca, which includes gazing into a black mirror or black-painted cauldron.[165] People can also focus their eyes on a bowl of water; a candle flame, bonfire, or smoke from incense or a campfire; mist, fog, rippling water, or water vapor; a plain mirror, window pane, ice, or any other smooth surface. Some of us even gaze into the popular crystal ball. Folklore tells of looking down a water well, at

---

165. Doreen Valiente, *Witchcraft for Tomorrow* (Wiltshire, UK: Crowood Press, 2018).

the water inside a rain barrel, or staring into a clear pool to see visions that represent the future. Images which have symbolic meanings are viewed in reflective surfaces like water and glass or in the movements of flame, smoke, or fog.

Procedures for scrying with a reflective device include darkening the room and placing the crystal ball, bowl of water, or mirror on a black cloth. Burning a candle nearby or shining a light onto the object's surface can help. The light source should be behind the practitioner, shining onto the reflective surface—some say the light must be projected over the person's left shoulder. Mirrors, water, and crystals can also be used under the beams of a full moon. Some magick users roll their eyes up as far as they can, then blink and glance at the source. Others stare directly at a flame or the rippling movements of water, fire, or smoke.

When scrying, people might see images that symbolize a particular condition, or they may simply use the movement or reflection to focus their own senses while allowing their mind to wander at the same time. Some practitioners believe there is a portal into another realm behind the vapor, flame, or reflection that is viewed as a gateway for energetic beings. The diviner may be utilizing their own powers of intuition and/or their subconscious to pick up on subtle pictures which have representational meaning, or messages that they can interpret.

The visions that are seen within a descrying tool have different connotations to each individual. For some a skull means death, while to others it denotes wisdom. A table of correspondence can help with interpretation.

A white or clear bowl of cold water is also used for divination by dropping liquids into it. Black ink, an egg white, or candle wax is slowly dripped into the water, forming patterns or shapes. These images represent certain objects or conditions. It is rather like the Rorschach test, which are inkblots used by psychologists. In the past, mercury or heated lead was dripped into the water, although we now know that these liquid metals are dangerous to humans. Images can also be seen in the shape of clouds, patterns in tree limbs, the embers of a bonfire, grain waving in the wind, and the splatter of a dropped egg.

Divination with Other Senses

Magick users can often hear sounds in nature that seem like voices imparting wisdom. The crackle, pop, and hiss of burning wood in a bonfire can seem like a whisper of advice. A ringing in the ears means someone is talking about you. Hearing a tone in the right ear means someone is saying good things, while hearing the ringing in the left ear means someone is badmouthing. Practitioners sometimes hear the voices of spirits or other beings on the wind, the singing of grain in a field, or the sound of a waterfall. An itching in the right palm means money is coming, but an itchy left palm means money is owed.

Splinter Spell

This divination spell originally used splinters pried from firewood, but flat wooden toothpicks work just as well. It helps to determine relationships and alliances amongst a group of people, such as coworkers or members of a town committee.

A number of splinters—between two and twenty—are marked with colors, numbers, or shapes and assigned names. A flat dinner plate (ceramic or china) is sprinkled with water, enough to cover its surface. A teaspoon of cooking oil or a squirt of liquid dish detergent is mixed in to make the plate slippery. The splinters are then dropped onto the plate, which is swirled counterclockwise three times while the user chants, "With me or ag'in me, who shall it be?" three times. The plate can also be left overnight in a place it will not be disturbed. Splinters that lean toward each other are allies. If their tops are just barely touching, they are talking about certain matters. If their bottoms are touching, they may have a more intimate relationship. Splinters that cross each other are opponents. A group of splinters are a clique. If one is standing all alone, it's the outcast. If there is a group clustered around the "boss" splinter, that might mean they are minions. If two splinters are standing side by side, they are working in harmony with one another.

Pendling

Using a pendulum for divination can answer binary, yes-or-no questions. For pendling, a magick user needs a string of some kind, such as the hair of a person or a horse's tail, a piece of yarn or cord nine inches long, or a thin, linked chain. The string is used to suspend a small object like a crystal, hagstone, coin, wedding ring, pointy stone, or metal pendulum constructed specifically for divination purposes. A back and forth motion of the pendulum means yes, while spinning around in circles means no. (Some practitioners assign different meanings.)

Other methods can also be used for pendling. An old-fashioned metal house key with a hole in the top, sometimes called a skeleton key, is strung on a cord or piece of yarn, then held between two virgin females, or two people who were in a loving relationship. They ask yes or no questions; the key spinning means yes, staying stationary means no, sliding right means yes, and sliding left means no. To determine the gender of an unborn baby, the mother's wedding ring is hung from a string over her stomach. A back and forth motion indicates a boy, while a circular motion means a girl.

Sieve and Shears

This older form of augury uses everyday household implements: a cooking sieve and an ordinary pair of sewing scissors.[166] This is another type of binary divination; it elicits a yes or no answer. The sieve is balanced atop the shears and fixed to them with a piece of thread, or the sieve is dangled, held in place between the blades of the shears. Questions are asked or names are spoken; the sieve will turn, vibrate, or drop at the correct answer.

Other Binary Divination

There are several other methods of binary divination such as a coin toss, with heads indicating a yes answer, while tails means a no answer. A dice throw that lands on an odd number means no, while even numbers indicate a yes. Rolling two ones, or "snake eyes," foretells bad luck, while two sixes, or "boxcars," is favorable. Nuts thrown into a bonfire can determine the likelihood of prosperity: if they pop, it means wealth; if they blacken and burn, it means poverty. Throwing a shoe over the house can give a yes or no answer, depending on which way it points.

Reading Tea Leaves

Although this divination custom arose in Asia, British folks love a cuppa afternoon tea, so the method of divination was imported along with the leaves of the chai, camellia, or tea plant. Herbal tea leaves can also be used.

Reading the patterns made by tea leaves in the bottom of a cup is called tasseography. The tea leaves are steeped in a pot of hot water and then poured into cups, which accumulates some grounds in the bottom of each cup. The person drinks the tea and can leave the grounds in the shapes they formed or swirl the grounds clockwise three times. If the person is right-handed, the cup handle faces to the right. Grounds stuck to the side of the cup facing the person indicate past

---

166. Muise, "Conjuring by Sieve and Scissors."

events, while leaves clinging to the far side of the cup mean future events. Grounds in the middle represent occurrences that are presently happening, or that influence the past and present. A flake of tea on the cup rim means something will occur very soon. Shapes created by the clumps of tea leaves symbolize life events or images relevant to the individual. For example, a kitten represents a birth; a hammer indicates work; a bird means a message; a heart means love; footprints and lines symbolize a journey; owls and snakes are bad luck; and anchors, trees, acorns, deer, and crescent moons signify good luck. The proximity of the symbols to one another shows their connection. Dots can mean months or years, depending on their size, which provides a time frame. Arrows pointing up means something is more likely to occur. Letters of the alphabet are related to people the individual knows.

Bones and Tell-Stones

This type of divination uses a number of small objects with written sigils, images, or letters of a magickal alphabet inscribed on them. Each of the letters or depictions has a symbolic meaning. The items are cast, thrown, or dropped onto a surface that may also have significant correspondences, such as colors, images, or words. The stones' relationship to one another, and to the background surface, has prophetic meaning.

Runes and Ogham

Both of these methods of divination utilize a magickal alphabet with symbolism ascribed to the various letters. The sigils are painted, burned, or carved onto objects that are then cast or released onto a surface. Like tell-stones or bones, the positions of the items, and the relationship between them, represents various states of being.

Ogham sticks, wands, or staves are constructed from long, thin twigs, with the ogham characters or letters inscribed on them. Ogham is possibly named for Ogma or Ogmios, the Celtic god of knowledge and storytelling. The letters originally came into existence in Ireland around the fifth or sixth century.[167] Some magick users believe that the wood of different trees should be used for each

---

167. Simon Ager, "Ogham," Omniglot, accessed April 6, 2020, https://www.omniglot.com /writing/ogham.htm.

ogham stick, while others prefer using only one type of wood, traditionally apple, yew, or elder. These are also called omen sticks, lots, tallies, sprigs, or tell-sticks. Some practitioners say that twenty ogham characters should be used, while others use twenty-one letters, including a blank. The sticks are held upright in the dominant hand with their ends against a flat surface, then released to fall in an arbitrary pattern. Another method is randomly choosing three ogham staves in a rite of divination called *coelbreni* in the Cymraeg language. The meaning of the letters, and the associations with the type of wood, are used for augury.

Rune sets are also used for divination, often made from the wood of trees that bear edible fruits or nuts, such as hazel and apple. Small limbs are cut into flat coin shapes and sigils are carved or burned into them. Rune sets can also be made of clay, small stones, or bones. Like tell-stones, they can be cast or dropped onto a surface, and their relationship determines the oracular meaning. One, three, or more runes can also be chosen at random for divination. The runes are also called the *fuðark* or *futhark*, for the first six letters of the alphabet, which comes from the Norse/Germanic tribes.[168]

Seekers can gaze at the limbs of bare winter trees to find runic and/or ogham letters in the shapes of the crossed branches. Runes and ogham can also be viewed in the flight of a large flock of birds. The letters may spell out a message or have a prophetic meaning, based on the association of certain conditions with the magickal alphabets.

Choosing a Method of Divination

The method of divination chosen by a practitioner depends on what information they wish to find out about. If it's a quick yes-or-no question, a binary augury, such as pendling, might be best. The sieve and shears and the splinter workings are good for finding a name—as long as the seeker is aware of the identities of the people involved. Runes, tell-stones, and ogham are good for discovering relationships between individuals and for learning how soon or how likely something will occur. Scrying takes longer, yet the visions may give more information to the magick user, as do the images seen in tea leaves. Conversely, it is up to the practitioner

---

168. Simon Ager, "Elder Futhark," Omniglot, accessed April 6, 2020, https://www.omniglot.com/writing/runic.htm#elder.

to consider and interpret the symbolic meaning of the pictures they envision during the rite.

There are many common magick divination rituals for the two very important human conditions of love and death. The binary "she loves me, she loves me not" rite of plucking petals from a daisy was described in folklore. Other divination rites for love include paring an apple carefully, leaving the skin in one long strip, and throwing the "whirlygirl" peeling over the left shoulder. It will land on the ground, spelling out the name or giving the initials of a potential beau. Twisting an apple stem while chanting the alphabet discloses the name of the intended, as the stem breaks on a particular initial. The first pea picked in the garden denotes relationship status. One pea alone in the pod means a spinster, two peas indicate a marriage partner, and further numbers equate to more marriages or the number of children the person will have. Young ladies chant to the full moon, "Mother moon, prithee, reveal to me who my husband shall be." They will then dream of their future spouse. Images of a love interest could also appear while scrying, especially when leaning backward over an open water well and gazing into a looking glass held over the left shoulder, aimed at the water. The full moon shining into a mirror can reveal the image of a future swain. Candle wax, egg white, or ink dripped into water can form an image that relates to the beau's profession, such as an anvil for a blacksmith, a computer for a technician, or a stethoscope for a doctor. A series of candles can be given names, then placed on the floor and lit. The first to blow out is the name of a potential spouse.

Many divination rituals are enacted at Hallowe'en, when the veils between this material realm and the otherworld are said to be thin, and the lines between the future, the present, and the past are blurred. A maiden can dream of the location of a ship on Hallowe'en night. Lovers can foretell the direction their relationship is taking by placing two hazelnuts near the fire; if the nuts move closer together, the pair will also. Young people can try to pull up a cabbage or kale by the roots with only one tug. If the root is long, the betrothed will be tall and lanky; if short, the loved one will be likewise. If a cat runs from a person during the last days of the harvest season, a secret will soon be revealed to them.

Of course, Hallowe'en rites are mostly associated with death. Hearing a pack of dogs howling around the house on this spirit night is an omen of death, as is hearing the Wild Hunt in the sky. Seeing a wraith or ghostlike image foretells death. Dreaming about a funeral on Hallowe'en is a death portent. People can write their initials on stones, place them into a bonfire, and then light the flame. On the following day, if a rock is broken, the person will be injured, and if the stone is missing, the person may die during the next year. Another augury rite done on Hallowe'en involves filling five bowls: one with clean water, another with used dishwater, one with grain, one with dirt, and leaving one bowl empty. A person is blindfolded and reaches out to touch just one of the bowls. Clean water means marrying a virgin, the dishwater means marrying a widow or widower, the bowl of grain means prosperity, while the empty bowl means never marrying. Touching the fateful bowl of dirt means a death.

Omens about mortality are not limited to Hallowe'en. If someone sees a funeral procession in a dream or vision at Beltane, it is an augury of death. Shadows cast on the wall by the Yule log fire show who will thrive and who might sicken and die. Long, stretched-out shadows are good fortune, while shadows without a head mean a death. Seeing a "corpse candle," or disembodied light, can foretell death. On New Year's Day, the Scots believe in performing the *frith*, or augury. The first thing seen outdoors predicted events for the rest of the year.

Beltane is also associated with a love prophesy. An initial in the morning dew can indicate the first letter of the future spouse's name. The song of a cuckoo bird on May Day tells how many years it will be until an individual is married, according to how many times the cuckoo calls. Seeing a hoot owl, or hearing it call a name, foretold an elder's passing.

Divination can also be done during meditation, journeying, and other rites of attunement.

Attunement

Attunement rituals are considered a passive form of magick because they do not involve making changes to the material world. However, nearly all attunement rites involve a deliberate, intentional change in consciousness. Meditation, trance working, and spirit communication are all conceptions of attunement rites. The goal of this type of magick is to gain understanding of, and to bring oneself into harmony with, the spirit world, energetic beings, the universe, and oneself. While other rituals can be done within a group or in the course of a holiday celebration, attunement rites are much more personal.

A Chance to Trance

Trance work is otherwise known as entering a trance state, spiritual journeying, remote viewing, spirit travelling, spirit projecting, astral projection or travel, having an out-of-body experience, transvection, and dreamworking. Psychologists may call it self-hypnosis.[169] In the common magick traditions of the British Isles, trance work is often called going out and about, riding the wind, sending a fetch, twilight sleep, leaping between, lifting, pathworking, or twinkling. Practitioners sometimes call it riding the hedge, crossing the hedge, or jumping the stile—metaphors that mean transcending this material plane. It connotes the spirit leaving the physical body and entering another realm. The hedge or stile represents the liminal place between the world of form and other worlds. Modern heathens call their shamanic practitioners *seiðr* workers, and they do nightwalkings and go fairing forth. British traditional witches sometimes call astral travel "walking the crooked path," since this representation emphasizes the journey rather than an ending goal. It also means awareness that the way is not always linear and can include detours. These are all metaphors for altering one's consciousness, leaving consensus reality behind, and entering a receptive state in order to gain knowledge and align oneself with magickal beings and powers.

Most British-based common magick practitioners simply say they are travelling to "the otherworld," but it is sometimes called the underworld, the shadowlands, hinterlands, borderlands, the other realm, or the otherside, while our earthly realm is called middle earth or the mundane world. British folktales tell us of a land of the dead, kingdom of the gods, Elfhame, Fairyland, or a dreamland. Some Irish magick users call it *Tír na' nÓg*, the land of youth, while Welsh folk call it *Annwn* or *Annwyn*, the realm of spirits, or *Caer Sidi*, the fairy fortress. The Norse divided the planes up into nine realms, including Asgard, home of the gods, Midgard, home of mortal humans, and Valhalla, the final home of honored warriors.

Different common magick users view the otherworld in various ways: as a castle of glass, a misty land with no up or down, an underwater kingdom, a beautiful forest, or an island such as Avalon. Some people believe that the planes are thinly

---

169. Beverly D. Flaxington, "Self-Hypnosis for Everyday Life," *Psychology Today*, September 13, 2013, https://www.psychologytoday.com/us/blog/understand-other-people /201309/self-hypnosis-everyday-life.

stacked, like pancakes, while others envision a series of interlocking spheres or a tree with far-reaching roots and branches. Many of us see the otherworld as a source for power and the location of our own magickal pool.

Some practitioners believe that dreaming accesses these other worlds, as does entering an alternate state of consciousness through use of mind-altering substances. Some traditional witches think that a portion of the soul is deliberately broken away and allowed to walk free as a fetch. The image of a fairy-tale witch riding a broomstick can be a metaphor for astral travel. Folk stories about people who were lost for a time and who danced and partied with the Fae might allude to those who underwent a prolonged spiritual journey.

Trance working can be equated with sacred quests, which are the subject of so much of British and Irish literature, featuring heroes such as Fionn MacCuimhal or King Arthur and his companions. *The Canterbury Tales* are a Christian allegorical quest. Fairy tales like "Jack and the Beanstalk," "Puss in Boots," and stories of any young person who went to "seek their fortune" seem like descriptions of magickal journeys. The heroes of folktales usually had to fight monsters, undergo trials to strengthen themselves, and answer philosophical questions in order to rescue a kidnapped child or to find a wondrous treasure. These might be metaphoric of conditions like understanding, fortitude, or wisdom. Sometimes the journey itself was the point; there was no reward at the end. The quest was undertaken to empower the protagonists, who would prove themselves worthy or align themselves with natural forces.

Like the quests of literature, a seeker who embarks on a spiritual journey can encounter darker forces, including their own "shadow" self. This was a concept discussed by Dr. Carl Jung, having to do with the hidden aspects of one's personality, the subconscious mind, and emotions such as anger, jealousy, and fear.[170] An astral traveler may encounter harsh truths about situations they thought were familiar and stable. Conversely, the trance work can be relaxing or invigorating, and it can help a person connect with a benevolent entity, including a deity, spirit, or animal guide. Folkloric traditionalists sometimes undergo spiritual alignment as if they were sitting down to the dinner table with a god for a lively discussion. A seeker may be granted insight into a cause-effect relationship by the voice of an ancestor. Common magick users who follow a shamanic path can learn the cause

---

170. C. G. Jung, *Psychology & Religion* (New Haven, CT: Yale University Press, 1938).

of an illness and methods for healing, discover information about plants and animals used as food and medicine, or find ways to enhance a natural habitat. The practitioner can visit alternate realities and play in the magickal pool.

As well as gaining knowledge, a magick user might do workings during astral travel, which can affect the physical world. Changes made on another plane of existence will reflect here in our material realm. For example, the practitioner could perceive an energy blockage and endeavor to redirect power. Shamans from around the world enact a rite called a "soul retrieval," meaning to heal the spirit of a person who has faced a traumatic event. People who are in a trance can sometimes divine the future and then take action in the material realm, to ensure the prediction becomes manifest or to prevent the prophecy from happening. This can involve doing a binding spell or performing another working. There is a legend about English witches who engaged in a ritual to stop Hitler from attacking Britain.[171] It is said that one of them had seen the invasion in a dream.

If a person has performed an active magick rite correctly—with all the proper steps taken—yet it does not seem to be making any difference, they can do a trance working to find out why. The seeker may discover that they are under the influence of a hex or spell. They may even comprehend that what they have asked for is not really in line with their own true will. Doing trance work can help a practitioner to gain wisdom about their own magickal capabilities.

Trance Steps

Shielding, grounding, and centering are necessary for most magick users before undertaking astral travel. Previous to a trance-working rite, a folk magick traditionalist often takes physical action to help purify their body and prepare their spirit, such as using a sweat lodge or sauna, smoke cleansing, or fasting. Some practitioners partake of an entheogen, a plant-based substance that can cause changes to perception, memory, and consciousness. A few witches really do use flying ointment to assist themselves in astral travel. Of course, using a substance is not necessary for entering an altered state of consciousness. People do it every night when they dream.

Anchoring is essential before doing any trance work. Astral travel can be disorienting or have an emotional impact, which anchoring can help to avoid. Some-

---

171. J. L. Bracelin, *Gerald Gardner: Witch* (London: Octagon Press, 1960).

one who is not anchored to their physical body may experience confusion, difficulty with memory, and problems orienting to time and place. (This is different than medical conditions or physical diseases that cause mental or memory problems, which may require the care of a professional.) Anchoring means tethering oneself to the material plane and/or keeping a part of oneself within consensus reality.

An anchoring technique used by Eastern mysticism is to envision a silver cord linking the heart chakra to the solar plexus, and in turn connecting the physical body to the "aura," or spirit. Common magick has a similar notion, but with different metaphors. People visualize a rope, or a ray of energy, attaching their inner being, or soul, to their physical body. As they journey, the cord unwinds (or the ray of light stretches), yet it still binds their essence to their material self. British traditional witchcraft sometimes uses an actual, physical red cord to symbolically attach the spirit to the body. At the conclusion of the rite, the symbolic anchor cord is reeled in, drawing the individual back to their physical body.

Other practitioners use touchstones, which means holding a real stone, a key, or some other material object that represents the physical plane. This item is believed to draw the spirit back to the physical world after the trance working is complete. A person may use the image of something stationary, like a tree or rock. Some magick users employ a type of mental roadmap with "landmarks" to find the location of their physical body relative to the location of the place their astral self or spirit is wandering, kind of like a cosmic GPS.

Other methods for anchoring include recalling attachments to the physical plane such as the names of loved ones, the location of one's home, or one's role in society. Common magick users may use a natural prompt to return from a spirit journey, such as the sunrise, a rooster crowing, or the regular rhythms of the body which awaken them from a dream state. Others rely on an intentional reminder, like an alarm set to music rather than a jarring noise. The flame of a candle or bonfire burning to ashes can also conclude a dreamworking. The plan for ending a trance should be arranged prior to the rite.

Folkloric traditionalists often isolate ourselves before embarking on a journey. This is to ensure no interruptions while entering a trance state. In past days, people may have sat within a dark cave, lain beside a bonfire all night, or covered themselves with an animal hide, as in the previously mentioned rite of *Taghairm*.

This type of ritual may not be possible during current times, so we must settle for a dark bedroom, a quiet fireplace, or a safe outdoor environment.

Meditation is usually undertaken to clear the mind and to focus before travelling the astral. Deep breathing exercises can help to relax the body. Prior to travel, concentrating on items such as an image or written statement can help us to remember the purpose of our journey. Putting a request into poetic form can help with recalling the reason for the working. Another function of the touchstone is using it as an emblem that symbolizes our desires. It may take practice before a person can do all of these steps and then recall their question or reason for their trance work. On the other hand, people might decide to just let go and experience the journey without expectations.

Trance working can require silence, so the practitioner may use earplugs or white noise, like the sound of a fan running. Sound might be needed to embark on a journey, so a chant or drumbeat can help. The tones should be low frequency, slow, rhythmic, and continuous. While recorded music can work, electronics might be compromised by an encounter with magickal energy, including batteries dying or a power surge. If it's possible to work outdoors, the lovely sounds of the breeze and singing birds are preferable.

Engaging the other senses is helpful as well. A practitioner can gaze at a pattern such as Celtic knotwork, a crystal, or a flame. A glain can be used as a center of focus, helpful for entering a trance state. Some traditionalists stare at the moon or the patterns in trees; others focus their eyes on a spot a few inches in front of them. Other magick users prefer darkness. Repetitive hand motions (tying knots, grinding a mill, or tracing a mazy stone with a finger) and movement (dancing, walking, or swaying) can help to occupy the body, thus helping the mind to enter a calm, receptive state. Some of us use ecstatic dance, which seems counterintuitive, but this type of motion can actually open the mind. The idea is to engross and occupy all of the senses, including hearing, vision, touch, smell, and taste, so that intuitive senses and dream vision can be attained.

The practitioner should feel themselves slipping into a trance. Magick users often describe this as crossing a symbolic boundary between this realm and the spirit world. Some people use imagery, like flying or walking toward a woodland. Like *Alice in Wonderland*, some seekers follow a spirit animal who escorts them to the otherworld. Folktales tell of entering Fairyland through a hole in a lake, through a burial mound, or in the midst of a fairy circle of mushrooms, trampled grass, or a ring of standing stones. Shamans sometimes describe astral projection as travelling beyond the dawn, or floating into a place where there is no time or physical objects. Other magickal people say that entering the astral realm is like falling asleep. In past times, the state between wakefulness and dreaming was called an "oneiric" state, which comes from the Greek *oneiros*. This has been used to describe the sense of dreamlike otherworldliness that comes from making a journey.

At the end of the working, the order of travel is reversed. Some common magick traditions employ a helper person whose job it is to return the practitioner from the dream realm to the physical world. This is done by calling their name, using words of power, or drumming. A series of drumbeats can signal that it's time to finish and return. The helper may hold the trance worker's hand and use the physical contact to draw the magick user's soul back into the body. Many shamans work with a spirit guide such as a bird or rabbit, which leads the astral body back to its physical home.

Shape-Shifting

Shape-shifting is also called shimmering, transformation, transmogrification, or werecasting. So many British Isles legends and folktales have to do with shape-shifting, from the Celtic stories of magickal transformation, to the witches who became cats, hares, or horses, to the hapless werewolf imported from the European continent. The old Welsh protagonist Gwion Bach turned into several animals to escape the goddess/witch Cerridwen after inadvertently drinking a drop of a magick potion intended for her son. Gwion finally turned into a kernel of barley, swallowed by Cerridwen as a black hen. She then became impregnated with Taliesin, the bard and magick user.

The wife of Fionn MacCumhil, called Savah, was turned into a white doe by either an evil Druid or jealous fairy. Fionn's hunting dogs, themselves shape-shifted from human form, recognized Savah as a person, refusing to kill her. She was brought back to Fionn's stronghold, where she regained her human body. Fionn and Savah soon had a child whom they named Ossian. In different versions, the wicked Druid changed Savah back into a doe, or she stepped outside of the boundaries of the fortress and was transformed. Years later, Ossian went hunting, found his mother as a deer, and recognized her. Following her beneath a fairy mound, he sat down to a sumptuous meal. When Ossian emerged three days later, he realized that he'd actually been gone for three years (or 300 years, depending on the version of the story).

Reynard the Fox is either an anthropomorphized animal or a were-creature. He is the antihero of a French folktale, later published in English by printer William Caxton, alluded to by both Shakespeare and Chaucer, and was the subject of a ballad included in the folk music collection of Ralph Vaughan Williams.[172; 173]

These tales could allude to shape-shifting rituals, in which a magick user undergoes a rite of spiritual transformation. A ceremony is performed to take on the aspect of an animal for the purposes of knowledge, attunement, and—in past times—for information related to hunting and herding. Shamans often allow themselves to become mentally and emotionally attuned with a spirit guide or animal totem while travelling to other realms. Some practitioners became adept at moving and acting like an animal. They were so convincing when they performed a shape-shifting rite that onlookers believed the magick user actually turned into a beast.

Assuming the consciousness of a deer, specifically, was called a *fith-fath* in Irish Gaelic (although this term could also mean a fetch or magickal fog). Traditional witches use the metaphor of inhabiting the body of a familiar spirit who appears in in the guise of an animal. Some researchers think that witches who gave testimony about shape-shifting during the witch trials were under the influence of psychoactive substances.[174]

A common magick user might use self-hypnosis to facilitate a transformation ritual. They can astrally project themselves into an animal's consciousness, attempt to take on the aspects of an animal, or even become an avatar for a spirit animal. More about the processes of aspecting and avataring will be explored in the next chapter.

Trance work, shape-shifting, and other attunement rites can promote beneficial internal changes for the common magick practitioner. A magick user can come to

172. *Encyclopaedia Britannica*, s.v. "Reynard the Fox," May 7, 2007, https://www.britannica.com/topic/Reynard-the-Fox-literary-character.

173. Imogen Holst and Ursula Vaughan Williams, eds., *A Yacre of Land: Sixteen Folk-Songs from the Manuscript Collection of Ralph Vaughan Williams* (Oxford: Oxford University Press, 1961).

174. H. Sidky, *Witchcraft, Lycanthropy, Drugs, and Disease: An Anthropological Study of the European Witch-Hunts* (Eugene, OR: Wipf & Stock, 1997).

intimately understand the nature of a spirit or being. They can feel the might of a thunderstorm or the fragile, ephemeral nature of a blossom. A shaman can experience the hunger, motherly instinct, and raw physical prowess of a bear.

Intellectual capacity might also be enhanced. A person can be granted wisdom by the voice of a deity, spirit, or ancestor. Guidance in life events might be provided.

There are emotional benefits as well. Trance working and attunement can inspire confidence. A magick user might experience incredible strength as they become united with the powers of nature or find themselves in the presence of a beloved deity. A journey can also be a playful, fun experience. A magick user can feel as if they are dancing with the fairies or soaring with the birds. All in all, attunement is a powerful, incredible part of folkloric magico-religions.

twelve
FOLK MAGICK RITUALS—
FOLKPLAYS, DANCES,
AND AVATARING

I n this chapter, we will explore some ceremonies that are the very heart of folk-loric magico-religions. In the British Isles, people often publicly perform folk dances such as the morris, jigs, and clogging. Folk dramas or street theater take place at seasonal gatherings. Traditional processionals such as Jack in the Green, the Straw Bear, and the Hobby Horse occur during holidays. The Mummers Parade in Philadelphia, or the Mummering Festival in Newfoundland, Canada, are examples of folk processions. Dances of Appalachia and the Ozarks, includ-ing flatfooting and square dancing, are performed at folk music festivals. All of these traditions come from the folkways of England, the Isle of Man, Ireland, Wales, Scotland, Cornwall, and Brittany.

What a Folk Ritual Is and What It Is Not

Folk rituals are developed by common working-class people, passed down from one generation to another. Folk customs can include dance and movement; instrumental music, traditional songs, and poems; street theater or folkplays; processions and parades; folk arts; and other activities. While they are entertain-ing, the rites can be done for more than amusement. Folk rituals have a profound emotional connection and deep personal meaning for participants and observers alike. Many of the practices are performed for cultural expression and/or magico-religious celebration.

Most folk rituals incorporate such elements as wearing costumes and playing a part to tell a story, although the characters may not have much depth and the plot can be very basic. The scripts or lyrics may vary from place to place, but many are recognizable as essentially the same ceremony or folktale. Some of the characters arise from folklore, represent summer and winter, or are archetypes of heroes or deities. Many folk rituals were, at one time, attached to an agricultural event (planting, hunting, the harvest, etc.) or a seasonal holiday (Beltane or Yuletide, for example). Many of them include—even require—audience participation. Spectators take part in various ways: yelling at the characters, singing along, or joining in with a gesture.

Folk rituals might have a magickal intention and purpose, or they might not. Some are simply an expression of ethnicity or heritage and are enjoyed by Christians and Pagans alike. Some folk rituals were adopted by modern Pagans, or "paganized," to seem older or more related to nature spirituality than they actually are. However, many of these folk traditions are authentically old, and have genuine pre-Christian origins. Many of them have ties to pre-Celtic, Scandinavian, or Teutonic folkways. Some folk customs were combined with each other and with Christianity. The folk rituals may have changed as a result, such as adding "Old Father Christmas" as a character in a Yuletide folkplay. This is a process called syncretization, when one or more cultures merge.

Other folkloric rites mutated in form over the years, making changes and adjustments to fit a particular era, location, or things like weather patterns. For example, Scandinavian people dance around a decorated pole at Midsummer in their native lands during June, but in the British Isles the ceremony is performed in early May. (It's colder in Norway than in England, so the springtime Maypole dance takes place in a warmer month.) The original meaning for a particular folk custom may have been modified or lost. Some traditions have continued unchanged, with brief interruptions during the Protestant Reformation and World Wars I and II. Several folk rituals died out and were revived in present times.

Many folkloric practices will be familiar to modern neo-Pagans and Wiccans; for example, ceremonially sweeping an area with a broom, enacting a symbolic battle between characters representing life and death, performing a circle dance, and portraying the deities involved in a sacred marriage. Anthropologist and author Sir James George Frazer speculated that folkdances and ritual dramas had to do with sacrifice, death, and rebirth.[175] Some folklorists have linked wearing animal disguises to shamanic practice.[176] Other rites may have to do with protecting a location from malevolent forces, summoning fair weather, or the fecundity of humans, crops, and animals.

Folk rituals raise energy, which can be directed with intent toward a goal. Dancing, acting in a drama, cavorting, and the laughter or surprise of the audience generates fuel for common magick workings and rites. Many rituals are performed as an expression of sympathetic magick, in an attempt to create change in the material world. These traditions are also enacted for personal empowerment, connection to universal forces, and spiritual well-being. Acting out a character and observing a rite engages the mind, body, heart, and spirit. Participants can avatar unseen beings and attune themselves with the entity's power, or they can draw upon their energies for a purpose. Some of the folk rituals have been performed for a long time and can use the principle of priordination. The ceremonies can withdraw from, or add power to, the magickal pool. Folk rituals are also a great deal of fun!

Most of these ceremonies require a group for optimal performance, so they can be done within a Wiccan Sabbat or a Pagan gathering. Anything that raises energy and empowers the participants is a genuine common magick ceremony.

Hooded Animal Traditions

Hooded animals are popular during certain seasonal celebrations in many locations of the British Isles. A hooded animal is a representation of a horse, bull, goat, sheep, or deer, which is used for a street performance. It can be a costume or a type of puppet figure. Various hooded animal rites are called hoodening, hodening, oodening, hop hoodening, guising, guizing, guise dancing, masking, mumming, an old horse play, a hunting ritual, a hunting dance, or a ritual dance. The hooded animal is sometimes called a hobby horse, hooden horse, hoden horse, the stag, the ram, the old horse, the bull, a beastie, a mascot, or they go by their own unique name, such as Mari Lwyd, Ol' Horney, or the Christmas Bull.

Many intact magico-religious societies or cultures worldwide have some type of hooded animal ritual dance or dramatization. Folklorists disagree on the origin

---

175. Frazer, *Magic Art and the Evolution of Kings*.

176. E. C. Cawte, *Ritual Animal Disguise* (Lanham, MD: Rowman and Littlefield, 1978).

and reason for hooded animal customs. Some think they are pre-Christian magico-religious rituals that represent fertility or death, depending on context.[177] Others believe the tradition is generally old but has no current religious significance.[178] British folklorist E. C. Cawte wrote that the hooded animal was a widespread practice throughout Britain, and he speculated that it might have magico-religious overtones.[179] Hooded animal rites were a continuous tradition in many villages in the British Isles right up until the 1930s.[180] Some have endured until the present day or have been revived. Several hooded animal costumes, masks, and figures are exhibited in museums, and some are still used during various holidays (or replicas of them are used instead).

During a hooded animal enactment, practitioners go in procession down the street, from house to house, or to public buildings, performing traditional songs, sometimes incorporating short dramatizations. Hooded animals and similar folk rituals are usually performed in conjunction with a seasonal holiday, especially around Oestara or Easter; Beltane, Mayday, or Witsunday; the autumn harvest and the hunting season; Samhain or Hallowe'en; and winter solstice, Yule, New Year's Eve, Twelfth Night, or Plough Monday. Some of these rites have been combined with folk dances such as the morris and street theater including mummers' plays. Other hooded animal ceremonies involve wassailing and traditional "begging" activities. Participants are usually rewarded with fruit, nuts, drinks, trinkets, or small change.

While many current hooded animal performances are done strictly for fun or cultural reasons, others seem to have religious or spiritual focus. Some common magick practitioners believe the hooded animals represent sacrifice, death, and rebirth, since many of the rites use an animal skull. Others believe that the

---

177. See Juliette Friedlander, "Ritual Dance in England, An Anthropological Study of the Evolution of Ritual Dance," (University of Winchester, 2009), https://www.academia.edu/7956588/030482_Ritual_Dance_in_England_An_Anthropological_study_of_the_Evolution_of_Ritual_Da; Ellen Ettlinger, "The Occasion and Purpose of the 'Mari Lwyd' Ceremony," *Man* 44 (July–Aug. 1944): 89–93, https://www.jstor.org/stable/2791738; and Christina Hole, *A Dictionary of British Folk Customs* (London: Paladin Grafton Books, 1986).

178. Trefor M. Owen, *Welsh Folk Customs* (Cardiff: National Museum of Wales, 1978).

179. Cawte, *Ritual Animal Disguise*.

180. Violet Alford, "Some Hobby Horses of Great Britain," *Journal of the English Folk Dance and Song Society* 3, no. 4 (Dec. 1939): 221–40, https://www.jstor.org/stable/4521156.

rituals bring fertility, as a ram or buck can symbolize male virility and the animal figures sometimes mime acts of sexuality. Some rites can be used for sympathetic magick for hunting and herding and, in current times, financial prosperity. The rituals may help people identify with spirit animals or totems for the purpose of manifesting an animal's qualities, like their strength. Other hooded animal rituals contain mock combat. In a Child ballad about Robin Hood from the 1600s, the hero fights a villain called Guy of Gisborne, who wears a "capull-hyde" [181] (horse-hide) cloak with the head, mane, and tail still attached. This could represent yet another symbolic battle between summer and winter.

The hooded animal can take several different forms.

Hooden Horses

In the southeast of England, especially in Kent, a folk ritual includes a wooden carving of a horse's head, with a skirting used as a costume. A performance with this animal figure is usually called hoodening. [182] The hooden horse often participates in a stylized dance or a comical folkplay where a blacksmith tries to put horseshoes on an obstinate steed. The ritual significance could have to do with blacksmith god-forms, such as Govannon, Goibniu, Wayland, Weyland, or Tubal Cain. However, the meaning has been lost to time, replaced with buffoonery and fun. Patting the horse brings good luck. While this rite usually occurs at Yuletide, hooden horses can be seen on other holidays as well.

Hobby Horses

The famous hobby horses, or "Obby Oss" like those found in Padstow in Cornwall, and Minehead in Summerset, England, are favorite May Day spectacles. The hobby horses have tiny heads carved from wood with jaws that snap, barrels constructed to look like a man is riding them, or big round cloth "skirts" covered with sheets of fabric, roundels, or streamers, used to sweep up young ladies for a mock fertility rite. The horses are accompanied by musicians, who sing traditional songs such as "Summer is a-Comin' In." Dancers and characters, such as a "teaser" or "groomsman," perform a short skit, while the horse cavorts (or rather

---

181. Francis J. Child, "Robin Hood and Guy of Gisborne," in *The English and Scottish Popular Ballads* (Boston: Houghton Mifflin, 1898), https://www.sacred-texts.com/neu/eng/child/ch118.htm.

182. Cawte, *Ritual Animal Disguise*.

glides) though the town. Some of the horses "smoot" participants with black soot, similar to smudging, to banish harmful energies. The hobby horse could have gotten its name from the hobnail boots worn by the rural practitioners, from a type of short, muscular working horse called a hobbie, or from Ol' Hob, another name for a woodland spirit being (or the devil).[183] These processions are believed to bring about fecundity, abundance, and good luck.

"Mast" Animals

Several areas in rural England, Wales, and Cornwall had or have processional rituals using a herd-animal skull or a fake head attached to a pole, staff, stang, or farming tool such as a hayrake, which is called a mast.

Mari Lywd

The tradition of the Mari Lwyd, or "old gray mare," is practiced in Wales. A horse skull is decorated with ribbons, beads, cloth flowers, bottle-glass eyes, and strings attached to the jaws to make them snap. Usually the Mari Lwyd has a white skirt or sackcloth to disguise the operator so that the horse seems to take on a life of its own. The skull is paraded through the town, falling or sinking to simulate dying, while participants sing songs, dance, and tell bad puns attributed to the dead horse. Call-and-response poems, songs, or *pwnco* (puns) are exchanged with homeowners, in the attempt to gain entry for the Mari and her company of "merrymen." The procession often culminates at the local pub or shares a wassail bowl with onlookers. While the Mari Lwyd originally appeared at Hallowe'en, the Celtic New Year, the rite is most often done around the winter solstice, Christmas, the New Year, or on January 6, which is Twelfth Night or the Christian Epiphany.[184]

The animal skull ritual also takes place in the north of England, where it's called the "old horse" procession. In Ireland it's called the *Láir Bhán*, and on the Isle of Man it's called the *Laare Vane*, both of which mean "white mare." Cornwall has a *Pen Kevyll*, "horse's head," whose skirts are black, and a *Penglaz*, which means "gray head," who cavorts around Penzance during Midsummer. Yorkshire has a hooded horse, constructed of a real horsehide, who dies on Christmas Eve

---

183. Ibid.

184. Ettlinger, "The Occasion and Purpose of the 'Mari Lwyd' Ceremony."

Figure 7: A Mari Lwyd

and is revived by the sound of a hunter's horn. The *Buca Llwyd,* or "gray buck," of the Welsh borderlands is a horse's head made from a feed bag stuffed with straw and attached to a rake or pitchfork. This hooded animal is seen at Hallowe'en, as is the Wild Horse of Cheshire, who accompanies "soulers" seeking treats. Around Derbyshire, a hooded horse called Ol' Ball, created from a horse skull with glass eyes on a pole, chases people and begs for money at Easter time. The horse's operator is covered by cloth and even has a horse tail. Six men with soot-blackened faces (as a disguise, *not* a racist display) accompany Ol' Ball in a procession. This ceremony is believed to bring good luck to observers and participants.[185]

The "poor ol' horse" could represent an equine deity (Rhiannon, Epona, or Equus) or a heroic mythological horse (Odin's Sleipnir or King Arthur's mare, Llamrei). It's also possible that the hooded horse has ties to blacksmith deities. Since the name *Lwyd* means "gray" in Cymraeg, I speculate that the gray mare might anthropomorphize death. In many Celtic societies, white or gray is the symbolic color of the dead.

Derby Tup

Another mast-type hooded animal is the Derby Tup, also called the Old Tup, Derby Ram, or Topsy. This is a carved wooden ram or goat head (or a ram skull with horns) stuck on top of a wooden pole, with a cloth covering to hide the Tup's operator. He is accompanied by a devil character, a cross-dressing male-female figure, and a butcher, who ultimately outwits the ram and kills him. In the town of Glouchestershire, the "Broad" is a bull's head on a pole, or a facsimile made of a carved rutabaga, decorated with ribbons. His attendants carry a wassail bowl as well as a carven turnip or rutabaga jack-o'-lantern. In the past, on the Isle of Lewis in the Hebrides of Scotland, a man wearing a bullhide cape was ritualistically ejected from the Christmas party at the manor house. In order to be allowed to reenter the building, the bull had to tell puns and jokes and sometimes engage in mock combat.[186] All of these rites occurred around the winter solstice, Christmas, or New Year's Day.

---

185. Cawte, *Ritual Animal Disguise.*
186. Brand and Ellis, *Popular Antiquities of Great Britain.*

Hooded Animals in Hunting Rituals

A hooded animal can also be a performer wearing animal hides, skulls, horns, antlers, or a costume or mask that represents an animal character during the course of a hunting ceremony or folkplay. In hunting dances and rituals worldwide, performers wearing deer masks, antlers, and costumes are sometimes ritually pursued and symbolically killed,[187] possibly as an act of attraction magick.

A similar rite was and is practiced by Welsh and Cornish immigrants to the US. It is called hoodening by my family, used during a ritual drama about a sacred hunt. A man named Herne, Cern, Buca, or the Buck shapeshifts into the form of a deer. He is hunted by a woman called Maid Marian, Maude, Maub, or Queen Mab. The stag is ritually sacrificed to feed a starving family during the hunger months of winter. Sometimes the character undergoes a symbolic rebirth. This rite, performed around the winter solstice, is believed to prevent famine and bring about prosperity. Traditional witches have a ceremony in which a priest wears a bullhide cape with a bull's head, sometimes familiarly called Ol' Horney, who represents both fertility and death. He is said to be another manifestation of the Horned Lord.

The Abbots Bromley Horn Dance of Staffordshire, England, contains elements of morris dances and mummers' plays, as well as hooded animal rituals. A hooden horse is present, as well as deermen who carry giant antlers attached to wooden stag's heads. A young hunter holding a bow and arrow accompanies the dancers and musicians. This ritual has been syncretized with Christianity, as the ancient horns are kept in a church and blessed each year by a minister. Those wishing to view the Horn Dance can attend it every September or see it online.[188]

A similar hunting ceremony could be the basis for the beast men depicted in prehistoric works of art throughout Europe.[189] There are speculations that animal skins and heads were worn for shamanic hunting rituals.[190] The folktales of

---

187. DK, *Dance: From Ballet to Breakin' Step into the Dazzling World of Dance* (New York: Dorling Kindersley, 2012).

188. *Revels*, "The Abbots Bromley Horn Dance."

189. Jean Clottes and David Lewis-Williams, *The Shamans of Prehistory: Trance and Magic in the Painted Caves* (New York: Harry N. Abrams Publishing, 1998).

190. See Friedlander, "Ritual Dance in England" and Nataliia Mykhailova, "Shaman-Hunter-Deer," *Adoranten* (2016), http://www.rockartscandinavia.com/images/articles/a16nataliia.pdf.

Herne the Hunter, the Buca, and the Wild Hunt could have come from this concept. It's possible that images of Cernunnos, Frey, or Pan as a horned god came from this concept as well.

The Ooser

The Dorset Ooser, also called the Grand Wooser, the Wooset, or the Christmas Bull, could have gotten his name from hoser, hooded, hoodener, or woodwose. He was mentioned by Wiccan author Gerald Gardner in his book *The Meaning of Witchcraft*.[191] The Ooser has the horns of a bull on his giant shaggy head, a mask that is worn balanced on the actor's shoulders. The current Ooser is a replica, as the last original one was lost during the late 1800s.[192] The hooded animal and his company march through the town along with morris dancers around May Day each year; they also perform at Yuletide.

While costumed animals are currently comical figures, they were not always so jovial. A frightening midnight visit from a masked character used to be a punishment for domestic abusers and unfaithful spouses.[193] During a ritual hazing, the hooded animal and his men would scatter straw across the criminal's doorstep, bang pots and pans, rattle cowbells, blow sheep's horns, holler invectives, shoot guns in the air, and even drag the offender from the house to be "ridden on a rail." This was called a *charivari*, or "skimmety riding." The modern chivaree, done for newlyweds as a good-natured prank, is quite similar to this rite. The animal figure might represent the wrath of an agricultural god, a woodland deity, or even the Christian devil. For the most part, however, hooded animals today are benevolent mascots.

Other Costumed Processions

Foliage Processions

As well as hooded animal characters, foliate figures appear in processional rites. Jack in the Green, introduced in chapter 8, was accompanied by milkmaids and chimney sweeps. The milkmaids wore a platter and piles of silver tableware on

---

191. Gerald Gardner, *The Meaning of Witchcraft* (Boston: Red Wheel/Weiser, 2004).

192. Ben Johnson, "Dorset Ooser," Historic UK, accessed April 6, 2020, https://www.historic-uk.com/CultureUK/Dorset-Ooser/.

193. Ibid.

their heads,[194] while the chimney sweeps wore top hats crowned with ribbons or feathers, blackened their faces to represent fireplace soot, and made a racket with their shovels and brushes. Academics disagree on whether or not this custom was authentically Pagan. However, the piles of silverware can be considered a way to bring about summertime by reflecting the light of the sun.

Dressing in costumes made of straw, called skeckling, was a Hallowe'en tradition in the Orkneys, Shetland Isles, and remote locations of Ireland. Skeckling may have come from Norse or Germanic settlers.[195] There are also skeck-lers, straw men, and straw bears in modern-day Britain and Germany that parade through villages on Hallowe'en, Twelfth Night, Imbolc, and on other traditional Pagan holidays. Bands of hay are tied around the arms, legs, and waists of marching harvesters. Straw costumes are also worn by wren boys or straw boys during the St. Stephen's Day custom of hunting the wren in Ireland.

The center of a folk festival in Edinburgh, Scotland, is a green man or fertility figure covered in cockleburs or prickly burdock seeds. The Burry Man troops through the town in mid-August to invoke good luck and a bountiful harvest. He stops at each tavern, pub, and government building to drink whiskey and accept the love of his entourage.[196]

Begging Rituals

There were and are many British costumed house-to-house procession rituals which involve ritualized begging for treats in exchange for prayers, blessings, good luck, or just plain entertainment. This is called cadging or busking. Some of these rituals are documented back to the early Middle Ages.[197]

The All Soul's Day, or All Saint's Day, souling tradition could have been the precursor to Hallowe'en trick-or-treating.[198] Around October 31, adult guisers,

194. Brand and Ellis, *Popular Antiquities of Great Britain*.

195. Samuel Hibbert, *A Description of the Shetland Islands: Comprising an Account of Their Scenery, Antiquities, and Superstitions* (Edinburgh: A. Constable, 1822).

196. Stuart Johnstone, "The Burry Man," *The Scots Magazine*, accessed April 7, 2020, https://www.scotsmagazine.com/articles/burry-man/.

197. Brand and Ellis, *Popular Antiquities of Great Britain*.

198. Rose Eveleth, "The History of Trick or Treating Is Weirder Than You Thought," *Smithsonian Magazine*, October 18, 2012, https://www.smithsonianmag.com/smart-news/the-history-of-trick-or-treating-is-weirder-than-you-thought.

soulers, or hoodeners went from door to door in disguises, singing a song or performing a skit. In return they asked for soul cakes, which are like a combination of a cookie and a biscuit. The soul cakes were marked with an equal-armed cross to designate them as alms for the poor, the same as hot cross buns on Easter. They might have originally been intended as Hallowe'en offerings for the departed.[199] Those who received a goodie were asked to bestow a blessing on the homeowner or pray for the souls of the dead.

Around Easter time in rural England and Ireland, pace eggers embark on a house-to-house procession, performing skits and soliciting for colored eggs, treats, drinks, or money. Pace egging may be based on a Pagan rite, although the word "pace" likely derived from "paschal."[200; 201] Some of the eggers originally wore animal skins,[202] similar to a hooded animal rite.

On the Isle of Man around Hallowe'en, children dress as Ginny the Witch and carry turnip lanterns from house to house, singing the "Hop Tu Na" song. Like American kids, they are rewarded with candy and treats.

Cross-dressers were and are involved in procession rituals, folk dances, and folkplays. Cross-dressing is practiced at Beltane, Hallowe'en, and other sacred days for the purpose of mixing traditional gender roles, creating change, and sowing confusion. Male cross-dressers can be called a man-woman, Maid Marian, a Bessie, Besom Betty, Ol' Bet, Dirty Bet, Lady Jane, Miss Funny, Molly or Moll, or simply Her Ladyship.

May Day processions usually involve young people wearing white or springtime pastel colors, flower crowns, and colorful ribbons. In many locations, a May King and May Queen are chosen to lead the troupe of revelers. Sometimes, a winter queen dressed in black is a cross-dressing male, while a queen of spring is a young girl wearing white with a laurel wreath or flower crown. Their factions engage in a mock battle, similar to the Oak King and Holly King struggle, oftentimes on a bridge. The losers fall into the water while the winning team

199. Brand and Ellis, *Popular Antiquities of Great Britain*.

200. Simon Thacker, "Nostalgia: Looking Back at Easter Pace Egg Plays in Rochdale," *Manchester Evening News*, March 28, 2016, https://www.manchestereveningnews.co.uk/in-your-area/nostalgia-looking-back-easter-pace-11103280.

201. Michael Haslam, "Pace-Egg: Notes for a History of Doggerel," *Northern Earth* 121 (Spring 2010): 12–16.

202. Castelow, "Pace Egging."

sings a victory song. Sometimes the skirmish ends with the May Queen being kidnapped and held for ransom, and her supporters have to raise funds for her release. The money is then donated to a charity. The May King and May Queen were also called Robin Hood and Maid Marian, or the Lord and Lady.[203]

Rush-bearing is a tradition that was Christianized and is closely related to harvest parades. Horse-drawn carts were decorated with streamers, flowers, bells, and/or woven wheat stems, then driven down the lanes of rural England. Rush carts bore the leaves of cattail and rush plants, used to cover the flagstone floors of homes, public buildings, and churches. Harvest parade floats were decorated with ribbons woven between the wheel spokes, and piled high with garden produce. Both customs had escorts of musicians, dancers, or costumed mummers. Harvesttime parades continue as a tradition for high school and college homecoming sports festivities in the US.

Folkplays and Mumming

Folkplays are just that—plays, dramatizations, or street theater performances put on by common folks. The performances are bawdy and full of slapstick humor, making them greatly entertaining. The costumed amateur actors go from house to house or perform in a town square, public building, or a local dignitary's manor. In current times, the plays are also presented at Renaissance fairs, town festivals, Pagan gatherings, holiday celebrations, and other public events. A folkplay is also called a mummer's play, mumming, mummering, mumping, mummery, guising, janneying, corning, a pantomime or panto, a folk drama, a ritual drama, or ritual theater. Participants are called mummers, players, guisards, guisers, mimes, rhymers, minstrels, tipteerers, hodeners, hoodeners, straw boys, younkers, and (comically) hams. A group of actors is called a company, troupe, team, or side. Street musicians may accompany the actors.

One purpose of a folkplay is to tell a rudimentary story with familiar, one-dimensional characters and a conflict that has a satisfactory resolution. Most of the performers' dialogue is delivered in rhyming couplets. The plot of a folkplay is simple: a character identified as a hero fights an antagonist or villain. The protagonist is vanquished, wounded, or killed. Often, the hero archetype is revived by a magic healer or doctor character. That's it—that's the entire plot. Other archetypical

---

203. Brand and Ellis, *Popular Antiquities of Great Britain*.

characters can appear, recite a poem, sing a song, or perform ritualistic actions. The folkplay audience participates by saying lines along with the beloved characters, singing along, cheering the hero, heckling the villain, and sometimes even taking a small part in the show. Since ritualized begging is a good portion of the fun, onlookers are encouraged to offer treats, money, and other rewards.

Mummers' plays are usually presented in conjunction with Beltane, May Day, or Yuletide through Twelfth Night. However, the folkplays' plots do not seem to have any relevance to the holiday itself, except for those that add Father Christmas as a character. The plays may be presented along with a hooded animal rite, folk dance, wassailing, or caroling. Some are unique to a particular event such as hunting the wren, wassailing the trees, or a plough play, performed on Plough Monday, which is the time to return to work after the Yuletide season ends. Interestingly, the actors in a plough play are sometimes called plow jacks or plow witches. Refusing to offer a treat to the actors meant they would retaliate with a trick—plowing up one's front yard.

Academics disagree on the age and origin of mummers' plays and if they have any real Pagan religious or spiritual content. Some argue that there are parallel traditions of ritualized dramas in intact pre-Abrahamic cultures as well as comparisons to various masking and theatrical traditions used for hunting, healing, and self-expression.[204] Folkplays were banned during the Reformation for being "heathenish," but they were revived after the Restoration.[205] Sir James George Frazer believed that most of the heroic characters represent a sacrificial king or god-form who dies and is revived. Frazer noted that the mock combat between the archetypical hero and villain might represent a battle between summer and winter or life and death.[206] There are characters who are healers, witches, a dragon, a cross-dressing man-woman, a comedic devil, and a fool, all of which have an esoteric connotation. A side plot (or sometimes a skit called a "wooing play") is a female character rejecting a series of suitors and finally running off with the fool, suggestive of a fertility metaphor. The practitioners of folkplays

---

204. Claire Schrader, *Ritual Theatre: The Power of Dramatic Ritual in Personal Development Groups and Clinical Practice* (London: Jessica Kingsley Publishers, 2012).

205. Martin Fitzpatrick, Peter Jones, Christa Knellwolf, and Ian McCalman, eds., *The Enlightenment World* (New York: Routledge, 2004).

206. Frazer, *Magic Art and the Evolution of Kings*.

may be seeking to cause a specific event by using the laws of sympathetic magick or priordination during their performances.

Ritualized actions of folkplays include going in one door of a building and out the other as well as sweeping the stage area before the play begins, both of which are believed to dissipate harmful energies. Characters announce themselves with "In comes I" and their name and role, rather like a magickal invocation. Noise is used to scare away malevolent influences, provided by bells on costumes, drumming, loud voices, the clashing of swords or staves during the mock battle, stamping feet, and "rough music," such as banging pots and pans. The sounds can also raise energy. As in many folktales, the warrior or hero is revived by a magic potion or a kiss. Characters make a toast, and actors cadge rewards from the audience in exchange for wishes of good luck and blessings. Turning away mummers from the door is said to cause bad luck, while welcoming them into the home and rewarding the actors brings good fortune to the household throughout the season.

The first known written reference to mummery in Britain is from the court of King Edward I in 1296.[207] There are records and citizen accounts of folkplays, mumming, and other forms of street theater right up until the early twentieth century,[208] when two world wars and a devastating flu epidemic wiped out many of the young male actors. Happily, folkplays began to be revived during the 1970s and 80s. There are many websites dedicated to mummery, some of which deny any Pagan connection, others which emphasize the plays' antiquity, overtones of nature spirituality, and magick.

Many folkplays have five, seven, or nine actors, as these numbers are considered to be good luck. Maid Marian was one of first identifiable folkplay characters, even before she appeared in literature about Robin Hood.[209] She represents springtime by often carrying a bouquet or nosegay of flowers. The familiar character of the fool is also called a dissard, jester, joker, Jack, knave, contrary, clown, juggler, tumbler, buffoon, Gill Finney, or squire. While they might perform juggling, gymnastics, and sleight of hand magic tricks for audience amusement, the fool also serves to distract the crowd if the other actors make a mistake. They also are in charge of the begging or cadging ritual. Like the famous court fools

---

207. E. K. Chambers, *The English Folk-Play* (Oxford: Clarendon Press, 1933).

208. Lilian J. Redstone, *Ipswich Through the Ages* (Suffolk: East Anglian Magazine, 1969).

209. Brand and Ellis, *Popular Antiquities of Great Britain*.

who performed for royalty, the folkplay fool could make political commentary or remarks about society for which ordinary people would be punished. The jester could also get away with vulgarity and annoying pranks, like pulling men's coats up over their heads. In some folkplays and folk dances, the fool is involved with leading or taming a hooded animal. The fool character represents discord, chaos, and the random factor so necessary for the generation of magickal energy.

In past days, a fool wore a whole cowhide or a calfskin coat called a buckram skin or a bullhide. They sported asses' ears, like the character Bottom the Tailor in Shakespeare's *A Midsummer Night's Dream*.[210] Sometimes a fool wears a rooster head, coxcomb hat, fox head and tail, or a calf's or lamb's tail. These animal symbols were replaced during the Renaissance by the popular fool's cap with several long, dangling cloth sections tipped by bells, or "younkers," and the patchwork, paisley, or "motley" tunic in bright primary colors.[41] Parti-colored leggings represent having one foot in the material world and the other foot in the spirit realm or otherworld. The fool carries a wand, scepter, bauble, or gam ornamented with ribbons, often topped with a pig's bladder for smacking other actors or a doll's head, representing a baby or one's conscience. A wand topped with a pinecone, acorn, or red tip represents a phallus. The fool's wand is a mockery of a monarch's scepter. Some fools held a soup ladle instead, although in many variations, a cross-dressing Molly was entrusted with this symbol of domestic abundance.[211]

Folkplay characters are frequently masked, not only to portray their archetype but also because mummery and begging were banned during the strict Protestant era, so secrecy had to be maintained.[212] Masks also add to the mystery of the performance rituals. Costumes can range from garments that actually portray the character, to tattercoats festooned with streamers, ribbons, and rags, to fluttering paper or straw outfits, to black clothing and blackened faces. Wearing chimney soot on one's face and hands was not intended as a racist statement; instead, it was to identify with chimney sweeps or factory laborers. However, most British mummers' guilds or teams currently omit "blacking up" as a disguise for reasons of cultural sensitivity. There are several costumes, masks, and artifacts found in British museums, village halls, or even churches which have been used in magico-

---

210. John Southworth, *Fools and Jesters at the English Court* (Gloucestershire, UK: Sutton Publishers, 1998).

211. Southworth, *Fools and Jesters*.

212. Fitzpatrick et al., *Enlightenment World*.

religious rites for centuries. Some masks, guises, and costumes seem to take on a life of their own. More about this topic will be explored in the section on avataring.

Folk Dancing

There are many folk dances of the British Isles that seem to have Pagan overtones, if not overt magico-religious themes. Of course, there is the celebrated Maypole dance, familiar to nearly everyone in England. Gerald Gardner, the founder of modern Wicca, made several mentions about the dances done by witches he was said to have encountered. These include a fertility dance done on broomsticks, dancing to help the gods, the sunwise Dance of the Wheel around a cauldron at Yule, and a spiral "meeting dance" for people to get acquainted.[213] Several of the previously mentioned folk customs contain a ritual dance, including the hobby horse and the Abbots Bromley Horn Dance. English country dances may include elements of magick, including one called the Witches Reel. A sun wheel dance can be performed to bring about the season of sunshine. British traditional witchcraft has a chain dance. There are sea chanteys and sailors' hornpipes, jigs, flings, clogging dances, circle dances, and the ever-popular morris.

Ritually speaking, dancing is done to tell a story, for raising power, for banishing harmful energies, and to bring about good luck during life events. Old-line Pagans have a saying about dancing a condition into existence. Woodcut art from the Middle Ages shows people dancing in a circle with demonic-looking entities, which was the imagined form of a witches' Sabbat. Many British dances resembled the Celtic knotwork pattern. Noisy bells on costumes and the music of horns, pipes, drums, and stomping feet are believed to repel malevolent beings. Dance is also an excellent way to connect with deities, heritage, and community.

The following are several types of British Isles folk dances.

Circle Dances

The Maypole dance could have begun as a magico-religious ritual of encircling a dolmen or sacred tree.[214] Ribbons were a later addition.[215] Dance participants stand face to face, each holding a ribbon, one group going deosil and the other

---

213. Gerald Gardner, *Witchcraft Today* (Lakemont, GA: Magickal Childe, 1982).

214. Jones and Pennick, *History of Pagan Europe*.

215. Brand and Ellis, *Popular Antiquities of Great Britain*.

going widdershins. The ribbons are woven in and out, back and forth, around the pole as the dancers skip or step and hop in a circular pattern. Dancing deosil raises beneficial energies, while going widdershins dispels that which no longer serves us. Sometimes a young person is tied to the Maypole to enhance fertility.

For a sun wheel dance, four participants stand in a square at the middle with their left hands on one another's left shoulders. Other dancers grasp their right hands, and more people grasp *their* right hands, forming lines resembling rays from the sun. Everyone moves forward, which forms a big revolving wheel. Dancers on the outside must move much more quickly than those at the center. This is done to raise power on the summer solstice.

Clogging

Clogging is a noisy, stomping dance from Wales, Northern England, and the borderlands. It is a form of step dancing similar to the dances of Ireland. In rural Britain, clogs or "clodhoppers" were everyday footwear of working-class people. The sycamore or alder wood soles make a clacking noise on floors and pavement, which is believed to drive away baleful spirits. Clogging, also called flatfooting, is a dance for holidays, life events, cultural festivals, and harvest celebrations. Music accompanies the dance, but no percussion is needed—the rhythmic sound of the clogs is drumming enough.

Clogging dances can be performed alone, with a partner, or in a group. Cloggers sometimes accompanied the rush carts during rush-bearing processions. They also gave performances around Yuletide because rural farmworkers and miners were laid off from work during the winter months. Clogging was sometimes a busking ritual. Routines included lines and circle formations. Ritual gestures can accompany the dance, or participants hold their arms still and at their sides. Clogging is also done by morris dancers, which we'll get to momentarily.

English Country Dance

This includes dozens of line, square, and circle dances. The number of formations and repeating movements can have ceremonial significance, as in circling clockwise three times. The dances are sometimes part of a courtship rite. A dance called Thread the Needle involves two parallel lines of dancers where a male and female partner dance together between them. This can symbolize fertility or rep-

Folk Magick Rituals—Folkplays, Dances, and Avataring — 261

resent birth. It might have a theme of finding balance and harmony between conflicting forces.

There are folk stories about dancers stepping on ley lines for energy. Garland dances were performed at Beltane and Yule after gathering foliage and creating long woven ropes of green branches. Hornpipes were done by bored sailors who also wanted to bring good luck to the ship. Jigs were not just for the Irish—there are British versions of the dance, whose name comes from the Old English *giga*, which simply means "old dance."[216] "Gigging" is a slang term for the sexual act. Scots and Brits enjoy a dance called a fling, which might be familiar from Highland dance. One legend says the arm was held above the head to represent the antlers of the Horned Lord.

The Mighty Morris

The morris dance is ubiquitous across Britain, and one of the main symbols of Merry Olde England. The jingling bells, leaping and prancing movements, waving handkerchiefs, and clashing swords of morris dances are fun, but they also have magickal connotations.

Academics disagree on the age, cultural context, and origins of the morris. The earliest known record of the dance dates from 1448.[217] Some scholars and dance teams' websites disavow any connection to old-line Paganism whatsoever, while others insist the custom was a form of ancient ritual dance. The morris is often performed on holidays that are traditionally Pagan, with Beltane, Whitsunday, and Yuletide the most celebrated days for dancing. The dance is accompanied by simple tunes played on old-fashioned instruments, including tabors, pipes, tin whistles, fiddles, and the accordion, which in present times is replaced by the melodion. Some of the songs are bawdy, while all are traditional. Most dancers wear leather pads covered by bells on their legs, which adds to the music, and the clanking sound is said to frighten off baleful entities.

There are many different kinds of morris dance, but the most common are Cotswolds, Border, Northwest, and Carnival. Some forms of the dance feature dandified clothing, bright-colored sashes, and baldrics or rosettes constructed of

---

216. Reneé Critcher Lyons, *The Revival of Banned Dances: A Worldwide Study* (Jefferson, NC: McFarland, 2012).

217. Michael Heaney, "The Earliest Reference to the Morris Dance?," *Folk Music Journal* 8, no. 4 (2004): 513–15, https://www.jstor.org/stable/4522721.

shiny ribbons. Ribbons and handkerchiefs are often tokens from favored ladies. The waving handkerchiefs have a symbolic purpose: they use ritualized movement to banish evil spirits and bad luck. Other forms of the dance have costumes that represent working-class outfits; the ragged, tattered clothing of the indigent; and footwear that resembles the clogs and boots used for work. Nowadays, this can mean Doc Martens. Several groups wear top hats with feathers, like huntsmen or chimney sweeps. Morris has attracted a lot of goth and neo-Pagan dancers, who have brought a magickal vitality to the art form. It is a more aggressive form of dance with lots of clashing batons, stomping, and hollering.

Like the mummers' play guilds, several town festivals and morris dance associations have banned "blacking up" because of cultural sensitivity. Many dancers today go barefaced, wear everyday makeup, or paint their faces in many colors. Black stripes or spots might be worn, in order to impart an air of mystery as well as to give a nod to the chimney-sweep tradition.

Many morris sides include characters such as the fool, a Molly or man dressed in women's clothes, and a person wearing an animal costume, called the beastie or mascot. This is sometimes a hobby horse or other hooded animal such as a stag. Other morris animals are merely fun, like a chicken or unicorn. Characters of Tom the Piper, the Captain, Bessie, or Betty are said to be the dancers' parents, and they often perform a comical side act. They may be responsible for "clearing the way" with a ritualistic sweeping before the dance ensued. As in the mummers' plays, the fool or captain is responsible for cadging from the audience.

Many morris dances reflect Pagan themes, including courtship and fertility, symbolic combat, and ritualized hunting. The clashing swords, stomping feet, rapping sticks, and noisy bells are believed to repel harmful energies. White clothing is said to represent purity and spring, while the darker costumes are symbolic of night and winter. Ribbons, rosettes, and colored cloth tatters are reminiscent of blooms. Most morris dancers walk in procession, which can have a magickal purpose in claiming a boundary or raising energy.

The dance movements, including circles, lines, squaring off, back-to-back steps, and crossing patterns, can all have ritual significance. The dance itself is said to awaken the earth, or to invoke or "dance in" the summer season. However high a dancer leaps represents the growth of the grain crop. Swords are interwoven together to form hexagrams and other geometric figures. An offering of spice cake or currant bread is impaled on the tip of a sword. Several of the dance troupes carried a Maypole, a small branch decorated with ribbons and tipped with garlic. The morris dance is certain to bring about a merry May or a joyful Yuletide for all.

Folkplays, folk dances, and procession rituals can be performed during a Wiccan Sabbat or circle, at a Pagan festival or convention, an ethnic celebration, a medieval period reenactment, or during an old-fashioned village holiday celebration. Our family has done a Maypole at our local community picnic, presented a stag hunt in our small town holiday parade and at a state university, offered instructions about the Mari Lwyd during Pagan Pride Day, done folkplays at regional Pagan gatherings, and taught folk dances on a Lake Michigan beach, not to mention hosting Beltane, Midsummer, Hallowe'en, and Yule celebrations featuring various folk rituals. We have conducted workshops where random people volunteered to portray folkplay characters, quickly assembled costumes and props, and read their lines from index cards. The acting was amateurish and the obligatory swordfight was clumsy, yet the effect was truly magickal.

These folkways are fun and enjoyable, and they also raise power to fuel a working. Dancing, singing, and parading through the town can banish harmful situations, increase beneficial circumstances, bring desired conditions into manifestation, and refill the magickal pool. However, that is not their only function. All of the common magick rituals that involve actors performing the role of a character have an important feature that is unique to folkloric magico-religions: folkplays offer an opportunity to interact closely with energetic beings through avataring.

The Rite of the Avatar

Common magick has two ways of enacting a communion with mystical entities, aspecting and avataring. To aspect an entity means to take on some of their characteristics, such as the bravery of the hero or the wisdom of a goddess. To avatar goes one step further; while portraying a deity, archetype, or other esoteric being, folk traditionalists believe we can accept their essence into our own consciousness for a brief period of time. We feel it is a spiritual union, in which we actually *become* a magickal entity. Avataring is also called channeling, incarnating, manifesting, communing with a being, spirit possession, hosting a spirit, being ridden by a spirit, or, from the perspective of the energetic being, descending into or alighting within the human recipient.

Of course, it's possible to act out the role of a character during a theatrical performance without avataring a spirit being. Nontheistic magick users can certainly participate (and raise and focus power) without belief in gods or other entities. However, some people who practice a folk magico-religion desire to serve as an avatar, for the reason of being touched by the divine. This entails allowing a being to temporarily inhabit or "possess" their mind, spirit, and sometimes even their physical body. It can help to fully attune oneself with an energetic being, to gain an intimate understanding of them, and to imbue oneself with the being's qualities.

Avataring a spirit animal is somewhat different from shape-shifting. Attuning to a bear means a person occupies the bear's space. However, as an avatar for the Great Bear, she occupies the person's space. Likewise, avataring a deity is different than aspecting. A practitioner who aspects a god-form retains their own personality and awareness even though they are taking on some of the deity's traits. Avataring a deity or archetype means manifesting that being within oneself, incorporating the entity's memories, emotions, consciousness, and thought processes into one's own personality. (Some traditions use the terms and definitions of avatar, aspect, attune, invoke, and manifest differently.) The goal is to become greater than oneself for a time.

Avataring requires a personal relationship with a magickal entity. Prior to avataring, practitioners strive to communicate with, work with, and understand a being's true nature. Other ceremonies, including journeying and aspecting, can help a person learn to avatar. The process includes the ritual steps that were outlined in chapter 6, such as shielding, grounding, and centering, as well as the technique of anchoring, which was discussed in chapter 11. Yet there are a few more considerations that are required before serving as an avatar.

Preparation

During the ritual step for voicing intent, a magick user should consider their reasons for avataring a magickal entity. This can include serving the community, creating positive change, gaining knowledge, and adopting the most beneficial aspects of the spiritual being. The practitioner may also request that a deity inhabit them to perform whatever working the god needs to accomplish. People can pick and choose specific characteristics of an entity to retain, like the courage to express themselves or skill in a profession, and then attempt to incorporate these qualities into their own personality. A deity can impart wisdom, nurturing, strength, and healing. Avataring can be a dynamic, transcendent experience.

However, some beings may have facets that aren't desirable all the time; for example, the sacred fool may point out fallacies by being sarcastic and, well, rude. A fool can also be quite entertaining. The same can be said of a hooded animal figure. While a herd animal can be very protective of their mates and offspring, they can also be prone to panic and fleeing. There is a legend related to the Stag Hunt where the Buca lost all human consciousness, and with it the noble ideal of sacrifice. He ran away from his loved ones, making them pursue him in a ritualized hunt. The avatar strives to retain the best portions of the entity, and to leave the not-so-nice ones out of their own personality.

This can come in handy while portraying a villain or an adversarial character in a folk drama. The role of an opponent is vital; in order to summon that which is positive and optimal, to manifest the very best circumstances for those attending the rite, the protagonist must have an opposing force. In order to appreciate summer, there must be a winter. Folkloric practitioners can handle this in several ways; some portray the villain as a buffoonish character, exaggerating their foibles and harmful behaviors with humor. Many prefer to just aspect the villain, rather than being their avatar. Or a magick user can go full-tilt nasty during the performance, becoming the meanest dragon or the cruelest winter character, confronting their shadow self, and then resuming their own personality afterward by engaging in rites to reconnect themselves with their true nature.

Shielding

Some folk traditionalists prefer to summon the entity they intend to host or portray before setting wards, shielding themselves, or otherwise creating a safe environment for magick. This is so that the being is not prevented from entering the ceremony and then descending into the individual. Other people simply allow the ancestor or deity to "drop in," which works if one has a long working relationship with the being.

Compartmentalizing

This step is designed to keep one's own essence separate from that of the spiritual being. The idea is to make room for the entity while still holding a secure place for one's own personality. The safe place can be visualized as external or internal, depending on whether the person wishes to astrally project their spirit else-where—allowing the being to take over their mind and body—or whether the person wants to be mentally present while the entity is within them. An individual's spirit can be kept within a symbolic compartment of the mind while the being has their own separate chamber within the practitioner's realm of consciousness. Those who are familiar with self-hypnosis, or who are adept at spiritual journeying, may already have a conception of how to compartmentalize.

One method of compartmentalizing used by common magick practitioners includes creating a metaphoric bubble, jar, or other container to keep themselves separate from the being. Another is to push one's personal life spark into a foot or hand, or to center one's conscious mind within the head or heart. This can be like cleaning out a spare room for a guest. If a god-form is one's own personal matron or patron, or if one is working with a being that can be implicitly trusted, this step may not be necessary. However, if a person suffers a great deal of confusion, nightmares, or personality dissociation, then compartmentalization is absolutely vital.

A Couple Other Arrangements

A magick user can establish boundaries when offering to serve as an avatar. A statement of parameters can be made, such as a time limit; this way, you can manifest through the duration of a performance and reestablish your own personality when removing a costume. This must happen before the ritual begins. Here is an example of how to set a boundary: "I, A.C. Aldag, will portray Besom Betty during this folkplay. When I take off the character's witch hat, I will resume being my own self."

The practitioner can also make a spirit pact while working with an entity, with terms and conditions that are mutually beneficial.

Avatar

This is the process of accepting a spiritual being into one's own consciousness. For some rituals, it may simply be a matter of preordination; the god-form has manifested within a human before and will be quite capable of doing it again. For others, there is more work to be done.

Many magick users use objects that represent a specific being, such as symbols of their culture, jewelry, ornaments, weapons, sigils, or other symbols, to summon that being into manifestation. As I mentioned, masks and costumes can help in avataring an entity. This is called guising or guizing in some British common magick traditions, but it goes beyond wearing a disguise. Donning a sacred mask, hooded animal outfit, dance kit, or ritual clothing can allow a person to do and experience things outside of their normal experience. It can bring a person into alignment with a deity or heroic figure.

In several folk magico-religions, the mask has a mystic transformative power. Sacred masks and costumes that have been used over time are believed to absorb some of the spirit of an entity. The being's consciousness is said to inhabit the object. Some cultures speak to their sacred masks, giving them offerings and venerating them as if they were the god-form that the mask represents. Intuitive people say that they can feel the vibe of the being in the costume. Merely donning the sacred clothing can help the practitioner to take on the power of the spirit being. The mask or costume is to be treated as an aspect of a magickal entity, spoken to and given honor. These objects should be thanked after a ritual performance.

Sometimes the practitioner must endeavor to manifest the entity. This can be done in several ways, including verbally summoning or requesting the being's presence by speaking their name and issuing an invitation. The being can be welcomed as an honored guest. In folkplays where the characters voice a line such as "In comes I, Little Jumping Jack, with my family on my back," this verbalization can actually invoke that particular spirit. Songs have the same effect. The magick worker can also create something to represent a character, make ritualized gestures, dance, and/or use a god-form's symbol or talismanic object to call them into the material plane through sympathetic magick.

Many folk magick practitioners use visualization to bring forth an entity. They can envision the deity or hero travelling from their realm, such as the otherworld, to the location of the common magick ceremony and entering the mind and body of the individual. The person can also imagine themselves as possessing the qualities of the being, while endeavoring to take on their persona.

Some magick users work with a partner to bring a spirit being's essence into their own consciousness. It is somewhat like the ritual that Wiccan author Gerald Gardner wrote about in his *Book of Shadows* called "Drawing Down the Moon."[218] This magico-religious rite, which likely came from the ancient

---

218. Gardner, *Gardnerian Book of Shadows*.

Greeks,[219] is when a priest summons or "pulls" lunar energies into a priestess, who then embodies the goddess Diana. A partner can request an entity to manifest and direct the being's energy into the recipient.

Magick users who have served as an avatar state that they could feel the energetic being filling them and that they were imbued with a sense of power, awe, and wonderment. They report a feeling of attunement with the spirit or god-form. Some say that they felt a deep connection to heritage, or to the circumstance that the being represents. The energy is so strong that it is almost overwhelming. This force can be used for healing, for fertility and growth, for knowledge, and for prosperity—not just for an individual, but a group. Once avataring has been successfully accomplished, it becomes progressively easier each time.

Banish, Disengage, or Devoke

This step is crucially important. The average human being cannot endure the power of a deity for very long. They would burn out. Other beings might feel restless, even annoyed, when confined within the body of a person and can cause mischief. Thus, the practitioner has to be able to let go of a god-form or spirit when it is appropriate to do so.

Sometimes the energetic being will automatically release the host at the conclusion of the ritual. Some spirits depart under natural conditions, such as when the sun rises and the rooster crows, or when the music stops and the folkplay or dance is over. The magick user may have made a covenant or agreement with an entity at the very onset of the ceremony, politely asking them to disengage when a ritual is finished. Other times, deities understand that their mission is completed and voluntarily leave.

However, sometimes a practitioner will have to intentionally banish or devoke a magickal being. This may entail a verbalization or another action that brings about the entity's dismissal. For example, an actor might say, "I am no longer the huntress, I am me, although I continue to embody the archetype's skills and bravery." A person can thank and dismiss the god-form or spirit as they would in any other rite. Words of power that cause an ending to a folkplay, such as "That's all there is, there ain't no more," can finalize an encounter with a magickal being.

---

219. Daniel Ogden, *Magic, Witchcraft, and Ghosts in the Greek and Roman Worlds: A Sourcebook* (Oxford: Oxford University Press, 2002).

Some older dramatizations really did use "Merry meet and merry part" to signal the end. Magick users can say "Return to your beauteous realm," reminding the entity that they have a lovely home of their own. (The statement used by many Wiccans, "Go if you must, stay if you will" is only recommended for dismissal if the deity is one's patron/matron, or if the entity is implicitly trusted.)

Other techniques for devoking include physically removing masks, clothing, ritual tools, or items representing the entity, thanking them, honoring them, and storing them away. Some magick users visualize a gateway or door opening in a boundary, such as the spirit realm. Others use a ritual gesture, which can be as simple as making the hand motion for "after you." While dismissing, the magick user can sense the entity's power receding and their own energy returning. Some say they feel the being's essence draining down and out through their feet, as when performing a grounding rite.

The process of devoking the entity and returning to one's own consciousness might not happen in that order. These steps can be simultaneous, or one's spirit might return to the body to "usher" the esoteric being politely away.

Return to Oneself

This is the reverse of whatever was done to anchor, compartmentalize, or astrally project. Some practitioners envision following a spirit animal or guide back to consensus reality, like the image of the white rabbit, deer, or bird found in many Celtic folktales. Magick users can ground, center, and do some of the steps outlined in chapter 6.

My advice to magickal practitioners who wish to avatar is to use care, but to have fun with it. In what other religion do you get to be God for a day?

After a ritual such as a folk dance, procession, or folkplay, the participants can help to direct the energy they have raised for a group purpose, such as prosperity for a community or healing for an individual. They can also each retain an equal portion of the energy for themselves and send magick to sustain a group energy pool.

Priordination and Energy Pools

As mentioned before, priordination is a magickal law that creates a beneficial condition in the present time by using the power of circumstances that previously occurred. Or, the short version: "As it was *then*, so it is *now*."

Although it works along the same lines as sympathetic magick, a rite that uses priordination does not have to resemble its intended outcome. Like attracts like, even though the ritual may have nothing to do with the desired condition...at least on the surface. However, the symbolic actions carry power into the material world. For example, when a hero character in a folkplay is resurrected by an archetypical healer, it is believed to cause the crops to grow. The wheat may seem dead and its straw is lying on the ground, but the grain plant will soon be reanimated and thrive, just like the hero. Verbalization of intent may not be required; it is implicit in the motion, activity, and sounds of song or spoken lines during the course of the ritual. Sometimes an optimal situation is "danced into being," brought into manifestation by participants' desires coupled with movement. A ritualized behavior, such as a gesture or using a power object, can also bring about priordination.

Priordination also means that folk magick traditionalists can tap in to a wellspring of energy which others have accumulated, including our ancestors and spiritual predecessors. Folk rituals have been performed so many times over the centuries that they have built up a tremendous reserve of power. Every time someone tells a story to an enraptured audience, performs a folk dance, sings a traditional song, or portrays an archetypical character in a ritual drama, they contribute energy to the magickal pool associated with that culture. The audience also plays a vital role: laughter at a fool's antics, enjoyment of a folktale, cheering a hero, or dancing along with a hobby horse causes a wonderful surge of power.

The energetic reserve of British folkloric magick is that of pre-Celtic stone-age tribes; the Bronze and Iron Age Celts/Brythonic people; the Romans; the Scandinavian, Teutonic, and/or Germanic tribes; Christians; and even the proto-humans who dwelt in the British Isles before human habitation. Anthropologists have discovered that Neanderthals performed ritualized actions.[220] In places where British people migrated, such as the US, the magickal pool merged with the collective energies of other immigrants and first nations. It has been added to ever since.

This reservoir of power can be accessed during other magickal rites, including personal healing and empowerment rituals. The modern medical establishment

220. Ker Than, "Neanderthal Burials Confirmed as Ancient Ritual," *National Geographic*, December 16, 2013, https://news.nationalgeographic.comnews/2013/12/131216 -la-chapelle-neanderthal-burials-graves/.

has learned that meditation and visualization have profound health benefits.[221] Focusing attention on a happy place, such as a tranquil beach or peaceful forest, can distract from the strain of childbirth, reduce pain, aid patients in physical rehabilitation, and have a calming effect. All of these practices utilize the same principle as tapping into the magickal pool.

Visiting an energy pool has pretty much the same steps as any other astral projection ritual or spiritual journey. The practitioner can use deep breathing techniques, ritualized movement, relaxation methods, visualization, and many of the other procedures mentioned in chapter 11. The difference is that the magickal pool is a unique, personalized place of safety and renewal.

Gathering energy from a magickal wellspring should feel invigorating, replenishing, and emotionally positive. Those individuals who are facing adversity can access a reserve of strength. People who are emotionally weary can feel energized. Seeking out an energetic wellspring can bring about feelings of happiness, peace, safety, tranquility, and love. Visiting a magickal pool is one of the most gratifying rituals within common magick.

---

221. Jeanne Achterberg, *Imagery in Healing: Shamanism and Modern Medicine* (Boston: Shambhala, 2002).

CONCLUSION

S ome recent books about folk magick present the beliefs, spells, and workings as grim, even frightening. Folkloric traditionalists are stereotyped as
dour, isolated eccentrics who throw curses around like confetti. While common
magick can be serious, many of the rituals are lighthearted, fun celebrations.
Workings and spells are often approached with pleasure because people enjoy
them as they do a favorite hobby, such as cooking or woodworking. Practitioners
can be farmers, nurses, plumbers, business owners, restaurant workers, military
service members, teachers, computer technicians, factory workers, electrical engi-
neers, and homemakers; people from all walks of life. (Okay, we'll own the part
about being eccentric.)

Folk magico-religions are designed to enhance the quality of life. Performing
spells and rituals is personally fulfilling and empowering. The results can create
major lifestyle changes, or simply augment small comforts. Chalking a hexfoil
above the bed can help one gain hours of restful sleep. Holiday celebrations not
only observe the cycle of the seasons, they can bring about an increase of well-being.
Interactions with nature cause satisfaction. Taking part in a folkplay, hooded animal ritual, or folkdance can connect participants to one another, to their culture,
to the audience, and to divine forces. The larger folkloric rites are often done on
two levels: a silly, funny, enjoyable time, which kids and non-Pagans can appreciate, and a deeper, more intense spiritual experience. The comical aspects can render Paganism and magick understandable in a nonthreatening manner. Interplay

with onlookers raises energy. The serious portions use symbolism to bring the will into manifestation. Participation draws on the magick of previous contributors, offers continuity, and can refill an energetic pool. Solemnity does the working, but entertainment fuels it.

Of course, neither our ancestors nor the common magick users of present times were/are likely to use some of the vocabulary I've used to convey esoteric concepts. For example, the word energy to describe the force of magick comes from the New Age movement. An energetic pool would have been labeled something like "the sacred wellspring of the otherworld." One's personal energy was called an essence, heart, soul, spirit, the Irish word *anam*, or the Welsh *enaid*. Working-class people were unlikely to have used terms such as astral projection, consciousness, ritual dramatization, entheogens, or magico-religion, as most of these words were coined by academics. Heck, we didn't even use the word "magick," which is attributed to British author and magician Aleister Crowley.[222] A common magick user would be more prone to say, "Stand back, I'm gonna throw a *cantrip* at this consarned tractor."

Nor did we call ourselves witches, or even magickal practitioners. A *dyn hysbys* is a wise man in Welsh, while *gwyddon* means a male witch or wizard, and a female witch is a *gwrach*. However, these terms could be pejorative. A magick user is called a *hudwr*, and a young female witch is called an *ellyllon* in Wales, after a type of fairy. In the olden days, elderly female witches were labeled hags, grannies, a *classap*, herb wives, old wives, and crones. A midwife was a *howdie* in Scotland, and a seer was a *spae*-wife. The term "biddy" for an older female witch came from the proper name Bridget and also means a hen. Males were called wizards, sages, and sorcerers. In Cornwall, a magick user is a *pellar*. In Irish Gaelic, a witch was called *crionna*, or wise; a male Druid a *drui*; and a female a *bandrui*. Cunning men and wise women provided magickal services such as spells, divination, herbal healing, and finding lost items.

It is unlikely that people in past days spoke in terms of earth religions, nature spirituality, or folkloric traditions. The word "witchcraft" was often an invective. However, the term "folk magic" can be traced back to Anglo-Saxon times.[223]

---

222. Crowley, Desti, and Waddell, *Magick*.

223. Sean MacLachlan, *British Folk Magic: The History of Magical Practices Across Great Britain* (Scotts Valley, CA: CreateSpace, 2017).

Many common magick rites survived right up until the modern era. For example, Cornish witches ritually buried pebbles, fertilized eggs, and sacrificed animals until the 1970s. Their coven was believed to have originated in the 1640s.[224] Popular literature, folklore, and nursery rhymes can contain spells. "Monday's child," which is from Devonshire, is an augury rhyme that predicts the fortune of babies born on a particular day. "One for sorrow, two for mirth" refers to the divination related to counting magpies (or crows, in the US) and dates to at least 1780.[225] Horseshoes are still viewed as lucky, although most people no longer have access to a horse. Originally, the iron in horseshoes was believed to frighten away witches and bad fairies. St. Dunstan, the Catholic patron of blacksmiths, was said to have nailed an iron horseshoe on the devil's hoof so that evil being would not dare to enter a building with a horseshoe above the door.[226] The Brothers Grimm wrote in the popular *Grimm's Fairy Tales* about a young woman who used "The Spindle, the Shuttle, and the Distaff," along with verbal spells and a blood offering, to attract prosperity and a handsome prince.[227] A similar type of tale is told in Britain. Folklorists now agree with Jacob Grimm, who theorized that these folk stories were thousands of years old, were handed down verbally through the generations, were shared throughout Europe, and arose from a common Indo-European language.[228]

The spindle or distaff, once used for creating yarn from wool or fiber from flax, is now almost obsolete, as is the horseshoe. Magick users today have been known to bespell their computers to prevent viruses and crashes, inscribe protective sigils on their power tools, and wear an amulet for safety while on a transatlantic journey on an airplane. Practitioners call upon an eclectic mix of historically Pagan deities, along with folk heroes, Catholic saints, and the Mother Goddess of Wicca. A funny, yet effective charm is "Hail Asphalta, full of grace, help me find

224. Martin Robinson, "Who Were the Modern Day Witches of Saveock?," *Daily Mail*, December 29, 2014, https://www.dailymail.co.uk/news/article-2889879/Archaeologists-reveal-Cornish-spinsters-using-witch-pits-recently-1970s-claim-practice-alive-today-discovering-scores-lined-swan-feathers-eggs.html/.

225. Brand and Ellis, *Popular Antiquities of Great Britain*.

226. "The Legend of the Horseshoe," Kentucky Derby Museum (blog), March 11, 2014, https://www.derbymuseum.org/Blog/Article/52/The-Legend-of-the-Horseshoe.

227. Jacob Grimm and Wilhelm Grimm, *Grimm's Fairy Tales* (Wolcott, NY: Scholar's Choice, 2015).

228. "Fairy Tale Origins Thousands of Years Old, Researchers Say," *BBC News*, January 20, 2016, https://www.bbc.com/news/uk-35358487.

a parking place," chanted while tossing pennies into a crowded parking lot. These newly discovered or created rituals work just as well as the old-fashioned ones.

Some purists act annoyed at the "diffusion" of folk traditions, complaining that magico-religions have been watered down, which means that they have been altered from their original form, combined with newer ideas, or cherry-picked from a multitude of cultures. However, I believe that eclectic practice is a good thing, and that to survive, our beloved folkways must change with the times and adapt to meet people's needs. As for cultural appropriation, I believe that my culture is awesome, and people are welcome to borrow from it.

Some of My Sources

There is considerable material written about older folk traditions of the British Isles, with varying degrees of accuracy. Many of the books were authored by academics, who used the writings of ancient historians and documentation of folk customs in municipal ledgers and church records. However, that means oral histories weren't considered. Sometimes the scholars held interviews with primary sources, common people who had participated in, or observed, the folkways. This could mean the writers interjected their own opinions about magickal practices. Several pamphlets about folk beliefs and customs were written by amateur anthropologists and members of the nobility for tourist amusement, some of which can now be found on British town websites and in museums. A few of the authors I've cited had actually witnessed or engaged in the folk practices themselves.

A fairly well-researched source is *The Book of Hallowe'en*, published in 1919 by a young librarian in Massachusetts called Ruth Edna Kelley.[229] Sir James George Frazer is often discounted, since some of his theories were disproven or found to be ethnocentric, but much of his work is (in my humble opinion) quite solid. Frazer's documentation of magico-religious rites was based on letters he'd received from missionaries, aid workers, and travelers who had actually observed the ceremonies of various cultures.[230] Other writers did a lot of speculating; for instance, James Bonwick interviewed people who had viewed or participated in Irish solar holiday gatherings, but then he compared the rituals to his interpre-

---

229. Kelley, *Book of Hallowe'en*.

230. Josipa Petrunic, "James George Frazer," The Gifford Lectures, accessed April 7, 2020, https://www.giffordlectures.org/lecturers/james-george-frazer.

tation of ancient Druidic ceremonies.[231] Some sources, like the dissertation written by Lyle Tompsen for the University of Wales, contain loads of information, yet the writer has drawn a few conclusions that cannot be proven (or disproven, either).[232]

Besides reading the works cited, I also looked at folk art and artifacts—both ancient and modern—housed in museums, private collections, and online. I read archeologists' and museum curators' opinions about the items, then checked out the energy field of several of the objects for myself. Some great resources include the British Museum in London, the Museum of Witchcraft and Magic in Boscastle, Cornwall, the National Museum of Wales, the Buckland Museum of Witchcraft and Magick in Cleveland, the Cornell University Witchcraft Collection, and the University of Michigan's Kelsey Museum of Archaeology.

Of course, I personally observed many of the rituals and workings mentioned in this book, or I discussed them with practitioners. Some of these were and are relatives, while others are members of groups who have varying levels of accessibility. (In my experience, folk magick users are more likely to talk with people who share their blue-collar background and political views.) I'd participated in some of the rites as a child, including a sacred hunt ritual, weather divination, healing and homemaking spells, spirit communication, and holiday celebrations. We put land snail shells in the cupboards to ensure plenty, looked for winter fairies when we saw frost etchings on the windows, and went fishing according to the most favorable days listed in the almanac. Our family still gardens by the moon, keeps bells on the doors to repel negative energies, makes offerings to ancestors, brings in the harvest before Hallowe'en so as not to annoy the puka, feeds the birds to honor a spirit pact, makes corn dolls to celebrate the harvest, and keeps real animals as familiars. These acts are magickal, and they are also fun family traditions.

It is my sincere hope that readers will try some of the common magick workings, rituals, and practices for themselves. Many of these rites can be seen in person

---

231. Bonwick, *Irish Druids and Old Irish Religions.*

232. Lyle Tompsen, "The Mari Lwyd and the Horse Queen: Palimpsests of Ancient Ideas" (master's thesis, University of Wales Trinity Saint David, 2012), https://www.academia.edu/5495517/The_Mari_Lwyd_and_the_Horse_Queen_Palimpsests_of_Ancient_ideas_Masters_Thesis_2011.

throughout the British Isles and Ireland. Our family and group will be performing some of the common magick rituals at Pagan conventions, gatherings, and festivals in the US. We'll be the ones running around with the decorated horse skull.

Bendythion!

A.C. Fisher Aldag

BIBLIOGRAPHY

"The Abbots Bromley Horn Dance." *Revels*. Accessed April 2, 2020. https://www.revels.org/experience-revels/cultural-traditions/abbots-bromley-horn-dance/.

"About Beltane Fire Festival." Beltane Fire Society. Accessed April 2, 2020. https://beltane.org/about/about-beltane/.

"About the Horn Dance." Abbots Bromley Horn Dance. Accessed April 2, 2020. https://www.abbotsbromley.com/horn_dance.

Achterberg, Jeanne. *Imagery in Healing: Shamanism and Modern Medicine.* Boston: Shambhala, 2002.

Aesop. *Aesop's Fables.* Translated by William Caxton. London: 1484.

Ager, Simon. "Elder Futhark." Omniglot. Accessed April 6, 2020. https://www.omniglot.com/writing/runic.htm#elder.

———. "Ogham." Omniglot. Accessed April 6, 2020. https://www.omniglot.com/writing/ogham.htm.

Alford, Violet. "Some Hobby Horses of Great Britain." *Journal of the English Folk Dance and Song Society* 3, no. 4 (Dec. 1939): 221–40. https://www.jstor.org/stable/4521156.

Armbruster, Barbara. "Gold and Gold Working of the Bronze Age." In *The Oxford Handbook of European Bronze Age.* Edited by Harry Fokkens and Anthony Harding. Oxford: Oxford University Press, 2013.

Barnhart, Robert K. *The Barnhart Concise Dictionary of Etymology*. New York: HarperCollins, 1995.

Beall, Abigail. "'Magic' Mesolithic Pendant is Oldest Art Ever Found in Britain: 11,000-Year-Old Jewellery May Have Been Worn by Shaman to Ward Off Evil Spirits." *Daily Mail*, February 25, 2016, https://www.dailymail.co.uk/sciencetech/article-3464192/Magic-Mesolithic-pendant-oldest-art-Britain-11-000-year-old-jewellery-worn-shaman-ward-evil-spirits.html.

Boeckmann, Catherine. "Predict the Temperature with Cricket Chirps." *The Old Farmer's Almanac*, June 24, 2019. https://www.almanac.com/content/predict-temperature-cricket-chirps.

Bonewits, P. E. Isaac. *Real Magic: An Introductory Treatise on the Basic Principles of Yellow Magic*. Newburyport, Massachusetts: Weiser Books, 1972.

Bonwick, James. *Irish Druids and Old Irish Religions*. New York: Hippocrene Books, 1986.

Borschel-Dan, Amanda. "The Pagan Goddess Behind the Holiday of 'Easter.'" *The Times of Israel*, April 5, 2015. https://www.timesofisrael.com/the-pagan-goddess-behind-the-holiday-of-easter/.

Bracelin, J. L. *Gerald Gardner: Witch*. London: Octagon Press, 1960.

Brand, John, and Henry Ellis. *Observations on the Popular Antiquities of Great Britain*. London: H. G. Bohn, 1853.

Brown, Evan Nicole. "Yes, It's a Witch Bottle Hunt." *Atlas Obscura*, April 23, 2019. https://www.atlasobscura.com/articles/witch-bottles-project-in-britain.

Burgess, Thornton W. *Old Mother West Wind*. New York: Grosset & Dunlap, 1910.

Carmichael, Alexander. *Carmina Gadelica*. Edinburgh: T. and A. Constable, 1900.

Carson, Ciaran, trans. *The Tain*. London: Penguin Books, 2007.

Castelow, Ellen. "Chalk Hill Figures." Historic UK. Accessed April 5, 2020. https://www.historic-uk.com/CultureUK/Chalk-Hill-Figures/.

———. "Pace Egging." Historic UK. Accessed April 2, 2020. https://www .historic-uk.com/CultureUK/Pace-Egging/.

Cawte, E. C. *Ritual Animal Disguise*. Lanham, MD: Rowman and Littlefield, 1978.

Chambers, E. K. *The English Folk-Play*. Oxford: Clarendon Press, 1933.

Champion, Matthew. *Medieval Graffiti: The Lost Voices of England's Churches*. London: Ebury Press, 2015.

Child, Francis J. "Robin Hood and Guy of Gisborne." In *The English and Scottish Popular Ballads*. Boston: Houghton Mifflin, 1898. https://www .sacred-texts.com/neu/eng/child/ch118.htm.

Clottes, Jean, and David Lewis-Williams. *The Shamans of Prehistory: Trance and Magic in the Painted Caves*. New York: Harry N. Abrams Publishing, 1998.

Connolly, S. J., ed. "Enech." In *The Oxford Companion to Irish History*. Oxford: Oxford University Press, 2002.

Corbin, Nicole. "Facing Death: Representations of the Ankou." *Celtic Breizh*, March 20, 2018. http://www.celticbreizh.com/facing-death-representations -of-the-ankou.

Coulthard, Sally. "6 Things You Need to Know About Witch Markings, According to an Ancient Graffiti Expert." *CountryLiving*. February 25, 2019. https://www.countryliving.com/uk/wildlife/countryside/a2021 /witch-markings/.

Crowley, Aleister, Mary Desti, and Leila Waddell. *Magick: Liber ABA, Book 4*. Edited by Hymenaeus Beta. Newburyport, Massachusetts: Weiser Books, 1998.

Cuncic, Arlin. "The Benefits of Burning Sage." *Verywell Mind*. Last modified March 18, 2020. https://www.verywellmind.com/the-benefits-of-burning -sage-4685244.

Cunningham, Scott. *Cunningham's Encyclopedia of Crystal, Gem & Metal Magic*. St. Paul, MN: Llewellyn Publications, 1988.

Davies, John, and Nigel Jenkins, Menna Baines, and Peredur I. Lynch. *The Welsh Academy Encyclopaedia of Wales*. Cardiff, UK: University of Wales Press, 2008.

Discover Boyne Valley. "Teltown; the Táilteann Games." Accessed April 2, 2020. http://www.discoverboynevalley.ie/boyne-valley-drive/heritage-sites/teltown-t%C3%A1ilteann-games.

DK. *Dance: From Ballet to Breakin' Step into the Dazzling World of Dance.* New York: Dorling Kindersley, 2012.

Dundes, Alan. "'Jumping the Broom': On the Origin and Meaning of an African American Wedding Custom." *The Journal of American Folklore* 109, no. 433 (Summer 1996): 324–29.

Evans-Wentz, W. Y. *The Fairy-Faith in Celtic Countries.* Mineola, NY: Dover Publications, 2002.

Edwards, Katie. "The Very Strange History of the Easter Bunny." *The Conversation*, March 24, 2016. http://theconversation.com/the-very-strange-history-of-the-easter-bunny-56690.

Ettlinger, Ellen. "The Occasion and Purpose of the 'Mari Lwyd' Ceremony." *Man* 44 (July–Aug. 1944): 89–93. https://www.jstor.org/stable/2791738.

Eveleth, Rose. "The History of Trick Or Treating Is Weirder Than You Thought." *Smithsonian Magazine*, October 18, 2012. https://www.smithsonianmag.com/smart-news/the-history-of-trick-or-treating-is-weirder-than-you-thought.

"Fairy Tale Origins Thousands of Years Old, Researchers Say." *BBC News*, January 20, 2016. https://www.bbc.com/news/uk-35358487.

Fitzpatrick, Martin Peter Jones, Christa Knellwolf, and Ian McCalman, eds. *The Enlightenment World.* New York: Routledge, 2004.

Flaxington, Beverly D. "Self-Hypnosis for Everyday Life." *Psychology Today*, September 13, 2013. https://www.psychologytoday.com/us/blog/understand-other-people/201309/self-hypnosis-everyday-life.

Foley, Ronan. *Healing Waters: Therapeutic Landscapes in Historic and Contemporary Ireland.* Farnham, UK: Ashgate Publishing, 2010.

"Fossil Agate Meaning and Properties." Fire Mountain Gems and Beads. Accessed April 5, 2020. https://www.firemountaingems.com/resources/encyclobeadia/gem-notes/gmstnprprtsfssl1.

Frazer, James George. *The Magic Art and the Evolution of Kings.* Vol. 1 of *The Golden Bough: A Study in Magic and Religion.* London: Macmillan, 1976.

Friedlander, Juliette. "Ritual Dance in England, An Anthropological Study of the Evolution of Ritual Dance." University of Winchester, 2009. https://www.academia.edu/7956588/030482_Ritual_Dance_in_England_An_Anthropological_study_of_the_Evolution_of_Ritual_Da.

Gardner, Gerald. *The Gardnerian Book of Shadows.* https://www.sacred-texts.com/pag/gbos/gbos38.htm.

———. *The Meaning of Witchcraft.* Boston: Red Wheel/Weiser, 2004.

———. *Witchcraft Today.* Lakemont, GA: Magickal Childe, 1982.

Gaspani, A. *Astronomy in the Celtic Culture.* Osservatorio Astronomico di Brerea. Accessed April 2, 2020. http://www.brera.mi.astro.it/~adriano.gaspani/celtcab.txt.

George. "Brigantia." *Brigantes Nation* (blog). Accessed April 2, 2020. https://brigantesnation.com/sites/brigantia.

Ginnell, Laurence. *The Brehon Laws: A Legal Handbook.* London: T. Fisher Unwin, 1894; Internet Archive, 2009. https://archive.org/details/brehonlawsalega00ginngoog/page/n5/mode/2up.

Goldstein, Jack. *10 Amazing Christmas Carols.* Vol. 2. Bedfordshire, UK: Andrews UK, 2013.

Graves, Robert. *The White Goddess: A Historical Grammar of Poetic Myth.* London: Faber & Faber, 1948.

Greer, John Michael. *The Coelbren Alphabet: The Forgotten Oracle of the Welsh Bards.* Woodbury, MN: Llewellyn Publications, 2017.

Grimm, Jacob and Wilhelm Grimm. *Grimm's Fairy Stories.* Wolcott, NY: Scholar's Choice, 2015.

Grimm, Jacob. *Teutonic Mythology.* Translated by James Steven Stallybrass. 4 vols. London: George Bell & Sons: 1882.

Haslam, Michael. "Pace-Egg: Notes for a History of Doggerel." *Northern Earth* 121 (Spring 2010): 12–16.

Heaney, Michael. "The Earliest Reference to the Morris Dance?" *Folk Music Journal* 8, no. 4 (2004): 513–15. https://www.jstor.org/stable/4522721.

Hibbert, Samuel. *A Description of the Shetland Islands: Comprising an Account of Their Geology, Scenery, Antiquities, and Superstitions.* Edinburgh: A. Constable, 1822.

"History of Freemasonry." Masonic Service Association of North America. Accessed March 30, 2020. http://www.msana.com/historyfm.asp.

Hole, Christina. *A Dictionary of British Folk Customs.* London: Paladin Grafton Books, 1986.

Holst, Imogen and Ursula Vaughan Williams, eds. *A Yacre of Land: Sixteen Folk-Songs from the Manuscript Collection of Ralph Vaughan Williams.* Oxford: Oxford University Press, 1961.

Homans, George C. *English Villagers of the Thirteenth Century.* Cambridge, MA: Harvard University Press, 2014.

Hope, Robert Charles. *The Legendary Lore of the Holy Wells of England: Including Rivers, Lakes, Fountains, and Springs.* London: Elliot Stock, 1893.

Hunt, Robert, ed. "Maddern or Madron Well." In *Popular Romances of the West of England: The Drolls, Traditions, and Superstitions of Old Cornwall.* London: Chatto and Windus, 1908. https://www.sacred-texts.com/neu/eng/prwe/prwe148.htm.

Jacobs, Joseph. "Gold-Tree and Silver-Tree." In *Celtic Fairy Tales.* London 1892. https://www.sacred-texts.com/neu/celt/cft/cft14.htm.

Johnson, Ben. "Dorset Ooser." Historic UK. Accessed April 6, 2020. https://www.historic-uk.com/CultureUK/Dorset-Ooser/.

Johnstone, Stuart. "The Burry Man." *The Scots Magazine.* Accessed April 7, 2020. https://www.scotsmagazine.com/articles/burry-man/.

Jones, Ben. "Traditions Similar to Hoodening." *Hoodening.* Last modified December 2019. http://hoodening.org.uk/hoodening-similar.html.

Jones, Bryn. "Names of Astronomical Objects Connected with Wales." *A History of Astronomy in Wales.* Last modified March 3, 2009. http://www.jonesbryn.plus.com/wastronhist/namesobjects.html.

Jones, Prudence and Nigel Pennick. *A History of Pagan Europe.* New York: Routledge, 1997.

Jung, C. G. *The Archetypes and the Collected Unconscious*. Vol. 9 of *Collected Works of C. G. Jung*. Translated by R. F. C. Hull. Princeton, NJ: Princeton University Press, 1969.

———. *Psychology & Religion*. New Haven, CT: Yale University Press, 1938.

Keightley, Thomas. *The Fairy Mythology: Illustrative of the Romance and Superstition of Various Countries*. London: George Bell & Sons, 1892. https://www.gutenberg.org/files/41006/41006-h/41006-h.htm.

Kelley, Ruth Edna. *The Book of Hallowe'en*. Whitefish, MT: Kessinger Publishing, 2008.

Kelly, Aidan A. *Crafting the Art of Magic, Book I: A History of Modern Witchcraft, 1939–1964*. St. Paul, MN: Llewellyn Publications, 1991.

Kipling, Rudyard. "A Tree Song." In *Puck of Pook's Hill*. Originally published 1906; Project Gutenberg, 2010. http://www.gutenberg.org/files/557/557-h/557-h.htm.

Laufer, Berthold. "Origin of the Word Shaman." *American Anthropologist New Series* 19, no. 3 (July–September 1917): 361–71. https://doi.org/10.1525/aa.1917.19.3.02a00020.

"The Legend of the Horseshoe." Kentucky Derby Museum (blog), March 11, 2014. https://www.derbymuseum.org/Blog/Article/52/The-Legend-of-the-Horseshoe.

Lyons, Reneé Critcher. *The Revival of Banned Dances: A Worldwide Study*. Jefferson, NC: McFarland, 2012.

Mabillard, Amanda. *Macbeth Glossary*. *Shakespeare Online*, August 20, 2009. http://www.shakespeare-online.com/plays/macbeth/macbethglossary/macbeth1_1/macbethglos_graymalkin.html.

MacCulloch, J. A. *The Religion of the Ancient Celts*. Edinburgh: T. & T. Clark, 1911; Project Gutenberg, 2005. https://www.gutenberg.org/files/14672/14672-h/14672-h.htm.

MacKillop, James. *A Dictionary of Celtic Mythology*. Oxford: Oxford University Press, 2004.

MacLachlan, Sean. *British Folk Magic: The History of Magical Practices Across Great Britain*. Scotts Valley, CA: CreateSpace, 2017.

Mark, Joshua J. "Boudicca." *Ancient History Encyclopedia*, November 8, 2013. https://www.ancient.eu/Boudicca/.

Marshall, Sybil. "Belling the Cat." In *The Book of English Folk Tales*. London: Duckworth Overlook, 1981.

Martin, Gary. "The Hair of the Dog." Phrasefinder. Accessed April 5, 2020. https://www.phrases.org.uk/meanings/hair-of-the-dog.html.

Martin, M. *A Description of the Western Islands of Scotland*. Originally published 1703; Internet Archive, 2009. https://archive.org/details/description ofwes00mart/page/n4.

McCarthy, James. *The Story of the First Woman in Wales to be Hanged for Witchcraft*. WalesOnline, October 30, 2017. https://www.walesonline. co.uk/news/wales-news/story-first-woman-hanged-wales-13816831.

Meier, Allison. "The First Known Depiction of a Witch on a Broomstick." Hyperallergic, October 24, 2016. https://hyperallergic.com/332222 /first-known-depiction-witch-broomstick/.

Merrifield, Ralph. "The Use of Bellarmines as Witch-Bottles." *Guildhall Miscellany*, no 3 (February 1954).

Milner, Nicky, Chantal Conneller, Barry Taylor, and R. T. Schadla-Hall. *The Story of Star Carr*. York: Council for British Archaeology, 2012.

Molyneux, Nicholas. "Discovering Witches' Marks." Historic England. Accessed April 5, 2020. https://historicengland.org.uk/whats-new /features/discovering-witches-marks/.

Muise, Peter. "Conjuring by Sieve and Scissors." *New England Folklore* (blog), November 30, 2014. http://newenglandfolklore.blogspot.com/2014/11 /conjuring-by-sieve-and-scissors.html.

Mykhailova, Nataliia. "Shaman-Hunter-Deer." *Adoranten* (2016). http:// www.rockartscandinavia.com/images/articles/a16nataliia.pdf.

"Newton's Third Law." The Physics Classroom. Accessed March 31, 2020. https://www.physicsclassroom.com/class/newtlaws/Lesson-4/Newton -s-Third-Law.

Ogden, Daniel. *Magic, Witchcraft, and Ghosts in the Greek and Roman Worlds: A Sourcebook*. Oxford: Oxford University Press, 2002.

Owen, Trefor M. *Welsh Folk Customs*. Cardiff: National Museum of Wales, 1978.

"Pace Egg Play." *World Wide Words*. Accessed April 2, 2020. http://www .worldwidewords.org/weirdwords/ww-pac1.htm.

Panati, Charles. *Panati's Extraordinary Origins of Everyday Things*. New York: William Morrow, 1989.

Paracelsus. *Four Treatises of Theophrastus Von Hohenheim Called Paracelsus*. Edited by Henry Sigerest. Baltimore, MD: Johns Hopkins University Press, 1996.

Parry, John Jay and Robert Caldwell. "Geoffrey of Monmouth." In *Arthurian Literature in the Middle Ages: A Collaborative History*. Edited by Roger Sherman Loomis. Oxford: Oxford University Press, 1959.

Petrunic, Josipa. "James George Frazer." The Gifford Lectures. Accessed April 7, 2020. https://www.giffordlectures.org/lecturers/james-george-frazer.

Pliny the Elder, *The Natural History*. London: Taylor and Francis, 1855.

Post, Emily. *Etiquette in Society, in Business, in Politics, and at Home*. New York: Funk & Wagnalls, 1922.

Potter, Beatrix. *The Tale of Peter Rabbit*. London: Frederick Warne, 1902.

Press Association. "Crows' Reasoning Ability Rivals that of Seven-Year-Old Humans." *The Guardian*, March 26, 2014. https://www.theguardian. com/science/2014/mar/26/crows-reasoning-ability-seven-year-old -humans.

Price, A. W. *Virtue and Reason in Plato and Aristotle*. Oxford: Oxford University Press, 2011.

Prickett, Katy. "The Shoes Hidden in Homes to Ward Off Evil." *BBC News*, December 10, 2017. https://www.bbc.com/news/uk-england-north amptonshire-41507752.

Ravenscroft, John. "The Helston Furry Dance." *Time Travel-Britain*, 2005. https://www.timetravel-britain.com/articles/history/helston.shtml.

Redstone, Lilian J. *Ipswich Through the Ages*. Suffolk: East Anglian Magazine, 1969.

Robinson, Martin. "Who Were the Modern Day Witches of Saveock?" *Daily Mail*, December 29, 2014. https://www.dailymail.co.uk/news /article-2889879/Archaeologists-reveal-Cornish-spinsters-using-witch -pits-recently-1970s-claim-practice-alive-today-discovering-scores-lined -swan-feathers-eggs.html/.

Roolf, Becka. "Healing Objects in Welsh Folk Medicine." *Proceedings of the Harvard Celtic Colloquium* 16/17 (1996/1997): 106–15. https://www .jstor.org/stable/20557317.

Ross, David. "Well Dressing in Derbyshire." *Britain Express*. Accessed April 2, 2020. https://www.britainexpress.com/counties/derbyshire /Well-Dressing.htm.

Rudd, Chris. "Horned God or Druid Priest?" *Celtic Coins*, December 2014. https://celticcoins.com/wp-content/uploads/2014/12/Horned-god.pdf.

Schrader, Claire. *Ritual Theatre: The Power of Dramatic Ritual in Personal Development Groups and Clinical Practice*. London: Jessica Kingsley Publishers, 2012.

Shakespeare, William. *A Midsummer Night's Dream*, 3.2.305. References are to act, scene, and line.

Sidky, H. *Witchcraft, Lycanthropy, Drugs, and Disease: An Anthropological Study of the European Witch-Hunts*. Eugene, OR: Wipf & Stock, 1997.

Simpson, John, and Jennifer Speake, eds. *The Oxford Dictionary of Proverbs*. 5th ed. Oxford: Oxford University Press, 2008.

Smith, William, ed. *Dictionary of Greek and Roman Biography and Mythology*. Boston: Little, Brown: 1867.

Southworth, John. *Fools and Jesters at the English Court*. Gloucestershire, UK: Sutton Publishers, 1998.

Thacker, Simon. "Nostalgia: Looking Back at Easter Pace Egg Plays in Rochdale." *Manchester Evening News*, March 28, 2016. https://www .manchestereveningnews.co.uk/in-your-area/nostalgia-looking-back -easter-pace-11103280.

Than, Ker. "Neanderthal Burials Confirmed as Ancient Ritual." *National Geographic*, December 16, 2013. https://news.nationalgeographic.com /news/2013/12/131216-la-chapelle-neanderthal-burials-graves/.

Thomas, William Jenkyn. "The Fairy Walking Stick" in *The Welsh Fairy Book*. New York: F. A. Stokes, 1908. https://www.sacred-texts.com/neu/celt/wfb/wfb26.htm.

Tompsen, Lyle. "The Mari Lwyd and the Horse Queen: Palimpsests of Ancient Ideas." Master's thesis, University of Wales Trinity Saint David, 2012. https://www.academia.edu/5495517/The_Mari_Lwyd_and_the_Horse_Queen_Palimpsests_of_Ancient_ideas_Masters_Thesis_2011.

Valiente, Doreen. *Witchcraft for Tomorrow*. Wiltshire, UK: Crowood Press, 2018.

Wallis, Faith, trans. *Bede: The Reckoning of Time*. Liverpool, UK: Liverpool University Press, 1999.

Watkins, Alfred. *The Old Straight Track*. New York: Ballantine, 1973.

Williams ab Ithel, J., ed. *The Barddas of Iolo Morganwg*. 2 vols. Abergavenny, Wales: Welsh Manuscripts Society, 1862.

Williams, Ralph Vaughan, and Albert Lancaster Lloyd, eds. *The Penguin Book of English Folk Songs*. New York: Penguin Books, 1990.

Winick, Stephen. "Ostara and the Hare: Not Ancient, but Not as Modern as Some Skeptics Think." *Folklife Today* (blog). Library of Congress, April 28, 2016. https://blogs.loc.gov/folklife/2016/04/ostara-and-the-hare/.

Zeyl, Donald, and Barbara Sattler. "Plato's *Timaeus*." *The Stanford Encyclopedia of Philosophy* (Summer 2019). Edited by Edward N. Zalta. https://plato.stanford.edu/archives/sum2019/entries/plato-timaeus/.

INDEX